SERVICE
LEADERSHIP

To the two people in our lives who really understand that once you have reached the mountain top, the climb only begins.

SERVICE LEADERSHIP

The *Quest* for Competitive Advantage

Svafa Grönfeldt
Actavis Group, University of Iceland

Judith Strother
Florida Institute of Technology

SAGE Publications
Thousand Oaks ■ London ■ New Delhi

For information:

Sage Publications, Inc.
2455 Teller Road
Thousand Oaks, California 91320
E-mail: order@sagepub.com

Sage Publications Ltd.
1 Oliver's Yard
55 City Road
London EC1Y 1SP
United Kingdom

Sage Publications India Pvt. Ltd.
B-42, Panchsheel Enclave
Post Box 4109
New Delhi 110 017 India

Printed in the United States of America

Library of Congress Cataloging-in-Publication Data

Grönfeldt, Svafa.
Service leadership: The quest for competitive advantage / Svafa Grönfeldt, Judith Banks Strother.
    p. cm.
Includes bibliographical references and index.
ISBN 1-4129-1374-8 (cloth) — ISBN 1-4129-1375-6 (pbk.)
   1. Customer services—Management. I. Strother, Judith B. II. Title.
HF5415.5.G756 2006
658.8′12—dc22   2005018321

This book is printed on acid-free paper.

05   06   07   08   09   8   7   6   5   4   3   2   1

Acquisitions Editor:	Al Bruckner
Editorial Assistant:	MaryAnn Vail
Production Editor:	Diane S. Foster
Copy Editor:	Catherine M. Chilton
Typesetter:	C&M Digitals (P) Ltd.
Proofreader:	Scott Oney
Indexer:	Molly Hall
Cover Designer:	Candice Harman

Contents

List of Leadership and Practical Insights

List of Figures

List of Tables

Foreword

The proverbial, but true, story: Marty and his wife were traveling recently from New York to New Orleans on a combined business trip and 25th anniversary long weekend. When they arrived at the ticket counter to obtain their boarding passes, they discovered that their reservations had been cancelled due to a data entry error made by the airline's reservations agent. Unfortunately, they were told, there were no seats available on their original flight, and the best the airline could do was to book them on a connecting flight that would get them to New Orleans around midnight, rather than midafternoon, on what already was going to be a rather quick trip. While the ticket counter attendant was shrugging his shoulders, a fellow attendant noticed the commotion and came over to inquire. When he learned of the problem, he began to make phone calls, at one point having two phones at work, one in each ear. He was making calls, working the computer, and asking the original attendant to help in various ways, all, it seemed, at the same time. It took him about 15 minutes, but he finally found two seats to New Orleans, in first class no less, and Marty and his wife were on their way to a well-deserved weekend celebration.

Now, what does another airline story have to do with this book? It's no secret that as we write, the airline industry is in dire financial straits. As every frequent flyer knows, for some time and for some airlines, the response has been to create cost savings by making service cuts of one kind or another. These cuts are felt directly by customers, thereby making driving, taking the train, videoconferencing, or vacationing close to home all increasingly attractive options, thus deepening the original troubles facing the industry.

The airlines should read this book. So should our bank. And maybe even our doctor.

Drs. Grönfeldt and Strother have melded nontraditional concepts of leadership with evolving business theory to create a new paradigm for what leadership looks like in a service industry environment.

From our perspective, as authors, teachers, and consultants on leadership development, there are three core leadership ideas that inform this powerful rethinking of the culture of a service firm. These are three of the essential elements of what we would call a *leadership culture* in a firm, an organization, or perhaps even a family.

First, in a firm with a leadership culture, every employee, no matter where he or she sits in the organization chart, with or without a corner office, believes and acts as if exercising leadership is an integral aspect of his or her job description. Exercising leadership is not the prerogative of those at the top.

Second, in a firm with a leadership culture, one of the ways that leadership is manifested is that individuals take responsibility for the firm as a whole, not just their individual silo. In the Grönfeldt-Strother context, that means that a service problem in one department has the constructive attention of everyone with some stake in it.

Third, in a firm with a leadership culture, leadership means exercising discretion, taking risks, and, again in this context, first meeting the customers' needs in ways that might well be beyond "standard operating procedure," job descriptions, and formal authorization, asking for forgiveness later rather than approval beforehand.

The significance of bringing together these two disciplines in this book goes beyond the service industry, and we expect that the model they have created will provide food for thought for practitioners and students in a wide range of business environments.

—Ronald A. Heifetz
Harvard University

—Marty Linsky
Harvard University

Acknowledgments

Like all explorers, we are drawn to discover what's waiting out there. We embarked on this journey without the slightest hesitation or thought of the road ahead, the obstacles we would meet, and the challenges we would face. We had *direction, purpose,* and *motivation.*

These binding elements made impossible schedules, thousands of miles, and the scarce resource of time look like bumps in the road on our way to accomplishing our mission. The thousands of minutes, hundreds of hours, days, and months spent on this project flew by. The result of our efforts is presented in this book. However, it is by no means only a result of our work and dreams but a collective effort of so many people we have met and worked with in the past.

We would like to express sincere appreciation to all those involved: our assistants Halla Jonsdottir and Ashildur Bragadottir who organized our world; the managers and CEOs who shared their experiences with us; all our talented friends at IMG Gallup and Deloitte—Gunnar Beinteinsson, Thor Karlsson, and Gunnar Haugen, to name only a few—who communicated their knowledge and insights; Jennee Saddorf and Michael Wahlgren at Florida Tech, who helped field test questions; and Edwin Strother, for his editorial expertise. We would also like to thank Al Bruckner at Sage for his helpful input and cheerful encouragement during the entire publishing process, Katja Fried for her developmental editorial expertise, and Catherine Chilton for her tireless copyediting. Without these valuable people, this book would not have been possible.

The Power of Leadership

Olaf Olafsson

Executive Vice President
Time Warner Inc.

As the towering skyscrapers of New York's Manhattan mysteriously disappear into the grey January sky, a tall and slender man steps into the executive meeting room on the 12th floor in Time Warner's headquarters on Columbus Circle. He is relaxed, his posture modest, and he almost appears shy if it were not for his sharp eyes. He is a physicist, a businessman, an executive, a renowned novelist, and the leading strategist for the global media and entertainment company Time Warner Inc. His name—Olaf Olafsson.

Whether measured by quality, popularity, or financial results, Time Warner companies are at the top of their game. America Online, Time Inc., Time Warner Cable, Home Box Office, New Line Cinema, Turner Broadcasting System, and Warner Bros. Entertainment maintain unrivaled reputations for creativity and excellence. Their purpose is to keep people informed, entertained, and connected in today's world of mass media and information obsession. In order for best-in-class businesses to maintain their position, constant reinvention needs to take place. The Company's culture needs to encourage prudent risk-taking and creativity. That does not happen without some core values that every employee understands," says Olafsson.

Since the merger of Time Warner and America Online (AOL) in 2000, the company has been undergoing a transformation of its culture and leadership style. The merger resulted in cultural upheaval for the company. The two cultures did not match. "I think the culture factor was certainly underestimated. Culture is serious stuff—you need to define it, hone it, cultivate it, and be clear about it if you are to expect competitive advantage to emerge from under its wing." Sometimes culture has been categorized as the soft stuff of business. In the opinion of the executive vice president of Time Warner, however, there is absolutely nothing soft about the success a collective culture can produce. "Any financial or other business metrics you can think of are indeed affected by the health of a company's exciting culture."

The company's values are the very foundation of any culture. They are usually developed by and communicated from the CEO and his closest team members and represent the management's beliefs and core understanding of how business should be run. "You need to value your values, and they need to be completely integrated with the way you manage." They can be used to change the current situation, or they simply reinforce values that have emerged from past practices and a consistent management style. Seven values outline and frame Time Warner's company culture: creativity, customer focus, agility, teamwork, integrity, diversity, and responsibility. They guide employee and manager behaviors and decision making. "We wanted the definitions to be simple and the message to be clear. This is not open-heart surgery—but it is equally important to the health of our company that they are respected, understood, and reinforced through our actions."

Time Warner Values

Creativity: We thrive on innovation and originality, encouraging risk taking and divergent voices.

Customer Focus: We value our customers, putting their needs and interests at the center of everything we do.

Agility: We move quickly, embracing change and seizing new opportunities.

Teamwork: We treat one another with respect, creating value by working together within and across our businesses.

Integrity: We rigorously uphold editorial independence and artistic expression, earning the trust of our readers, viewers, listeners, members, and subscribers.

Diversity: We attract and develop the world's best talent, seeking to include the broadest range of people and perspectives.

Responsibility: We work to improve our communities, taking pride in serving the public interest as well as the interests of our shareholders.

In addition to the values, Time Warner's board of directors has adopted *Standards of Business Conduct,* which applies to all corporate employees of Time Warner Inc. This code has served as a model for similar codes of conduct that have been adopted at each of the company's businesses. Also, *Code of Ethics for Senior Executives and Senior Financial Officers* has been developed and implemented at the company and its businesses.

The cultural no-man's-land Time Warner found itself in after the biggest merger in recent U.S. history had a tremendous impact on the company's performance. It finally resulted in transformation of the top of the pyramid as well as on various levels at the corporate headquarters. When Richard D. Parsons became the CEO of Time Warner Inc. in 2002, Olaf Olafsson returned to Time Warner as executive vice president, after having been away from the company for some time. After the merger, he left his position as vice chairman of Time Warner Digital Media, where he had been responsible for developing strategic business plans and identifying emerging growth opportunities for Time Warner's diverse digital media businesses.

"When I returned and joined the new corporate team, the company had all kinds of issues, many of them stemming from some core cultural problems. Given the health of our balance sheet today, it's actually quite amazing that it was only two years ago that some analysts were wondering if Time Warner would even make it over the mountain of debt left by the AOL merger. The new management's first task was to make some drastic changes at the corporate level and begin articulating and reinforcing the type of culture we were convinced the company needed. Well, it is as simple as this: The head leads the way. The top management must not only wish for the values to be true—they must make them true by leading by example.

Time Warner began hunting for *creative, customer-focused,* and *agile* people for most top management positions—*responsible* men and women known by reputation to have *integrity* and live those values the company now embraced. The company then trusted them to deliver the level of business results the company's shareholders looked for. "If you have the right people on board, life is easy."

The values are communicated by day-to-day actions and special value and training programs. They are reinforced without exception. "There is very little tolerance for managers who do not exhibit the underlying values in the way they approach the job and their staff." The entertainment and media industry is known for big personalities, high self-esteem, and numerous prima donnas. At Time Warner, however, people from every walk of life can be expected to receive equal treatment. "Here the best argument wins—not rank or fame," says Olafsson, and smiles. "We all deserve to be treated with integrity and respect, no matter where we come from or what we do for a living within the company."

Time Warner relies on people's leadership at every level. "We are innovators in technology, products, and services. Our people's leadership—their creativity, talent, and commitment to excellence—ensures that Time Warner continues to provide the high-performance service, trustworthy information, and enjoyable entertainment our audiences, members, and customers expect." This definition of leadership fits well with the company's values. When asked what leadership is, Olafsson concludes: "It is about inspiration and motivation. About a belief. About respect and courage to challenge ideas, performance, and rank. It can be found wherever you look—it is by no means restricted to a job description or corporate level. With more than 80,000 employees across continents, in numerous business divisions, and with a network of strategic alliances—the ability to work with others is a determining factor for success. "The most important element is *ability to work with others.* I am convinced that over 40% of people's success in today's businesses comes from one's ability to work with people of all shapes and sizes. It is simply a prerequisite for almost anything else. It requires self-confidence and respect. The company's culture has to nurture both."

For people who engage in leadership, Olafsson emphasizes the importance of a clear, simple, and consistent way of communicating ideas, thoughts, and strategies. These qualities should be displayed through both verbal and written communication and even more so through nonverbal behaviors and actions. His belief in clarity, simplicity, and consistency is as obvious when he turns to talk to people suddenly standing in the doorway of the meeting room as it was when he initially entered this room an hour ago: He practices what he preaches in the way he talks. It is apparent in his body language and voice—and in the way he works. "Leading needs to be personal. The work needs to be fun, not only business. Only that way can we harvest the power of the soul, not only the mind. I believe that's how you win."

1

Introduction

If it's to be, it's up to me.

—William H. Johnson

*S*ervice leadership is the culture that empowers the organization to strategize its promises, design its processes, and engage its people in a proactive quest for competitive advantage. When an entire organization has a service leadership mind-set, every employee-customer encounter is considered to be an invaluable opportunity to improve customer service and engender customer loyalty. Under these conditions, every individual takes responsibility and pride in creating or protecting the organization's leading position in service quality or in designated markets by carefully observing and communicating customer needs through the organization.

Changes in our daily lives and corporate environments continuously force organizations to reexamine their strategy concerning their markets, their employees, and their customers. Globalization, advanced technology, and communication compel all organizations to acquire a competitive advantage by placing an emphasis on a factor that is not as easy to copy as price or technology—namely, the quality of service they give to customers. Furthermore, increased competition has called attention to the growing importance of employee initiative, innovation, flexibility, and productivity as a response to pressures to adapt to external changes in the corporate environment. If organizations are to be expected to successfully plan and carry out continuous cycles of change to survive in today's service-driven economy, the exciting question of *leadership in service* arises.

Leadership

There is no universal definition of leadership, in spite of a growing number of studies on the topic. Leadership principles and themes can be found in such diverse ancient texts as Egyptian hieroglyphics (2300 BC), the writings of 6th-century Chinese philosophers, the Bible, and sagas of Viking heroes and villains.

In Greek political thought, each citizen was a potential leader and had an equal right to have his voice heard. Over the centuries, definitions of leadership developed from the democratic ideas of the Greeks to ideas and images of the "Great Man," one individual who leads. This is the person "who steps in and leads those who cannot or do not want to assume the responsibility into battle, into safety, into new territory, into new heights of accomplishment."[277] Note that the assumption of the person stepping in is that others do not want to.

Only in recent years have the old ideas of the Greek political philosophy of every citizen's leadership powers begun to emerge again, this time in the form of collective leadership efforts on the part of every organizational member. Now, in the early 21st century, leadership is viewed as "the capacity of a human community to shape its future, and specifically to sustain the significant processes of change required to do so."[276] Leadership no longer applies just to each manager's ability to lead. Now it also applies to the whole organization and its ability to develop a *leadership mind-set* for an entire organization.[72]

Service Leadership and Sustainable Competitive Advantage

The challenges are great for today's service organizations, but the opportunities for those who master the science of leadership in the service sector are also tremendous. The act of leadership can be integrated into the marketing and operational strategies of any service organization. In fact, in today's service-driven economy, you cannot expect to achieve leadership without service. The common denominator is the focus on assuming a leadership role—either as a company in the marketplace or as an individual within the organization, regardless of formal authority or power.

The concept of service leadership builds on ideas of strategy as perspective or culture and theories of leadership as a collective mind-set. Henry Mintzberg, one of the leading contemporary scholars in strategic management, has identified various approaches to strategy formulation and application. One of those strategies is the cultivation of a strong organizational culture. This kind of culture centers on strong organizational values and norms, reinforcing certain sets of behaviors needed to give the organization a competitive edge. The concept of service leadership suggests that the desired behaviors in today's service settings are collective leadership acts and that all organizational members share in protecting and preserving their organization. It takes the management practice of empowerment a step further in an attempt to overcome the disadvantages associated with power transfer and to capitalize fully on investments in higher labor and training costs. In service organizations aiming for service excellence, employees must have not only the authority to point out issues or to watch and wait for things to happen; they must also *crave* service excellence and regard it as their *responsibility* to be proactive to protect and preserve their organization and collectively shape their future working environment and organizational success.

There is no doubt that, when an entire organization considers each encounter between an employee and a customer to be a rich opportunity to improve customer service and build customer loyalty, a leadership mind-set is in place. In this situation, *every employee takes responsibility and pride* in helping the organization reach a high level of service quality. Employees do this by carefully observing and communicating customer needs through organizational channels. Of course, this calls for a change in employee and managerial roles. It also calls for a reversal in the traditional relationship between service provider and customer. Instead of the employee just doing what the manager dictates, he or she must do what the customer wants and needs.

This new view of roles and relationships empowers the entire organization to streamline its strategies and processes accurately and in a timely manner and thus to achieve *continuous service adaptation.* This ability gives the organization a solid competitive advantage in the marketplace, where reactive behaviors are more common than proactive ones.

Traditionally, leadership theory has focused on various traits and behaviors of individual leaders and the circumstances in which they find themselves, causing us to overlook the real leadership potential all around us. A definition of leadership that fits this book is best reflected in the words of George Bernard Shaw, who said: "The people who get on in this world are they who get up and look for the circumstances they want, and, if they can't find them, make them."[74]

What relevance does this notion have in a service context? One of a service organization's key performance indicators is the level of customer satisfaction it has obtained. Understanding and fulfillment of needs creates perceived value to customers and subsequently translates into customer satisfaction. In today's business environment, this is simply a prerequisite in the service industry. It is essential for the organization striving for service leadership to *expect* and foresee changes and to use the power of a collective leadership mind-set to be able to go further and faster to obtain the organizational goals of growth, profits, and service quality. The organization can obtain sustainable competitive advantages through service leadership—in other words, it has to dare *not to* do what it has always done, both at the organizational level and on each employee's individual level of responsibility. Standardized procedures and carefully laid-out processes ensure speed and accuracy of service.[117] However, if an organization is going to use customer service as its primary weapon in the battle for market superiority, it must learn to use proven methods of success and simultaneously dare to be different. It must position itself differently and manage its human resources to foster initiative, helping behaviors, and continuous improvement efforts.[117] This is in line not only with marketing thoughts in the past two decades but also with the core of leadership science and human resources theory and research. In short, a service leadership mind-set inspires each person to dare to use his or her brain to break market, organizational, or

> *Service leadership is the culture that empowers the organization to strategize its promises, design its processes, and engage its people in a proactive quest for competitive advantage.*

personal barriers that are holding the organization back. In this way, the organization can be expected to obtain what can be called *proactive service adaptation.*

The Theoretical Framework of the Book

Service is composed of *intentions, interactions,* and *impacts.* In other words, a service organization *intends* to provide a certain set of services, based on the organization's corporate and service strategies. These strategies are carefully formulated to optimize the organization's operational efficiency and to fulfill expected customer needs. The intended services, or the *service promise,* are then delivered through *interactions* with the customers. The interactions are regulated by service processes that may be automated, technologically assisted, or totally dependent on human contact. The *impact* of an interaction depends on how well the customers' expectations are met, which in turn affects their level of satisfaction. The impact is delivered through people and processes and determines customers' loyalty and, thus, ultimately, the organization's profitability.

The velocity of change in our service-driven economy calls for a new approach to service management. Organizations that used to be scared to death of the uncertainty of change are now faced with the daunting uncertainty of the dangers associated with staying the same.[57] Changes must be implemented for the service *promise,* the service design *process,* and the use of human resources embedded in the *people* of the organization.

In this book, you will see that, for the service industry, the traditional idea of a corporate culture must be expanded to the new paradigm of a service leadership culture. Service leadership concepts are based on three assumptions:

Assumption 1: Organizations can achieve competitive advantage in service through a collective leadership mind-set based in strategic application of processes and people to design and deliver the service *promise.*

Assumption 2: The *process* ensures competitive advantage through speed, accuracy, and adaptability of service delivery and enhances organizational efficiency by maximization of both internal and external resources.

Assumption 3: The *people* ensure competitive advantage through proactive adaptability to change by employing innovation, flexibility, and motivation to move the organization forward.

The concept of service leadership is based on a multidisciplinary approach that draws on leadership theories and principal methods of strategic management, service management, and human resources management, as shown in Figure 1.1. The theoretical framework suggests that (a) the leadership mind-set of organizational members is powerful and (b) leadership mind-set can be a driving force for sustainable competitive advantage. Therefore, *service leadership* is defined as *the culture that empowers the organization to strategize its promises, design its processes, and engage its people in a proactive quest for competitive advantage.*

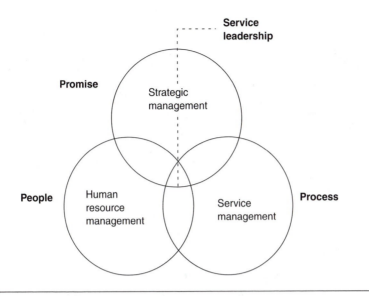

Figure 1.1   Multidisciplinary Approach to Service Leadership

A *service leadership culture* is a strategy designed to (a) carefully select and design service processes with active participation of customers and employees in the design processes and (b) strategically build on collective leadership efforts at every level of the organization to fully benefit from an organization's investment in its human resources. This paradigm shift requires changes in traditional management practices and demands more from employees. The manager's role becomes one of creating the framework within which the organizational members will work and cultivating an environment with which people can identify and to which they can commit their skills, ideas, and knowledge.

Figure 1.2 emphasizes the three key elements of service leadership. First, strategies are crucial for developing the service promise, which has to be tied to the organization's goals and mission. Second, the service process must deliver the services in the most efficient manner to enhance profitability. The service providers (people) are then the key ingredient in making the service unique and difficult to imitate.

The Power of People

For the last decade, strong organizational cultures have been believed to be critical to bottom-line performance in large organizations.[67] Commitment-based organizations that are packed with people who fit the organizations' values perfectly have repeatedly outperformed other organizations.

The implementation of service leadership culture is meant to create harmony between customers, employees, and organizational structure. An organization can create a competitive advantage by fully using its investment in the "best of the best" through employee selection, continuous learning and training, and cultivation of employees' sense of responsibility through leadership. The organization's services

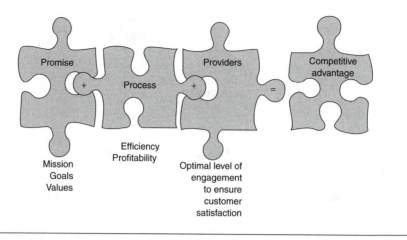

Figure 1.2   Service Leadership Culture

can become strategically unique by emphasizing those features of the organizational capabilities that create the best results and are hard for competitors to copy. This type of culture encompasses all the characteristics of a *competency culture* (see Chapter 9 for details). To ensure the accomplishment of unparalleled products or services, the successful organization applies a strategy of superiority, excellence, creation of market niches, and constant innovation.[271] This success depends on a strong, service-oriented corporate culture with superior goals. To reach those goals, the organization must fully use its employees' competence and find the correct balance between standardization, customization, and automation of processes. In such cultures, the function of leadership is to challenge others, to set standards, and to persuade others to believe that carrying out their role helps the organization fulfill its vision and purpose. The fundamental issue is the realization of superior goals. Through that culture, both the full use of employees' competence and a strategic balance of resources can be reached to ensure the best service delivery.

The Customer

Who are an organization's customers? In today's complex environment, the answer to that question is more complicated than ever. Most people immediately think of a retail customer or end user of a product as the typical customer. However, we have to look at a number of other groups if we truly want to identify the full range of customers.

Any organization has both external and internal customers. External customers are those to whom the organization sells its products or services. These external customers can take a variety of forms. They can range from a single individual shopping in a department store to a large multinational corporation that is buying machine parts for its assembly plants. An external customer could be a person buying a service, such as automobile repair, or a group of corporations contracting for health insurance for their employees.

Defining an organization's internal customers is often more challenging. An internal customer is one within the organization itself—employees who are served by other employees. A department that provides a service to another department is taking care of one of its internal customers. For example, the purchasing department has the production department as an internal customer when it is responsible for acquiring the parts and materials for the assembly line. Also, all employees are the internal customers of their company's human resources department and its services.

The larger and more complex the organization, the more complicated the definition of internal customer becomes. A company's call center employees are customers of the training department, which prepares them for their jobs, and of the payroll department, which prepares their paychecks. What about a company that outsources some of these services? Is the outsourcing organization an internal customer or vice versa? Think about some services that are frequently outsourced. For example, a small company may outsource its bookkeeping and payroll operations. Although the employees who perform the bookkeeping and payroll operations actually work for another company, they are providing services for the small company. Thus, there is an internal customer relationship between the two organizations. This is a complex relationship, which will be discussed further in Chapter 6.

Framing the customer service strategy and designing the appropriate process for service delivery will depend on the characteristics of both an organization's internal and external customers. Chapter 6 covers this topic in more detail.

The Purpose of Process

Standardization and customization of processes must carefully match the needs of the customer as well as the organizational strategy if the design is to create a competitive advantage. The benefits of standardization are speed, accuracy, and cost reduction. Some organizational processes can be standardized, but which processes to choose and how the required changes should be implemented depend on their role in differentiating the organization's services from the services of their competitors. Service processes should be designed to enhance efficiency and maximize customer satisfaction. Customer satisfaction does not depend on the quality of the service alone but on the fit between the customer's needs and expectations and the services that are delivered in a particular situation. In other words, the environment determines the process design through active participation of customers and employees in the design process.

Three dimensions must be considered in strategic decisions in process design: (a) the environment, (b) the strategic approaches, and (c) the characteristics of the service itself. Stable environments allow for more static approaches to the process design and provide the possibility for more standardization. Unstable environments such as highly competitive markets or changing needs of customers require more dynamic approaches to the service delivery, calling for more innovation, customization, and changes in at least some parts of the delivery process, as illustrated in Figure 1.3.

The design of the processes helps organizations tailor their promise to customers' needs in a timely and proactive manner and deliver the services with optimal efficiency. Good process design allows organizations to deliver their

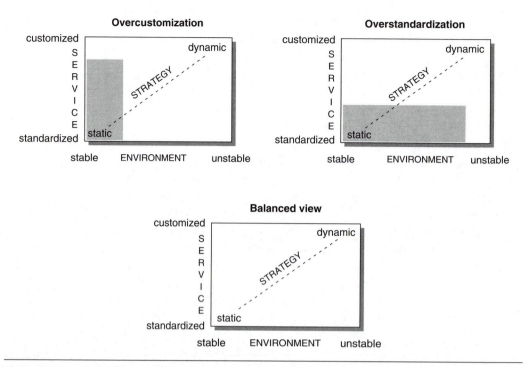

Figure 1.3   Three Dimensions of Service Strategy and Design

services faster, cheaper, and better, depending on customer preferences (see Figure 1.4). According to research, this enhances customer satisfaction and, consequently, loyalty—the generator of organizational profitability. The concept of service leadership is discussed in detail in Chapters 3 and 4, and the building and maintenance of service leadership cultures are outlined in Chapter 9.

Purpose and Overview of the Book

The purpose of this book is to provide a comprehensive theoretical framework as well as practical strategies—not just for survival but for a true search for excellence in the uncertain and ever-changing world of customer service management. The theoretical framework is based on the notion that customer service contains three key variables: a promise, a process, and people. The book is organized around those variables. It provides insight into (a) strategic schools of thought and practices needed to determine the service promise, (b) an overview of service process design principles, and (c) management and human resources practices needed to implement the service strategy through the service providers—that is, the people. In addition, we take a close look at how the outcome of the applied service strategies can be measured and how the results of the measurement can be used to enhance service performance.

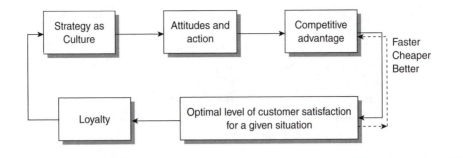

Figure 1.4   Service Leadership Action Chain

The book takes the reader step by step through the service management process. After going through the book, the reader will have the necessary understanding and skill to choose the right strategy for the right circumstances, to design service processes, to identify the means and methods to implement them, and to measure the outcome. Furthermore, the reader will have a new understanding of the importance of leadership, which is embedded in all members of an organization, for organizational success in a service context.

This text provides a comprehensive view of the *whats* and *whys* of service behaviors and actions, in addition to the *hows* of process implementation. There is evidence of a growing consensus among managers that the path for future organizational success calls for rethinking their strategies. In most industries, the trend has been moving away from top-down control, formal planning, and the kind of industry analysis frequently associated with traditional prescriptive strategic planning. This trend has also been evident in the service industry, where organizations no longer believe that rigid structures and bureaucratic solutions are the key to customer satisfaction. In this turmoil of change, organizations—many of which are struggling with delivering their promises to customers—are engaging in "strategic experiments without the guidance of appropriate theories of strategic management."[313] Thus the need for strategic theory in the 21st century is greater than ever.

This text makes a number of significant contributions to the field. First, it incorporates a thorough discussion of the development and application of strategies and how they may be applied to enhance organizational performance. Second, it includes a discussion on both quantitative and qualitative methods in a service context. However, the most important contribution to the study and practice of service management is the conceptualization of the new paradigm of *service leadership* and the development of a multidisciplinary approach to the topic.

Content Outline

The text is organized into 12 Chapters and divided into three main sections. Part I addresses the service *promise.* The chapters in this section introduce various definitions of the service concept, discuss the industry's growing global economic importance, and provide insight into the different ways that service strategy can be determined and applied. The key decisions addressed are *where to go* and *why.* The aim of the first section of this book is to discuss how service leadership can be fostered from within to enhance organizational success.

Once an organization knows *where to go* and *why,* the question of *how to get there* immediately arises. The purpose of the second section of the book is to discuss various ways of designing and mapping the service *process.* Implementation of the service process is another essential part of successful service management. This section of the book provides valuable and practical insights into what to look for among the dragons and dungeons of the service implementation process. An essential part of this process is to know and understand customer needs, attitudes, and expectations. Therefore, one chapter (Chapter 8) in this part of the book is dedicated to the question of how to monitor and measure customers' perspectives and expectations. The logistics of continuous improvement and service recovery are also discussed.

Part III of the book deals with the human element of service. The focus is on what can easily make or break any effort to operationalize a service strategy or process—the *people.* What makes people behave the way they do toward their customers? Any organization that depends on obtaining customer satisfaction and loyalty for survival must know how to answer this crucial question. Various aspects of employee service orientation, as well as the roles of employees and managers, are examined to help answer this vital question. This part of the book also addresses the human resources management (HRM) practices of selection, socialization, and training of frontline staff. Successful HRM practices can modify, adapt, and align employee behaviors with organizational goals. In addition, ways to achieve a collective service leadership culture are introduced. Throughout the text, the application of service leadership strategies and methods of data use, which are needed for strategic and operational practices in service, are highlighted.

The methods discussed in this book can be applied to various industries around the world, provided there is careful consideration of local and company cultures. Each chapter is organized in the same manner, starting with learning objectives, to direct the reader's attention, followed by a theoretical overview and practical applications of the relevant topic. The chapters provide a comprehensive overview of the theory and research associated with each topic. Furthermore, each chapter provides practical insights and the application of step-by-step methods regarding strategies, processes, or people.

Each of the three parts of the book starts with an interview with a top executive of a company that depends on the delivery of impeccable service for its success. These leading service strategists were asked to reflect on the unique elements of their organization's success, as well as probable future challenges and trends in the service industry. The interviews provide an opportunity to examine past practices and emerging trends through the eyes of high-level executives of large multinational corporations. These interviews are designed to engage the reader in a structured application of the tools of the trade and to promote out-of-the-box thinking concepts and viewpoints related to service leadership. Throughout each chapter, practical insights from a variety of corporations and their executives demonstrate how these organizations implement service strategies and deal with specific service leadership issues. At the end of each of the three sections, a summary of data management and research methods needed for strategy formulation, process design, and service performance evaluation is provided. Chapter review questions and topics for discussion are given at the end of each chapter.

Key Concepts

Directions: The following are key concepts presented in this chapter. Write a complete definition for each one.

Service leadership

Service leadership mind-set

Proactive service adaptation

PART

one

Strategizing the Promise

T his first section provides insight into the changing world of the service industry. First, we take a look at how the concept of service has evolved and the importance of service in today's marketplace. Second, we introduce the concept of collective leadership of all organizational members in a service setting. Finally, we provide a theoretical framework of a new concept, *service leadership*.

The Power of the Strategist

The Strategic Application of Culture

Robert Wessman

Chief Executive
Actavis Group

R obert Wessman, CEO of Actavis, one of the world's fastest growing generic pharmaceutical companies, talks about his experiences building an international company through an application of strategic mergers and acquisitions and a unique company culture.

Our company had a little over 100 employees 5 years ago. Today we have an army of about 7000 dedicated employees operating in 25 countries. Our market value has grown 50-fold. What we have achieved during those years is obviously something which I'm personally extremely proud of, and all of us should be proud of, because everybody within our group has been contributing to this success.

We are actually being seen as one of the best companies developing generic products due to our capability to develop high-quality generic drugs faster and cheaper than our competitors. We have very strong sales and marketing units all over the world and we are continuing to build that up to be able to enter into more markets. We have low-cost production with very strategic location of our manufacturing sites.

We are growing very fast by the power of organic growth, but we are also making a lot of acquisitions. We have basically been starting up or acquiring companies every third month now for more than 4 years. Consolidation and integration has been our major challenge in all of this. Consolidation means that every single local unit has a role in the overall strategy of the company. Our people are critical to our growth. We need to have a shared vision and common core values. The culture needs to be clear, simple, and consistent.

Our name, Actavis, was selected because we wanted it to represent some of the key drivers behind our competitiveness and our vision for building a unique company culture that would be extremely difficult for competitors to copy. Actually, the name consists of two Latin words, *acta*, which means *action*, and *vis*, which means *strength*. Building and maintaining a culture where all organizational members ambitiously seek ways to continuously improve our performance has been our top priority. The energy created by our culture in the past has provided the drive and resourcefulness needed to operate in this highly competitive industry. To strengthen our culture even further, we have launched a program we call "one company, one vision."

The objective of the project is to raise the awareness of the company values and to identify ways for us to live those values to the fullest every day. The six values— ambition, flexibility, proactiveness, efficiency, teamwork, and customer care—are the framework that guides our behaviors and actions. They are the common thread between the different locations and operations of Actavis. They bind us together while we use and welcome our differences and local strengths. They identify how we should work in order to achieve Actavis's ambitious goal of becoming a world-leading generic pharmaceutical company. The project has three main phases, carried out in each country of operation: In the first phase, a *survey* was conducted to measure current awareness and employees' perceptions of how well we all live the values today. In the second phase, *workshops* were held in each location to discuss and identify ways to raise awareness and improve our practices. In the third phase, the *suggestions made in the workshops were implemented,* accompanied by local *training* for employees and managers.

Managers must be role models if our core values are to be consistent and efficient. In addition to raising awareness of our company values and identifying ways of living them in our everyday practices, all our HR and management practices are tailored to those values. The aim is to create a dynamic workplace where proactiveness and accountability for results are high. Recruitment and selection of new staff aim to find ambitious, proactive, and flexible individuals who can efficiently work in teams to provide the level of customer care we seek. Our management team operates on the assumption that everyone has the freedom to act but not to neglect. The best argument at the table wins—not rank. The only victory is to be successful. We expect our management team to lead by example, and therefore our performance appraisal system is focused on the performance of our top 100 managers. Their performance is vigorously monitored, where they are expected to reach ambitious business objectives and deliver bottom-line results. However, it matters tremendously to us how that success is achieved, so we measure regularly other key performance indicators, based on how well they manage through our values and provide our staff with direction, purpose, and motivation. With a clear strategic vision, few rules, and strong values accompanied by a flexible structure, excellent teams of managers and scientists, and a unique mind-set of our staff, we face the future with confidence.

These are my rules of thumb: (1) Select the best people, (2) expect nothing but the best from them, (3) never expect less from yourself, and (4) never take no for an answer.

Looking Back on Service

In manufacturing, a product is composed of hundreds or thousands of components. Similarly, services consist of hundreds or thousands of components. However, unlike a product, service components are usually not physical entities, but rather are a combination of processes, people skills, and materials that must be appropriately integrated to yield the "planned" or "designed" service.

—Goldstein, Johnston, Duffy, and Rao[111]

Objectives

After completing this chapter, you should be able to

1. Identify key characteristics of service phenomena

2. Understand how service differs from manufacturing

3. Understand the importance of service for Western societies

4. Realize managerial implications of service organizations

The Importance of Service

Well into the second half of the 20th century, the industrial structure of Western societies was dominated by production of goods from the agriculture and manufacturing sectors. Our domestic production was dependent on steady increases in productivity, and our national resources were used for consumption or production of those goods. However, a new wave was on the horizon—a wave of intangible, value-adding tasks and interactions in unprecedented quantity. This was the rise of the service industry.

> We become just by performing just actions, temperate by performing temperate actions, brave by performing brave actions.
>
> —Aristotle

By the 1980s, it had become apparent through development of the quality movement in management that the level of service in the United States was lower than desirable. This needed to be addressed, because service was no longer the *least* important industry sector of the economy.[125] In the new economy, corporate focus began to turn toward managing these new service challenges.

In today's economy, service has become the foundation on which postindustrial societies are firmly based. The importance of the service industry in Western societies is beyond dispute because it is such a powerful vehicle of economic growth. The vast majority of our labor force works in services, through which it creates over two thirds of our gross domestic product (GDP). Organizations increasingly depend on their level of service to differentiate themselves from their competitors as they seek competitive advantage in the marketplace.

Although the importance of service is undisputed, managing these intangible assets is challenging. Services are designed to make our lives easier and to add value to our being. However, in spite of their importance, services often are major sources of frustration and disappointment to customers, because a mismatch occurs between what was promised or expected and what was actually received. When so much is at stake, why does this occur? The answer to this question lies in the intangible and elusive nature of the service phenomenon itself. The purpose of this chapter is to shed some light on the characteristics of service and to discuss why its very nature has made all of the attempts to apply traditional management and production methods—which were so useful in the era of manufacturing and mass production—problematic in a service context.

Service Defined

The characteristics of service make it difficult to define. Service has been defined in a variety of ways, ranging from broad generic definitions encompassing the entire service process to highly specific descriptions of the value created by particular services. For example, services are "economic activities that produce time, place, form, or psychological utilities. Services are acts, deeds, or performances that are intangible."[326] The following is a more descriptive definition of service:

Service includes all economic activities whose output is not a physical product or construction, is generally consumed at the time it is produced, and provides added value in forms (such as convenience, amusement, timeliness, comfort, or health) that are essentially intangible concerns of its first purchaser.[248]

Zeithaml and Bitner[326] argue for the importance of making a distinction between *services* and *customer service*. Services, as defined in the broadest of terms, include a wider rage of industries—each providing a set of services needed or wanted by their customers. Similarly, customer service is usually provided by all industries, but it is the service provided in support of an organization's core products. Customers are usually not charged directly for customer service. Typically, those working in customer service positions perform such tasks as answering phones, answering questions, dealing with billing issues, and handling service breakdowns.

It is easy to see that service has different characteristics from goods or tangible products, which are specific objects that are manufactured at one time and then sold or used later. In contrast, service is intangible and perishable. It is created and consumed simultaneously (or nearly simultaneously). This suggests that service cannot be stocked or easily demonstrated beforehand. Contrary to selling tangible goods, change of ownership does not take place as services are being bought and sold. In fact, services consist of acts and interactions that often can be described as social events.[218a]

The Art and Science of Service

Is service a science or an art? Many attempts have been made to apply science in the regulation and control of the provision of service, to standardize transactions and enhance the speed and accuracy of the process. However, the process of dealing with human beings servicing other human beings in different circumstances, different times, and different places is often extremely difficult to regulate. It is the human factor that determines that service can never be, however necessary from an operational perspective, only regarded as science.

Delivering quality service and becoming a service leader is truly an art. Service is intangible, unpredictable, and difficult to reproduce. Its delivery often depends on each individual situation, relationship, and circumstance. In addition, the customer plays an important role in the service process, both as the receiver of service and as a provider of self-service.

Driven by the trend toward self-service—for example, ATMs, online banking, ordering, and bill paying—customers have, to a great extent, become both the producers and consumers of service: They are "prosumers."[217, 218b, 306] Customers are now better informed about the choices they make and have higher expectations concerning the quality of the services being offered. As a result, organizations have had to increase their level of competition in virtually all service sectors by providing better information for their customers.

For a service organization to be truly successful, it has to anticipate expected customer needs and wants and establish appropriate responses to them. Thus successful service provision often requires patience, insight, and understanding of needs that are often based on incomplete or imperfect sets of information. Gathering, analyzing, and updating this information are other challenging tasks facing service organizations today.

Most essential information about customers' wants and needs is gathered through direct contact with customers. This can be done in face-to-face contact during a transaction or through simultaneous data collection during an electronic transaction. Even in this age of technological innovations, we are still mostly dependent on the human element to interpret, understand, and take action on the information before us. Science and technology are involved in the collection and calculation processes, but it is in the interpretation, projection, and action that *art* enters into play.

> *To command is to serve, nothing more and nothing less.*
>
> —Andre Malraux

Service Management

Because of the unique characteristics of service, managing the service process can be a daunting task. Due to the *intangibility* of service, it cannot be inventoried, patented, or readily displayed or communicated. Pricing can be difficult due to the difficulty in determining the actual costs incurred by the provider or the value of the service to the customer.

In spite of efforts to standardize services, it is obvious that it is impossible to plan or regulate every action taken in the employee-customer contact. Most services are performed by people for the consumption or use of other people—a process that can never be fully foreseen or standardized. The result is a heterogeneous set of characteristics of the interaction. Quality of service delivery and customer satisfaction depend heavily on employee actions. Service quality depends on many *often uncontrollable* factors, such as prior experiences, expectations, and, in some cases, the particular mood or psychological motivation of the individual service provider or customer. Furthermore, the way customers react, behave, or communicate can affect the employee. All of this adds to the management challenge. In fact, there is no guarantee that the service delivered will match what was planned or promoted by the organization.

The *perishable* nature of service makes it hard to manage, both from a marketing and from an operational point of view. It is difficult to synchronize supply and demand for service. Failure to do so, however, can result in overstaffed or understaffed operations. Obviously, operational efficiency is highly dependent on successful achievement of the proper balance between supply and demand. The fact that the production and consumption of services are *simultaneous* events implies that the customer is, in effect, a participant in the transaction.

From this it is apparent that service can be both difficult to define and even more difficult to manage. Hence, we choose to define service in broad practical terms, where the focus is on the key players in the service process—namely, the service organization and the customers, their intentions, and what they derive from the transaction. For the purposes of this book, we define service in terms of *intentions*, *interactions*, and *impacts*. In other words, a service organization *intends* to provide a certain set of services. The intent is usually based on the organization's corporate and service strategies and is tailored to leverage the organization's operational efficiency and fulfillment of expected customer needs. The intended services are then delivered through *interactions* with customers. The interaction can be automated, technologically assisted, or carried out through human contact. The *impact* of that interaction, however, is a result of (a) the match with the customers' expectations regarding the intended or promised services, (b) the perception and satisfaction customers experience in the interaction with the organization, and (c) the value they perceive before, during, and after the service has been delivered.

The Intention

Service organizations' intent is to provide the best possible match with customers' needs for the least amount of the organizations' resources. In a perfect world, organizations' intentions are perfectly leveraged by customers' needs and organizational goals, whatever those goals may be—for example, profit, social justice, quality, or market leadership.

A corporation must choose a market or a market segment and then carefully lay out a plan of service promises based on the following:

- Data collection and knowledge of customer needs and expectations
- Market segment analysis
- Organizational strengths and weaknesses
- Competitors' strengths and weaknesses

The promise or intention is expected to be a perfect match of organizational strengths that fit the needs of a particular market or segment efficiently and strategically. However, in the turmoil of competition and changing customer needs, service intentions can sometimes be hard to formulate and even more difficult to live up to. The result can be inefficiency in the operation and dissatisfied customers. An inefficiency can occur when an organization applies too many resources to satisfy particular wants or needs; for example, an organization may hire too many employees, or its staff may be overqualified to handle service delivery tasks. In those particular circumstances, the level of service is, in fact, too high. This is a classic case of "overkill," in which the balance in the value-to-cost relationship is off. However, this is a very thin line to walk. Research has shown a positive relationship between exceeding customer expectations and customer loyalty.[326] Thus the aim is to find the exact spot where the two lines of optimization of resources and customers' expectations cross. You want to spend only the amount you feel is justifiable to attract and retain loyal customers. There can, however, be circumstances in which an organization decides for strategic reasons to operate inefficient service units. It might do so to support its main service lines, to win a new set of customers, or to outperform and eliminate the competitors.

From the organization's point of view, the bottom line is that if service intentions are not based on the corporate strategies, the level of service and the amount of resources put into providing the service cannot be efficiently determined. For example, the service level must be coordinated with the organization's goals. The goal might be to "*simply be better,*" as stated by the pharmaceutical giant SmithKline Beecham, or to become market leader in a certain segment within 3 years. It might be to compete on prices, which requires the organization to "buy" the customers' time in some way. For example, the customers participate in the process through self-service, or they will accept lower service levels because customers in that particular market segment are not ready to pay for something they either believe they can do themselves or they know will save them money.

Whatever the goal, the organization must tailor the promise made to the customer. Organizational resources have to be put in place or taken out of the existing process for the organization to achieve its objectives and simultaneously meet the needs and expectations of its customer base. In other words, the organization must match resources, such as people, technologies, and facilities, with optimal outcome or return on that investment. From the customers' point of view, if the resources are not sufficient to meet their expectations, the customers will ultimately be dissatisfied or disappointed by what they perceive as the organization's *broken promise.*

The implications of good or poor service management are apparent. The characteristics of service, such as its perishability and the simultaneous production and consumption of service, make an even stronger case for a timely and flexible strategy on which managers can base their decisions about efficient distribution of resources. There are in fact three key elements. An organization must know (a) what its customers want, (b) what it has to offer, and (c) what it needs to *efficiently and profitably* meet the customers' needs. The importance and different methods of formulating a service strategy are discussed in Chapter 3.

The Interaction

Every service encounter involves an interaction between the organization and its customers. The contact may be through humans or through technology, or it may simply be interactions with tangible objects within the organization's facilities, regardless of whether the contact is through what is usually referred to as the *front line* or through what can be called the *second front line* or *metallic* or *electronic front line* (Figure 2.1).

The line of human contact with the customer has in some cases been moved backward, out of sight of the customer. The second front line may be composed of some form of automation, self-service, or new technology applications. The second front line is then serviced by the personnel responsible for technology, maintenance, service design, and the appearance of tangible items at the place of customer contact.

Online Service Interactions

There is no doubt that the Web is transforming all facets of business, and the impact on customer service has been significant. Many customers deal with a company's metallic or electronic front line—and online business is exactly that

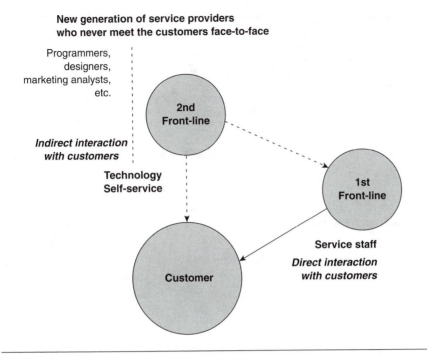

**New generation of service providers
who never meet the customers face-to-face**

Programmers,
designers,
marketing analysts,
etc.

**2nd
Front-line**

*Indirect interaction
with customers*

**Technology
Self-service**

**1st
Front-line**

Customer

Service staff

*Direct interaction
with customers*

Figure 2.1   The Second Front Line

for many companies. For some, such as amazon.com, the Internet is the only way they conduct business. For other companies, such as Land's End, online shopping is simply an additional way for customers to purchase products. Pure service organizations, such as banks, provide electronic services to their customers. Because of the ever-increasing revenues generated by online services, it is essential that companies using this avenue get it right. When they do not, they risk losing a major source of income.

Hewson, Meekings, and Russell[144] reported the results of a major research project, using a research base of more than 10,000 "eMysteryShopper" surveys, more than 500,000 consumer opinion surveys, quotations, and findings from a global panel of 1750 Internet users and 3.7 million customer service requests made to more than 200 U.S. businesses. Their conclusion is that "there is now compelling, indisputable evidence that improving the end-to-end user experience is hard-wired to bottom line results."

For example, according to their results, 28% of people who want to buy something online or use an online service find the process too difficult or too time-consuming. This means those customers or potential customers are frustrated—and their frustration connects directly to the company. This translates into lost revenues, not just for one particular sale but for each frustrated customer. The company with poor online service is guaranteed to lose its competitive edge to those companies who invest in the process of making their services carefully designed, well organized, and smoothly delivered.

Hewson et al.[144] conclude that their research has identified key opportunities by which managers can become heroes through advocating the following improvements to end-to-end user experience:

1. Making self-service as good as it can be

2. Actively striving to eliminate unwanted calls and e-mails into the contact center

3. Designing the contact center to deliver value rather than just being an expensive resource to compensate for poor Web site design

These improvements can directly affect a company's bottom line by increasing sales and satisfaction by about 11% and dramatically reduce the costs of Web support, typically by as much as 70%. It is interesting that Hewson et al.[144] found these results consistent across business sectors. They identified some clear, best-practice guidelines for integrating self-service into the overall site design summarized generally above. For example, the German airline Lufthansa, by making some of these suggested improvements, reported that their e-mail volume was reduced by 75%; self-service user numbers increased by 500%. This allowed Lufthansa to improve its e-mail response time to less than 24 hours. As another example, Belgacom Skynet reduced total operational costs by 30%, and its customer satisfaction increased by 18%.[144]

How do companies achieve high levels of customer satisfaction through online service delivery? Amazon.com, the world's largest online retailer, has clearly discovered the way to do this. In 1995, it first began to sell only books entirely online; now, it offers a wide variety of products and its sales of electronics outperform its book sales. Throughout its expansion, Jeff Bezos, its founder, continually emphasized amazon.com's "Six Core Values: customer obsession, ownership, bias for action, frugality, high hiring bar and innovation."[164] Note that obsession with customers is the number one core value. In addition to having customer satisfaction as its number one goal, the company also clearly recognizes the value of having employees who know how to deliver on that goal.

In contrast to amazon.com, other companies allow their customers to use their Web sites to supplement store and catalog sales. Land's End is a good example of a retailer that has long had solid catalog sales as its primary income producer. When it added online ordering capabilities, its customers were able to move seamlessly between shopping online or from the latest catalog using phone, fax, or regular mail. This kind of choice helps guarantee customer satisfaction if the delivery process is well strategized and effectively implemented. Land's End does this well.[144]

Through automation and self-service, organizations have managed to involve the customer physically in the process itself whenever appropriate, using *customer labor* or input in many cases in return for faster service or lower prices. The customer *sells* his or her spare time to obtain a desired outcome of the transaction. In many service sectors, such as banking and retail sales, this trend, together with technological advances, has increasingly been replacing the human contact between service employees and their customers. However, that is not to say that service organizations' dependence on their human capital is diminishing, as is sometimes thought. Quite the contrary. Where the needs and wants of the customers call for self-service capability or automation of the transaction, an application of the human element in the service process changes. The frontline employees move backward from the first point of entry of the customers, who now serve themselves or are served by new technology applications. Under these conditions, the efforts of the staff become focused on coming up with new and improved ways of providing the service. Direct personal contact with customers, where the aim of the service provider is to fulfill the needs of a particular customer, transitions into efforts to find innovative solutions to how the organization can better foresee and meet all customers' needs. This transition from the front line to the *second front line* does not diminish the reliance on human capital. In fact, it escalates the need for more advanced intellectual capital in the service industry. For example, employees now would need to focus on the design of more user-friendly technology, more accessible user interfaces, or better access to the point of transaction, in addition to looking for ways to improve the variety and quality of services being offered. The result is even greater dependence on human capital to achieve competitive advantage, even though the first front line has in fact been replaced by machinery or self-service. The *metallic* or *electronic* front line still depends on the brainpower and insights of those behind the scenes.

The location of the human front line is thus simply a matter of how, when, and where you serve customers. One thing is clear: Service must be tailored to the needs of the customer. Ideally, the organization is able to predict customer wants and needs and then design the services accordingly.

The humanization of service is necessary in spite of technology and the changing ways of the world. There is now a need for a new breed of service provider, because where and how people apply their skills and ability to provide service is definitely changing. However, in spite of the rise of the "prosumer" and parts of the service process being technologically automated, services will still be designed and produced for people by people.

Both customers and employees have their own agenda. It is not the same agenda, but both are centered on need fulfillment. The employee's aim is to satisfy customers' needs to create repeat business, thus strengthening the organization and protecting jobs. Every customer is an individual with his or her own set of expectations, experiences, and needs. In most cases, the customer is not likely to care much or even think about the success or future of the service provider, only about fulfilling a particular and immediate need. The customer may have chosen the service provider casually or even randomly, or the choice could have been made after careful consideration of when, where, and by whom the customer's needs could best be met. An interaction is inevitable, both to provide and to receive the service. In most cases, the customer expects the service to be within a certain range of acceptability, based either on his or her image of the service or on previous experiences. Research has shown that the interaction has a strong impact on customer satisfaction and even more on employees' perception of important service dimensions, such as empathy and how personal they feel the service is.[117, 118]

Service success depends on how well the customers' needs were met and the manner in which the perceived promise was met and delivered. The perception and satisfaction of the interaction has a tremendous impact on a customer's decision to do repeat business with the organization. Due to the unpredictability and variance of each interaction, only a part of the process can be successfully standardized to minimize the heterogeneous nature of the service process. Therefore, a heavy responsibility is placed on the organization's point of contact—the person, the technology, or the facilities with which the customer interacts. The responsibility ultimately lies with the human element of service, the people at the front line and, in fact, the people in the second front line, who are just as important. Normann[218] believes that the positive or negative performance by the employee or employees involved may have a tremendous and immediate impact on how individual customers will perceive the quality of what they have been given. There are relatively few ways of covering up lack of enthusiasm or the absence of a decent performance on the part of the service provider. The effect and the feedback are immediate and striking. Furthermore, research has shown an important link between customer satisfaction and customer loyalty.[326] Therefore, it is apparent that how the interaction is planned and carried out has an enormous impact on organizational success.

The Impact

The interaction between an organization and its customers has an impact not only on the organization's success but on the customer as well. From an organizational point of view, the impact is activated through the customer satisfaction associated with the interaction and perceptions of the fulfillment of the service promise (intention).

Arguments for the importance of customer satisfaction are overwhelming. For example, work sponsored by the Marketing Science Institute[261] suggests that corporate strategies focused on customer satisfaction, revenue generation, and service quality are in fact more profitable than strategies focused on cost cutting or strategies that attempt to do both. Today, profitability and growth come mostly from skillful management of intangible customer relationships—intangible assets that are not reflected in the accountant's balance sheet.[218]

Evidence suggests that higher customer satisfaction should increase customer loyalty, insulate a company's current market share from competitors, lower transaction costs, reduce failure costs and thus the cost of attracting new customers, and help build a firm's reputation in the marketplace.[7] Extensive research efforts, both in Europe and in the United States, have shown strong links between customer satisfaction and customer value,[141] profits,[8] and shareholder value.[100]

Customer Satisfaction Index

Measures of customer satisfaction on a national level have been conducted in the United States since 1994, in Sweden since 1989, and in Germany since 1992. Currently, efforts are under way to further develop a European customer satisfaction index.

Such measures monitor service organizations' most fundamental asset—their customers. The American Customer Satisfaction Index (ACSI) was started in 1994 and has grown to a comprehensive national study, administered on a quarterly basis. It includes a large number of industries, as well as numerous public sector activities. The ACSI (shown in Figure 2.2) is in fact a market-based measure for organizations, industries, economic sectors, and national economies (examine their Web site at http://www.theacsi.com/overview.htm).

Measures of customer satisfaction represent a cumulative evaluation of market offerings rather than a person's evaluation of a specific transaction. "Although transaction-specific satisfaction measures may provide specific diagnostic information about a particular product or service encounter, overall customer satisfaction is a more fundamental indicator of the firm's past, current, and future performance."[7] The arguments of more consistent measures of customer satisfaction suggest that conventional quality measures of economic performance, such as productivity, probably tell us less than they used to do. Fornell, Johnson, Anderson, Cha, and Bryant,[98] the founders of the ACSI, state that in the new economy, producing more—however efficiently it may be done—is not necessarily better. More important, they stress that we must measure the *quality* as well as the *quantity* of economic output.

According to ACSI data, customers are generally more satisfied with the goods they buy than with the services they receive.[125] The Customer Satisfaction Indexes are reported on a scale from 0 to 100, where 0 means the lowest possible

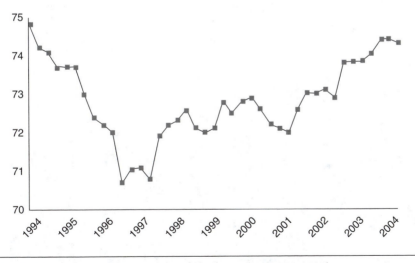

Figure 2.2   American Customer Satisfaction Index (1994–2004)

SOURCE: American Customer Satisfaction Index Web site (http://www.theacsi.com/).

NOTE: The American Customer Satisfaction Index (ACSI) is the national index of satisfaction with quality. It is compiled by measuring customer satisfaction with a representative 38 industries in nine sectors of the economy and is updated on a rolling basis, with new data for one or two sectors each quarter replacing data collected in the previous year. This graph shows ACSI numbers for 1994 through the third quarter of 2004.

level of satisfaction and 100 the highest possible. As a rule, a difference between two observations of two or more percentage points is statistically significant.

The results in America have increased from about 71% to 74% since 1996. This is higher than in most European countries. The Customer Satisfaction Index (CSI) is a study conducted in nine European countries (Denmark, Finland, Greece, Iceland, Ireland, Norway, Portugal, Russia, and Sweden). The study has been conducted annually since 1999. Only the top five European countries— Finland, Ireland, Iceland, Greece, and Portugal—stand up to the United States' improvement level. The lowest three are Denmark, Sweden, and Russia, as shown in Figure 2.3.

Although customer satisfaction may vary between national cultures, the more important factor is how the service organizations themselves measure up over time. It is absolutely crucial for organizations to measure their own customer satisfaction levels and trends, because the decline of overall customer satisfaction usually indicates that a company has deeper problems.[98] A study in the retail industry on customer satisfaction and sales volume[6] suggested a lag time of 6 months between declining customer satisfaction and buying behavior. In other words, on average, customers began to change their buying behavior 6 months after a decline in customer service was first detected in customer satisfaction measures. This suggests that regular service measures can serve as an important defense mechanism that can flag potential internal problems and give advance notice that allows the organization to take appropriate corrective actions in time. Furthermore, customer satisfaction measures have been associated with increased return on investment (ROI) in terms of market value (see the Swedish CSI). Ittner and Larcker[161] estimate that in terms of market value, a one-unit change in ACSI is associated with a

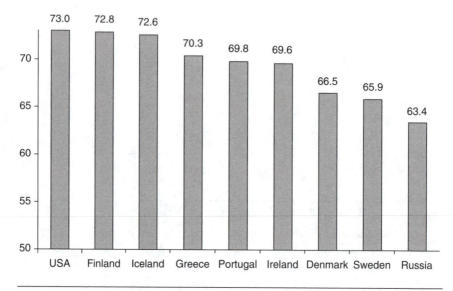

Figure 2.3   Customer Satisfaction Indexes for the United States and Europe

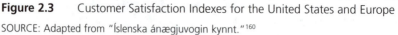

SOURCE: Adapted from "Íslenska ánægjuvogin kynnt."[160]

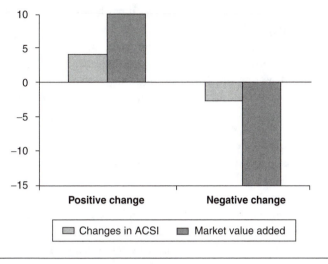

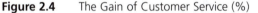

Figure 2.4   The Gain of Customer Service (%)

SOURCE: American Customer Satisfaction Index Web site (http://www.theacsi.com/).

$654 million increase in the market value of equity, above and beyond the accounting-book value of assets and liabilities.

Studies have shown a correlation between scores in the satisfaction indexes and overall performance of service organizations. A Swedish study[91] divided participating organizations into two groups. One group contained organizations whose scores had declined, and the other group contained those whose scores had increased. In group one, customer satisfaction had risen an average of 4.2%, but in group two it had declined about 3%. Market Value Added (MVA) was, on average, 10% in the first group but –15% in the second group. This relationship between satisfaction and operational performance is shown in Figure 2.4. Notice that, with the same amount of change in customer satisfaction (according to the ACSI), the market value added is dramatically different. With about a 3% increase in customer satisfaction, the market value added jumps about 10%. However, when customer satisfaction drops by about 3%, the negative influence on market value is about 15%, a significantly greater loss for the company.

Why does customer satisfaction have a tendency to decline in spite of its apparent importance for organizational profitability and overall success? Various theories have emerged. Zeithaml and Bitner[326] suggest the following possible explanations:

- Organizations' emphasis on calculated profitability results in customers getting less service than they received in the past.
- Increased use of self-service and technology-based services can be perceived as less service because of the lack of human interaction.
- Failures have been frequent in implementation of new technology-based services.
- More intense competition usually results in higher customer expectations.
- Cost cutting, in some cases, has gone too far, and as a result, some service organizations have become too lean and understaffed.

- Competition in the labor market makes it harder to find qualified employees for frontline service jobs.
- There is a lack of commitment to training and other human resources (HR) practices that are crucial to success. Frontline staff are often not carefully selected and are untrained, overworked, and underpaid.
- A gap between promise and performance appears too frequently. Organizations cannot or do not deliver what they say they will.

Why, then, does anyone buy services? In general, we buy a service that in some way has a positive impact on our lives. It can be because the service saves us time or money. It can be a matter of convenience, or the purchase may allow us to do more fun or fruitful things with our time. The service can make us physically feel better about ourselves, our health, or the way we look. Research suggests that (a) customization of services is now becoming more important than reliability in determining customer satisfaction, (b) customer expectations play a greater role in sectors in which there is a low variance in production and consumption, and (c) customer satisfaction is more quality driven than value or price driven.[98] Whatever the reason or need underlying the service purchase, one thing is apparent—a customer's satisfaction with the interaction and how well the organization succeeds in positively affecting that customer's life has an important impact on overall organizational success. Much rides on the *intention* to serve and the *interactions* needed to deliver on the promise: first, the customer's understanding of that promise (customer satisfaction), and second, the alignment between the organizational strategy and the amount of resources put in place to carry the *intention* forward (efficiency).

The Macro Impact of Service

As discussed in the beginning of the chapter, our economy is constantly changing, and services now account for about two thirds of Organization for Economic Cooperation and Development (OECD) economies.[239] A change this large has significant impacts.

Employment. The impact of the service sector on the United States economy is great. Now the majority of the workforce is employed in the service sector, and the U.S. economy is often referred to as a service economy. "Almost all of the absolute growth in number of jobs and the fastest growth rates in job formation are in service industries."[326a] This is, however, a fairly new development. In the 1930s, roughly half of the working population was employed in the service industry. In 1956, white-collar workers outnumbered blue-collar workers for the first time in American history,[217] but by the year 2000, roughly 7 of every 10 working men and women in the United States held service-related jobs, and this number is now approaching 80%.[326b]

Gross Domestic Product. The Statistical Yearbook of the Economic Commission for Europe 2003[309] shows the enormous impact service has on national economies in Western societies. Figure 2.5 shows that, on average, service accounts for 63% to 72% of the national GDP in Western and Northern Europe, compared with 67% in Canada and 75% in the United States. This is an enormous change from the early

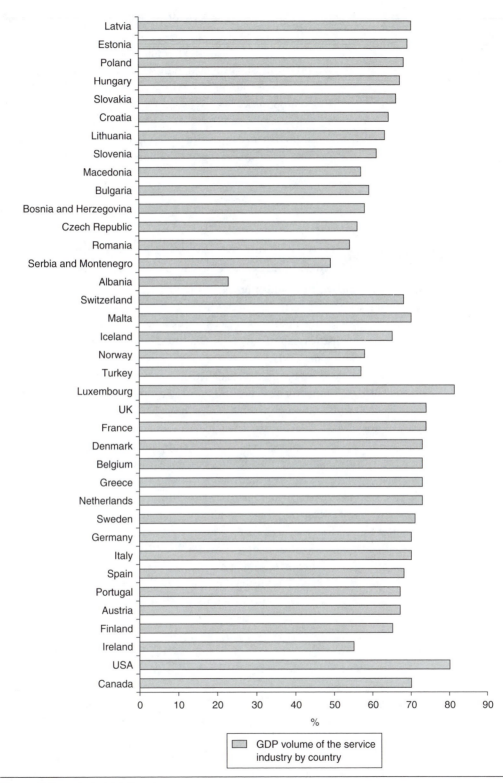

Figure 2.5   Industrial Structures

SOURCE: United Nations Economic Commission for Europe.[309]

> One must learn by doing the thing; though you think you know it, you have no certainty until you try.
>
> —Sophocles

1950s, when only 54% of the U.S. gross national product (GNP, the term used at that time) was generated by service.

The highest reported volume of service in the GDP of the countries exhibited in the table is in Luxembourg (81%). The contribution of service is lower in Central and Eastern European societies (47%-65%).

International Trade. The importance of service in the global economy is also changing. The U.S. trade surplus from services was $81 billion in the year 2000, when the overall balance showed a deficit.[18]

Managerial Implications in Service Organizations

Research has shown time and time again the positive relationship between customer satisfaction and customer loyalty. The good news is that if an organization manages to provide the desired services, the customers will probably reward that organization with their repeat visits and loyalty. The bad news is that it is not enough just to provide satisfactory service to obtain loyalty. Loyalty is a result of a *superior* satisfaction (see Figure 2.6). Satisfied customers are just as likely to wander off and fall for a competitor's offers as they are to be loyal to the company they were just satisfied with. Although nothing may have been wrong with the service received, they simply were not satisfied *enough* to be committed to one organization. Later, the customers may return to the company they were satisfied with if they experience dissatisfaction with the one they went to. However, in the meantime, the organization has lost the revenues it otherwise could have earned if the customer had been satisfied enough to become or remain loyal.

Deciding what level of service to offer to gain customer loyalty is a major challenge for service managers. As noted earlier, the characteristics of service and changing customer needs and desires make it difficult for companies to meet customers' expectations and ensure operational efficiency.

Operational efficiency calls for standardization of the service processes. However, the market is moving toward personalization. An organization that can provide personal service that is perfectly suited to customers' needs and, at the same time, manages to efficiently maximize its use of resources will win the service game. However, the need for standardization and the need for personalization are at opposite ends of a continuum and, are in fact contradictory, thereby creating yet another management challenge.

Another challenge is the image problem of the service industry. Some have claimed that service organizations lack the status associated with manufacturing and that these image-generating factors tend to reflect on the whole industry—a sort of "anti-halo effect"[218c] in which all service jobs are seen as low level and poorly paid, and frontline service providers are often poorly selected and get limited training before they enter the trenches. Employees for the second front line

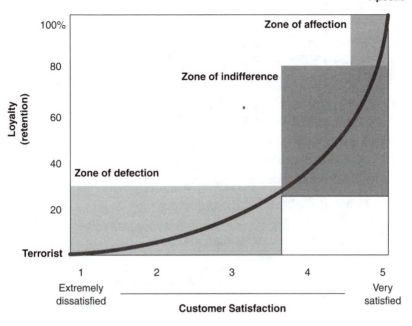

Figure 2.6   Loyalty and Service Perception

SOURCE: From Heskett, Jones, Loveman, Sasser, & Schlessinger, Putting the service profit chain to work, in *Harvard Business Review*, March-April, 2004, reprinted with permission of Harvard Business School Publishing Corporation. All rights reserved.

are usually selected for their task capacity or particular expertise or education, not because they are good service providers. This creates conflict and role ambiguity, which ultimately results in the service not being as good as it could be.

The misperception is that service providers in general are not very dynamic or productive and that they are poorly paid. Furthermore, it is felt that most service jobs offer little potential for growth or advancement. Recent data has shown, however, that the service industry has been highly innovative and has also experienced rapid productivity growth in the last decade. Studies have shown that some service sectors are even more innovative than manufacturing. As just one example, in 1997, 55% of all firms in knowledge-intensive services in France showed evidence of innovation, compared with 45% in manufacturing firms.[239] Figure 2.7 gives an overview of innovation in the service industry compared with manufacturing for some European and Scandinavian countries.

In addition, there are fast-growing services that can be characterized as the *new service industry.* Here, the services are in areas of scarce expertise and knowledge, performed by individuals with a high level of education, and are considered anything but low status. Few industries exhibit such a wide range of employee status. This makes the service industry one of the most challenging to manage from both an operational and a human resources perspective.[218d]

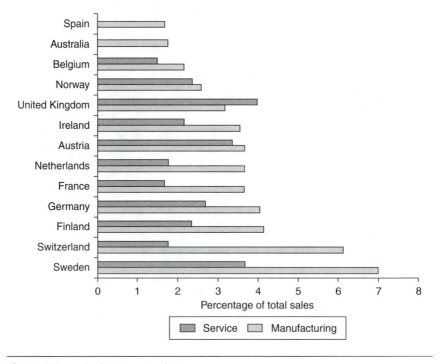

Figure 2.7   Business Innovations

SOURCE: *Business expenditure on innovation as percentage of total sales, 1996* (partly based on data from Eurostat), table from: Pilat D. (2000), "No longer services as usual," *The OECD Observer,* N°223, OECD, Paris, p. 52.

NOTE: Business expenditure on innovation as a percentage of total sales, 1996 (partly based on data from Eurostat).

The major managerial challenge is to maximize resources. To do so, a manager needs to be able to predict what customers need and where and when they will need it, as well as foreseeing possible changes in their behavior. On top of that, the manager also needs to leverage the human resources at his or her disposal. This means that the right number of people are working at the right time at each location; are properly trained; are skilled and knowledgeable; and show the right attitude to do the job at the "moment of truth"—when facing the customer. Sound easy? Far from it! With the increase in customers' choices and changing needs, this leveraging act is only going to become more important and more challenging for overall organizational success.

The world is too complex for one manager to be able to hear, see, and know everything. It is virtually impossible for a manager to prescribe when and how to act in every given situation. That is why service organizations need to rely on employee participation, imagination, and skill if they are to provide their services better, faster, and cheaper than the competitors do. The frontline employees are constantly interacting with customers, so they hear and see what is going on "out there." Individually, they can perform at the "moment of truth," but their scope can be narrow and, often, focused on their particular task, workplace, or customer. Collectively, they can see the full view and should be expected and allowed to provide feedback, which can be very useful for both strategic and tactical decision making. The following facts are becoming more and more obvious:

- The world has become too complex for one person to be able to know everything.
- Speed has become so important that the traditional communication and decision-making processes are often inadequate.

Employee roles have changed from "doing what I am told by the manager" to "*doing what I am told by the customer*." Now, employees are expected to actively listen, watch, and act on the judgment they make from the service interaction. *Managerial roles* have changed as a result of this. Instead of controlling and taking disciplinary actions, managers now use role modeling, motivation, inspiration, and team-building activities. In fact, greater emphasis has been placed on developing the leadership behaviors of managers over the last few years not only in the service industry, but across other industries as well. What would happen if everyone in the organization engaged in *acts of leadership* and shared a common interest in protecting and preserving the organization? What would be the cumulative effect of a collective leadership effort on the part of every organizational member serving on both the front and second front lines?

The role of each employee in such settings is to do everything in his or her power to ensure the appropriate service level in line with and governed by the organizational vision, mission, and goals. The manager's role is to communicate the shared vision and cultivate the conditions necessary for every individual to be able to make decisions that will be in the best interests of both the customer and the organization. The job of management now requires skills and abilities that are quite different from those we have seen in the past

> I like the dreams of the future better than the history of the past.
> —Thomas Jefferson

(discussed in Chapter 3), and all of the jobs throughout the organization require that a collective leadership mind-set be established (discussed in Chapter 4).

The Future of Service

The need for speed and quality in Western societies and maximization of resources has created a platform for the *science of service*. Various ways of process engineering, technology applications, and need identification techniques, to give only a few examples, have enhanced the ability of managers to anticipate and prepare for meeting customer needs in an efficient manner. Such techniques make it possible for organizations to better use their resources and streamline their operations in accordance with their customers' buying behaviors. They are also increasingly playing a role in the interaction of customers with the organization as a result of more self-service application and electronic service options. However, as long as services are designed *by* people *for* people, the *art of service* will never be fully replaced by machinery; in other words, the process will never be completely standardized. In fact, recent evidence suggests that customer satisfaction is now increasingly related to customization of the service.[98] Where the employees are stationed and how they provide their services may change in some service sectors, but the interpretation of the data and the insight needed to interact with the customer quickly and properly in this complex and often unpredictable process is embedded in people (discussed in Chapter 11).

With the creation of the second front line, we are seeing an increased need for "service-minded" people with a broad range of expertise and skills. The engineer whose responsibility is to design a customer interface needs to think, breathe, and feel like the potential customer and regard it as his or her job not only to know the technical aspects of the task but to regard his or her technical skills, education, and know-how as a means to meeting customers' needs. This trend is already beginning with a higher demand for technical people who speak the "language of business"; for example, surgeons and teachers often recognize their patients and students as customers with certain needs and expectations. Service has become an inseparable part of almost any task. Normann[218e] puts it well when he says:

> What we see today is a gigantic reshuffling of activities between different types of units in society, creating a new specialization pattern in which one type of specialization may create opportunities for other units to in fact desterilize and perform a broader range of activities than in the past.

Can service be improved indefinitely? Will customers' needs change continuously? These are compelling questions. Without a doubt, the evolution of service and its importance will continue to grow hand in hand with its increasing impact on our lives and organizations. There is a parallel here with the earlier shift from agriculture to manufacturing, which was associated with an increased productivity in agriculture that left people free to do other things. The trend seems clear, but figures can be deceptive. It has been argued that the rise of the service sector has become possible largely as a result of increasing effectiveness in the goods-production sector. Therefore, it is also argued that we cannot afford an increase in the service sector, unless productivity in the manufacturing sector continues to grow.[218f] One may agree or disagree with that statement; however, the need for effective strategies in service organizations is greater than ever before.

Competition raises customers' expectations and demands more of service organizations. Today, companies have less time to plan and act. They need all of their resources to stay on top and cannot afford to waste money in the process. At the same time, innovative ways are needed to formulate successful service strategies. The same pressures that are placing new demands on strategic management in service organizations are forcing them to rethink their processes and their use of human resources (see Chapter 3). Stanley M. Davis, in his book *Future Perfect*,[82] states:

> Present-day goods and services are designed in such a way that the individual can save time, become more and more independent of location restrictions, squeeze more accumulated knowledge into every time-location unit, and be better able to use his own knowledge and resources for things he could not do before.

This future vision not only places demands on the service industry but also provides exciting opportunities. Without a doubt, services will continue to affect our lives—both professionally and personally—as never before. Hence, if a service organization wants to create and deliver added value for its customers in an efficient, effective, and timely manner, it needs to (a) formulate its intentions in tune with evolving customer demands (the service promise), (b) strategize about the most effective way to incorporate automation and self-service to the extent possible (the service process), and (c) continue to rely on the quality of its human capital (the service provider).

> *We have met the enemy, and he is us.*
>
> —Walt Kelly

Summary

The importance of the service sector for Western societies and the reliance we as individuals place on access to and consumption of services has become a fact of life in today's service-driven economies. Services account for 60% to 70% of OECD's economies, where the greatest absolute growth in number of jobs and the fastest growth rates in job formation are in service industries. In the United States, up to 80% of the working population is employed in the service sector.

In spite of its importance, the service industry remains an elusive and under-researched phenomenon. We do not fully understand how it works, what drives productivity in this industry, or, indeed, even how it is defined. What remains undisputed is that the service process, in most cases, involves a combination of tangible and intangible components. Service is difficult to manage due to its intangibility, variability, and heterogeneity. In addition, the fact that it is produced at the same time that it is delivered or consumed makes it even more challenging.

Service is, for the purposes of this book, defined in terms of *intent, interactions,* and *impacts.* It applies to both actors in the service process—the customer and the service organization. Both have certain intentions that are not necessarily the same. However, their common interest is to fulfill or satisfy the needs of the customer through their mutual interaction. Through that process, the impact of the interaction depends on how successfully the interaction took place. The impact of a successful interaction for the organization is a satisfied customer who is likely to return and repeat his or her purchase. That in turn affects the overall performance of the organization, its profits, and shareholder value. The impact on customers is that the service makes their lives easier in some respect. It may save time or money, it may allow customers more free time to do something they value more, or it may make them feel better about themselves.

No matter what need the service is supposed to fill, the organization needs to be vigilant regarding the timing and appropriateness of its service strategy and the impact of this strategy on resource allocation. The current and future success of the organization may very well depend on the match of a particular promise with customers' expectations and the delivery of that promise through the customer interaction.

The U.S. Army on Leadership

Eric K. Shinseki, a general in the United States Army and its chief of staff, states:

We call on our leaders to translate character and competence into leader actions. Army leaders influence people—by providing purpose, direction, and motivation—while operating to accomplish the mission and improving the organization. Leaders inspire others toward uncommon goals and never lose sight of the future even as they labor tirelessly for the demands of today. That is what we expect our leaders to do. The Army's foundation is confident and competent leaders of character.

The *U.S. Army Leadership Field Manual* is a single-source reference for all Army leaders. Its purpose is threefold:

- To provide leadership doctrine for meeting mission requirements under all conditions
- To establish a unified leadership theory for all Army leaders: military and civilian, active and reserve, officer and enlisted
- To provide a comprehensive and adaptable leadership resource for the Army of the 21st century

On the first page of the first chapter, the manual states: "Leadership starts at the top, with the character of the leader, with your character. In order to lead others, you must first make sure your own house is in order." The Army leadership framework contains three categories on what a leader must be able to *be, do,* and *know.* This definition not only applies to officers of various ranks but also to all subordinates. According to the *Army Leadership Field Manual,* everyone is a part of the team, and part of being a good subordinate is being a good leader.

What Leaders of All Sizes and Shapes Must Have

Who a leader must *be,* according to the *U.S. Army Leadership Field Manual,* is a person who lives according to certain values and allows them to shape his or her character. To achieve excellence, a person must be *loyal,* have a sense of *duty,* show *respect* for him- or herself and others, and have *honor, integrity,* and *courage.* This set of values is essential to any organization. It can create a driving force like no other if truly lived by and implemented throughout the organization. Furthermore, a leader must have certain mental, physical, and emotional attributes to achieve excellence. The combination of these values and attributes is the essence of how to be a leader. In addition, every leader needs knowledge, ranging from technical skills to people skills, to effectively do his or her job. Most important, these attributes and skills must be translated into action if the leader is to effectively have an impact on other people and bring about change. It is through the action of *influencing* (which includes communication, decision making, and motivation), *operating* (planning, executing, assessing), and *improving* (developing, building, learning) that a leader truly achieves excellence.

Key Points

- You must have your own house in order if you are to effectively lead others.
- Leaders must. have loyalty, a sense of duty, respect, honor, integrity, and courage.
- Leaders must live by their values at all times.
- True excellence is achieved through influencing and improving yourself and others.

SOURCE: Center for Army Leadership, Department of the Army.[60]

Key Concepts

Directions: The following are key concepts presented in this chapter. Write a complete definition for each one.

Service

Service management

Second front line

Customer satisfaction index

Questions

1. Think of one business that specializes in service and one that delivers customer service along with its main product. Use these two to explain Ziethaml and Bitner's concept of difference between service and customer service. Do you think this is an important distinction?

2. Briefly define the three key elements embedded in the definition of service. Using your own company or a local company as an example, describe how each element is implemented.

3. Does the increasing use of a metallic or electronic front line decrease the need for human capital to achieve customer satisfaction? Why or why not?

4. The service industry has employees at quite a variety of educational and skill levels. Briefly describe service jobs that require low, medium, and high levels of specialized education. What effect does this diversity have on quality of service delivery?

5. There are a number of reasons for the decline of customer satisfaction. Eight are listed in this chapter. Select three of these reasons, then choose one company in your area to illustrate each of your choices. Explain why you think each may have let to declining customer satisfaction.

6. What are several tangible results of customer satisfaction on the organization?

7. Why is it so crucial for companies to use their own customer service measures in addition to following the ACSI data?

8. What do statistics show about the role of service in the United States as compared with the global market?

9. In trying to optimize service levels, some organizations consider standardizing service to reduce costs as well as personalizing service to increase customer satisfaction. Why is this a contradiction? How should an organization decide to resolve it?

10. How has the role of the employee changed in helping the organization decide on the kinds and quality of services to be delivered?

Advanced Activity

Go to the library or search the Web and find examples of newspaper or magazine advertisements for service from the last 20 years. Bring examples to class and discuss how service has been presented over the years. Analyze the commonalities you notice as well as how images of service have changed over the years. Summarize your findings and be prepared to present them to the class.

Search the Web

Find data on the service industry in your state or your country.

   a. How many people now earn their living in the service industry?
   b. How much has service grown in the past 20 years?
   c. What are the most important service industries in your state or country? Has this shifted over the 20-year period?
   d. Write a brief report summarizing your findings.

Suggested Readings

Heskett, J. L., Jones, T. O., Loveman, G. W., Sasser, L. W., Jr., & Schlesinger, L. A. (1994, March-April). Putting the service-profit chain to work. *Harvard Business Review, 72,* 164–174.

Hewson, W., Meekings, A., & Russell, C. (2003). *Beyond philanthropy: How improved service contributes to efficiency and profitability.* Retrieved June 13, 2005, from http://64.233.179.104/search?q=cache:qqQahoXYhgMJ:webdesign.ittoolbox.com/browse.asp%3Fc%3DWD PeerPublishing%26r%3D%252Fpub%252FSF070903.pdf+%2Bhewson+%2 Bmeekings+%2B%22beyond+philanthropy%22&hl=en

Leading the Service Wave

If you want to build a ship, don't herd people together to collect wood and don't assign them tasks and work, but rather teach them to long for the endless immensity of the sea.

—Antoine de Saint-Exupery

Objectives

After completing this chapter, you should be able to

1. Understand the role of leadership in service

2. Identify characteristics of leadership behaviors

3. Understand why organizations often fail to involve and empower employees

4. Realize the importance of collective leadership for organizational success

5. Understand the changing role of management in service

Leadership

Changes in our daily lives and corporate environments force organizations to reexamine their strategy toward their markets, their employees, and their customers. Globalization, advanced technology, and communication compel all organizations to acquire a competitive advantage by placing an emphasis on a factor that is not as easy to duplicate as price or technology—namely, the quality of service they give their customers. Furthermore, increased competition has called attention to the growing importance of employee initiative, innovation, flexibility, and productivity as a response to pressures to adapt to external changes in the corporate environment. If organizations are expected to successfully plan and carry out continuous cycles of change to survive in today's service-driven economy, then the importance of *leadership in service* arises.

> *Your future depends on many things, but mostly on you.*
> —Frank Tyger

The purpose of this chapter is to examine an application of the concept of leadership in a service context. The question is, can a changed view of the role and mind-set of employees and managers aid service organizations in the difficult task of leading the service wave?

Leadership is a dynamic and evolving phenomenon. History has shown that leadership and our view of it has changed over time, depending on the time, place, actors, and conditions; therefore, the concept of leadership needs to be continuously reexamined. To put it into perspective, we take a brief overview of leadership theory and highlight various definitions of the concept. Next, we discuss the characteristics of leadership and then turn the focus away from the traditional discussion of a single "great leader" toward a new look at the power derived from a collective leadership mind-set that includes all organizational members.

The concept of leadership does not have a single definition, despite a continued interest in military and organizational leadership and a growing number of studies on the topic. Although the word *leadership* first appeared in the English language in the first half of the 19th century in writings about the British parliament, the word *leader* had appeared much earlier, around the year 1300.[28] Leadership principles and themes can also be found in such diverse ancient texts as Egyptian hieroglyphics (2300 BC), the writings of 6th-century Chinese philosophers, the Bible, and the Icelandic sagas of Viking heroes and villains.[246]

In Greek political thought, each citizen was a potential leader and each had an equal right to have his voice heard. Over the centuries, early definitions of leadership drifted away from the romantic ideas of the Greeks into more authoritarian definitions of "great man" theories. The emphasis was on control and centralization of power. Although the concept of leadership has been around since the earliest days of our existence, a systematic study of the concept did not begin until the 1930s. Traditionally, leadership theories have been based on the notion that leadership involves one leader and a group of followers and that dominance, motivation, and influence are the primary tools of leadership. Leadership has typically been associated with certain traits, qualities, and behaviors of the person we label a *leader*.[12, 151a]

Around the middle of the 20th century, definitions of leadership had become increasingly understood as an influencing process toward achievement of shared, group-related goals. It has become increasingly difficult to separate who leaders are from what they do,[205] and the focus has been shifting away from the person to the process of leadership, involving entire organizations in the act of leadership.

Today, in the early 21st century, leadership is closely associated with people's ability to shape their own future and to cope with the changes that are part of it.[276] In recent years, the term *leadership* has been more broadly defined, so that it no longer applies solely to a single manager's ability to lead. Now it applies as well to the whole organization and its ability to develop a *leadership mind-set* for all the members of the organization.[72]

Over the last eight decades, several trends have emerged in the leadership literature. The first systematic research on the topic examined the individual characteristics that universally differentiated leaders from nonleaders. Researchers tried to identify the attributes of great leaders under the assumption that leadership could be explained by the internal qualities with which a person is born.[38] They examined hundreds of psychological, physical, and personality traits and published their results mainly between 1930 and 1959. The thought was that if the traits that differentiated leaders from followers could be identified, then potential leaders could be quickly assessed and put into positions of leadership.[151b]

Second, a new trend began to emerge after researchers had spent almost 30 years of studying leaders, either by observing them in laboratory settings or by asking individuals who worked with them to describe people in leadership roles.[153a] The attention shifted from finding universal traits common among leaders to a more direct approach of monitoring leadership behavior. The focus was on looking at the behaviors leaders exhibit, to try to determine what successful leaders actually *do*.[126, 138] In these studies, the leader's behavior was examined in relationship to the impact of his or her actions on organizational effectiveness.

Not unlike the approach that had searched for universal internal traits, this behavioralist movement, which began in the 1950s, looked for some universally effective leadership behaviors. Although little thought was given to the context in which leaders operate, their role demands, or possible differences in dispositions of leaders and followers, this search managed to identify two general types of leadership behaviors—task oriented and person oriented. However, one important element was missing from the equation: namely, what impact did circumstances and the environment have on the behaviors and effectiveness of individuals in leadership positions?

Continuing efforts to answer the question *What is the best way to lead?* resulted in the development of the third trend in leadership theory 10 to 15 years later. For the first time, researchers examined the interaction between the leader's traits, the leader's behaviors, and the situation in which the leader found him- or herself.[151c] The main contribution of these situational theories was that they led to better, empirically supported theories of leadership, because they explained, described, and predicted important leadership-related phenomena.[153b]

A fourth major paradigm shift occurred in the mid-1970s with the emergence of the so-called New Leadership Theories.[54] In these theories, the attention is shifted toward the relationship between leadership and change. Major concepts included Burns's theory of transformational leadership,[56] Bass's revised version,[27] and House and Adity's theories of the importance and role of charisma in organizational settings.[152] According to House and Aditya,[153] these theories all have several common characteristics. They all attempt to explain

> how leaders are able to lead organizations to attain outstanding accomplishments such as the founding and growing of successful entrepreneurial firms, corporate turnarounds in the face of overwhelming competition, military victories in the face of superior forces, and leadership of successful social reform for independence from colonial rule or political tyranny.

The latest trend, reflected in recent definitions of leadership, suggests that leadership can and should be regarded as an even broader phenomenon. The concept should not be isolated to a single person, labeled *the leader*, but should fully use and focus on the fulfillment of group goals. In this approach, leadership is defined as "the accomplishment of group purpose, which is furthered not only by effective leaders but also by innovators, entrepreneurs, and thinkers; by the availability of resources; by questions of value and social cohesion."[106] This approach boldly challenges the traditional view that leadership is always found within one individual in a given situation. Instead, leadership is aimed at achieving a group goal, not just because of the efforts of one skilled person called the leader but because of the contributions of group members.[151]

On this note, the concept of "SuperLeadership" began to emerge. Manz and Sims[199a] moved away from the long-held belief that leadership was in fact "one person's doing something to other people" and suggested that "the most appropriate leader is one who can lead others to lead themselves." This constitutes a profound change in the way researchers and practitioners had previously viewed leadership. Suddenly leaders become great by tapping into or releasing the potential and abilities of others. As a result, they benefit from the knowledge of many people instead of relying solely on their own knowledge and skills.

This approach has now been taken even further. Today, most definitions of leadership regard the act of leadership as a process. The focus is less on the characteristics of the leader and his or her greatness and more on his or her ability to coordinate the efforts of a group or an organization. Thus the concept of leadership has become closely associated with the theory of corporate culture, such that the leader no longer takes center stage. In this process view of leadership, leaders become members of a *community of practice*, which is identified as a group's shared history, values, beliefs, language, and way of doing things.[87]

This focus on "self-leadership," within each individual—instead of an examination of the behaviors and actions of a few select individuals formally labeled as leaders—represents dramatically different dynamics not seen before in traditional leadership theories. A particular group or an organization may include a leader, but when everyone is involved and expected to play an active role in moving the organization forward through his or her own leadership efforts, no one needs to be motivated or dominated by that leader. In this view, many individuals can exert small degrees of leadership, regardless of their personal power or their position within the organization. A similar concept is peer leadership, which argues for the distribution of leadership behaviors throughout the

> *If you do what you have always done, at best you get what you have always gotten.*
>
> —Anonymous

organization or group. Evidence suggests that this approach is associated with a high level of organizational performance.[48, 89, 151, 199, 205]

Leadership Can Be a Risky Business

U.S. General Willard W. Scott stated: "Any fool can keep a rule. God gave him a brain to know when to break the rule."[157] This quote reflects one of leadership's greatest contributions to service management. Using a leadership mind-set in a service context demands that organizations, managers, and employees alike have the courage to go beyond what is expected of them. Marty Linsky and Ronald Heifetz, from the Kennedy School at Harvard University, have recently introduced a new thought-provoking idea into the leadership debate.

Traditionally, leadership theory has focused on various traits and behaviors of individual leaders and the circumstances they find themselves in, causing us to overlook the real leadership potential all around us. Scholars have now begun to recognize that we know a lot about leaders but too little about leadership and its collective power. Linsky and Heifetz[195] suggest that successful individuals, both in corporate settings and in the political arena, whom we so often tend to label *leaders,* cannot automatically attribute their success to leadership. Linsky and Heifetz claim that those individuals have mastered the art of monitoring and fulfilling the needs of those around them, causing them to focus all their efforts on performing anticipated or expected acts. This means the organization keeps the self-proclaimed leader safely tucked away within his or her "scope of authority." That, according to these Harvard professors, is not leadership. To them, the act of leadership demands courage to go beyond the safe zone of anticipated acts. Their definition of leadership is perhaps best reflected in the words of George Bernard Shaw: "The people who get on in this world are they who get up and look for the circumstances they want, and, if they can't find them, make them."[74]

What relevance does this notion have in a service context? One of a service organization's key performance indicators is the level of customer satisfaction it has obtained. As discussed earlier, the understanding and fulfillment of needs creates perceived value in customers and subsequently translates into customer satisfaction. In today's business environment, this is simply a prerequisite in the service industry. It is worth repeating that *you get what you've always gotten when you do what you've always done.* Therefore, *current* customer satisfaction can be achieved by working within the organizational or personal scope of authority. All behaviors and acts are then designed to satisfy well-known customer needs through proven methods or processes. This approach can be expected to work best in stable or highly regulated environments and during times of low levels of competition. Under more challenging conditions, the approach undoubtedly contributes to short-term organizational success, but it does not reflect a leadership mind-set in the organization, nor does it engender a competitive advantage. This is the safe, comfortable approach to customer service. It does not stretch or push the limits. It does not encourage employees to think outside the box—to use creative solutions, to shape the desired future of the organization.

> *People prefer to follow those who help them, not those who intimidate them.*
> —C. Gene Wilkes

This is not a leadership approach aimed at meeting the customer's needs. Aiming and acting to please within one's scope of authority can best be described as *passive service adaptation.*

International Perspective

The development of our understanding of leadership has changed in line with changes in our societal structure, industrial characteristics, and business philosophies, but is the leadership phenomenon constant across cultures? Is leadership understood and expected in the same manner in different countries and industries?

Let's explore these points further. Theories state, and empirical evidence of cross-cultural leadership indicates, that people's expectations and acceptance of leadership, as well as what constitutes effective leader behavior, vary across cultures. However, the leadership literature mostly reflects Western industrialized society. About 98% of the empirical evidence supporting various leadership theories is distinctly American in character. American leadership can be characterized as "individualistic rather than collectivistic, stressing follower responsibilities rather than rights, assuming hedonism rather than commitment to duty or altruistic motivation, assuming centrality of work and democratic value orientation, and emphasizing assumptions of rationality rather than asceticism, religion, or superstition."[153c] However, there are studies based on the charisma scale of the Multifaceted Leadership Questionnaire (MLQ)[30] that have examined if and to what extent one leadership trait (e.g., a leader's charisma) affects organizational effectiveness. Evidence from India,[232] Singapore,[185] the Netherlands,[184] China and Japan,[29] Canada,[316] and Iceland[17] suggests that the effects of certain characteristics of leadership are, in fact, rather widely generalizable.

> *Never tell people how to do things. Tell them what to do and they will surprise you with their ingenuity.*
>
> —General George S. Patton

Another interesting view on this topic is the impact of changes in our service-driven economy on the application of traditional leadership theory. Hogan, Curphy, and Hogan[148] have argued that current leadership models have been designed for the typical American worker, who, at one time, could be described as a white male with a high school education working in manufacturing. In reality, today's "typical worker" is rapidly moving toward an older and more ethnically diverse demographic working in service. Within the service economy, the competition for highly educated, talented people is steadily increasing. Hence, along with a changing workforce, we have to change our perceptions about leadership in today's more competitive, service-oriented environment.

Why Leaders Succeed

As discussed earlier, the idea of *leadership as a person* has been changing. In the complex and competitive environment of the 21st century, it would appear to be more appropriate to look at leadership not as a position a person holds but as *a process;* namely, the *act* of leadership. In this view, anyone and everyone can rise to the challenge. However, although there are many popular trade publications on leadership, solid research on what makes people successful in their leadership activities is extremely slim. This is in part because measures of effectiveness are very difficult to identify and isolate.[148] Nevertheless, some general attributes have been identified. In line with trait theory, the Center for Creative Leadership has identified several characteristics of effective leaders. They discovered that leaders are generally hardworking, emotionally stable, self-confident, and very self-controlled. In addition, they usually have integrity, are power and results oriented, and have a hunger for learning.[157]

Although trust is considered to be a critical leadership element, a leader's ability to inspire others through value-related activities or empowerment (believed to be necessary in today's working environment) appears to be largely a function of personality and the intangible phenomenon we call charisma.[205] Bennis[35] suggests that leaders are "people who know what they want and why they want it, and have the skills to communicate that to others in a way that gains their support."

Leaders really *mentor* leadership. They accomplish this by setting examples of the behaviors they seek in others and by being consistent in their own words and actions. In other words, leaders take a personal interest in the leadership behaviors of others and teach leadership as they practice it. Furthermore, they encourage others from the heart and promote collaboration by giving power away.[205] These acts of leadership foster a leadership mind-set throughout the entire organization.

Why Leaders Fail

According to research by Charan and Colvin,[64] 30% to 50% of leaders fail to achieve what they set out to accomplish. The limited research that exists on why leaders fail seems to suggest that leadership success depends on a combination of exhibiting positive behaviors (as mentioned earlier) and not exhibiting negative or derailing behaviors.[157] Negative behaviors include arrogance, untrustworthiness, moodiness, insensitivity, compulsiveness, and abrasiveness. Of course, no one formula exists to measure leadership success, and no one leader embraces all the traits or qualities suggested in the literature.

Every man is the architect of his own future.

—Appius Claudius Caecus

Apparently those who fail and those who succeed share many of the same qualities. However, research has found five common characteristics and behaviors among those who have failed to achieve what they set out to do. First, they are less emotionally stable than those who succeeded. Second, they are apologetic and frequently show more signs of being defensive. Third, they tend to have less integrity. Fourth, their communication skills are inferior to those who are more successful. Fifth, they often appear arrogant and tend to overestimate their own power.[12, 37, 148, 157]

Empowerment

In the new organizational structure, where employee participation is expected and, indeed, needed, the term *empowerment* is typically used to describe management's efforts to involve employees in decision making. Initiatives to involve employees in organizational decision making are as old as industrial democracy,[129, 193] and the last in a long line of such efforts is employee empowerment. Based on research over the past 40 years on delegation of authority and participation management, the concept of employee empowerment emerged from total quality management (TQM) programs, which grew out of the work of quality gurus such as Deming and management visionaries such as Peters and Waterman, who emphasized pushing decision-making authority to the lowest possible level. Since 1990, there have been countless empirical and applied research studies dealing with employee empowerment. In fact, the 1990s were labeled the *empowerment era*.[12] What does the term *empowerment* actually mean? How has it been applied, and can it be applied successfully in a service context?

Empowerment Defined

To empower simply means to give power to someone. Power, however, can have several meanings. In the literal or legal meaning of the word, power is authority, so empowerment means authorization. Power also may be used to describe capacity, as in the self-efficacy definition of Conger and Kanungo.[73] In this definition, self-efficacy, or competence, is a belief that one has the skills and abilities necessary to perform a job well. However, power also implies energy. Thus to empower can mean to energize.[130, 304]

In an organizational context, empowerment suggests that employees at any level can show initiative to successfully complete a task or service or to support the corporate mission. Also, as Appelbaum and Honeggar[13] advised, "When you see something that needs to be done, do it! Don't wait to be told to do it, don't sweep the problem under the rug, and don't blame it on someone else."

No consensus has been reached regarding the concept of empowerment or how far organizations should take it. Some definitions of empowerment suggest complete and almost uncontrolled power in the hands of employees. Although many managers recognize the importance of fast decision making and flexibility, the dictate "If something needs to be done, then go ahead and do it" goes a bit too far for most. To them, this is almost a license to act irresponsibly. To achieve its purpose, empowerment, in their view, might be reflected in the words of a Fortune 500 manager who said, "Real empowerment is telling the people what you want from them, giving them the tools to do it, and leaving them alone."[12, 70] This way, the management team still initiates communication, sets the task, determines the relevant resources and tools, and assigns people to the job. In fact, the different approaches to empowerment can be viewed as a continuum, as shown in Figure 3.1. On the far right, there is the full license to act, and on the other end, the limited or controlled empowerment suggested by critical theory.

Critical theory suggests that empowerment programs should make it possible for disenfranchised members to overcome being dominated by others. To do this, these programs have to identify the way the disenfranchised are being dominated, as well as who is controlling their behavior. In this concept, for individuals or

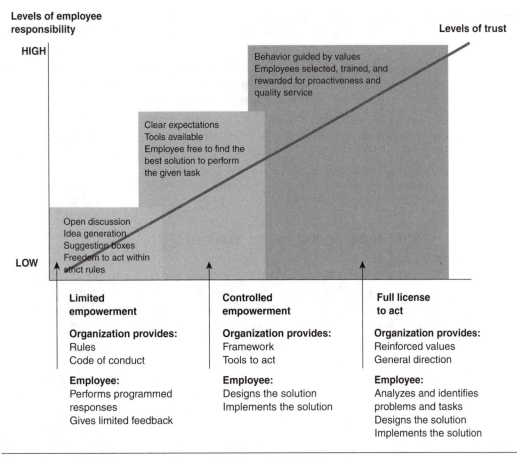

Levels of employee responsibility

Levels of trust

HIGH

Behavior guided by values
Employees selected, trained, and
rewarded for proactiveness and
quality service

Clear expectations
Tools available
Employee free to find the
best solution to perform
the given task

Open discussion
Idea generation
Suggestion boxes
Freedom to act within
strict rules

LOW

Limited empowerment	Controlled empowerment	Full license to act
Organization provides: Rules Code of conduct	**Organization provides:** Framework Tools to act	**Organization provides:** Reinforced values General direction
Employee: Performs programmed responses Gives limited feedback	**Employee:** Designs the solution Implements the solution	**Employee:** Analyzes and identifies problems and tasks Designs the solution Implements the solution

Figure 3.1   The Empowerment Continuum

organizations, empowerment is a process of gaining control over one's own situation. Such critical forms of empowerment are typically outside the field of management, where they have been applied to a broad spectrum of groups, such as women, ethnic minorities, and consumers.[4, 49, 99, 130, 251, 259, 287]

The problem with a phenomenon as intangible as empowerment is that each person involved begins to envision what it means for him or her and attaches a personal meaning to the concept. In fact, empowerment means something quite different to most managers than it does to critical theorists. Cullen and Townley[79] argue that managers in an organizational context have emphasized a transitive use of *empower* as a verb: *to grant or bestow power;* critical theorists, however, have adopted the reflexive usage: *to gain or assume power over someone else.* The second view sees power as domination; the first sees endless motivating resources to be shared by everyone. Some theories of organizational behavior suggest that empowerment can create beliefs and expectations that the organization simply cannot meet. If it is not managed carefully, it can actually lead to the destruction of the entire power structure.[230]

With this controversy in mind, and with the tremendous changes needed in organizations to bring about empowerment and demolish the traditional hierarchical structure, we have to raise the following question: Why on earth would anyone embark on such a journey?—especially within the service industry, which has such an elusive and intangible nature. There are many who point out possible risks associated with such a change and choose to ignore its potentials.[105, 308] However, to deal with today's challenges and stay competitive, organizations need to look beyond traditional directive management. Today's environment requires the contribution of more than a single individual, and employees are not only expected but need to assume an active rather than a passive role in the organization. To do this effectively, the organization must develop a structure that emphasizes collective leadership roles.[198, 293]

How Has Empowerment Worked?

To facilitate employee participation and empowerment, organizations must foster openness, teamwork, support, and security. However, attempts to empower employees have been met with varying degrees of success. There is little evidence to show that a large number of organizations is truly empowered. In fact, few empowerment programs have been successful, despite the popularity of the employee empowerment movement in the literature.[12]

According to a survey of Fortune 1000 companies, employees in only 10% of these companies can be said to be truly empowered.[166] Furthermore, employees and management do not agree on the extent to which empowerment has been applied and implemented. A study of 200 managers in North America showed that 88% believed that they were giving employees more authority to make decisions and take actions than they had done in the years before. However, another study conducted at the same time revealed that only 64% of employees from a nationally representative sample believed that management was giving them more authority to make decisions and take action than previously.[207] The results of another American study revealed that employees surveyed "felt empowerment was more myth than reality in the so-called empowered organizations."[80]

These results are somewhat surprising. One would imagine that the overwhelming evidence of benefits attributed to empowerment at both the individual and organizational levels should *inspire* organizations to go the extra mile in attempts to achieve this objective. Suggested gains include

- Increased productivity
- Greater employee enthusiasm
- Increased morale and creativity
- Higher quality products and services
- Improved teamwork
- Improved customer service and competitive position
- Increased speed and responsiveness
- Lessened emotional impact of demoralizing organizational changes and restructuring.[13, 51, 278, 308, 314]

It is easy to see why the idea of empowerment has enjoyed such popularity. However, any transformation of power has been limited to lower level managers and their subordinates, with most of the control over the extent of the power transfer still firmly in the hands of top management. At the end of the day, upper level managers still decide who, what, and when certain actions are appropriate, although the execution of those actions usually rests in the hands of employees.[21, 130, 220, 229]

The critical approach symbolizes the unwillingness of most organizations to go the distance really needed to succeed. They fail to deliver on the matter of power transfer where it really matters and thereby undermine their success. Koch and Godden[150] go even further, proclaiming that employee empowerment is unworkable and that empowerment is incompatible with strong leadership, as well as being an inefficient way to control an organization. However, it is no longer conceivable for managers to be the source of all knowledge; therefore, managers need to consult and involve those around them in intelligence gathering, communicating the information gathered, and decision making, as opposed to simply expecting workers to comply with their commands. Today, managers must decide, within each particular situation, how much authority and responsibility to give to each individual employee.

Sociological and psychological theories of motivation and leadership generally provide support for empowerment approaches. However, there are also theories that suggest that, in the final analysis, empowerment creates dissatisfaction. Perhaps the solution lies somewhere in the middle. A more workable solution may be reached simply by limiting the amount of autonomy granted to the employees.

Cost-benefit analysis from economic theory has provided arguments for what can be characterized as *controlled empowerment.*[230] The key ingredient is structured teamwork through careful experimental design, structured meetings, and strict goal setting and measurement. The emphasis of the power transfer is on work process improvement and planning and targeting specific missions. Training and carefully managed creativity sessions are used to support the process.

To fully benefit from any effort to transfer power, organizations must create a supportive climate based on trust where two-way communication, risk taking, and initiative are encouraged. Appelbaum et al.[12] have argued that individuals must feel liberated rather than constrained by their working environment if they are to feel empowered. However, the concept of empowerment implies certain promises of authority. Failure to meet employee beliefs and expectations can result in dysfunctional employee behavior.

The benefits of employee participation and initiative are apparent, but the disadvantages and failure to implement are equally apparent. How then can organizations take advantage of the benefits yet manage the disadvantages of empowerment? There are a number of ways to manage the dilemma. In fact, most of them just involve good human resources management practices. The focus is on "managing the contract formation process, adjusting and maintaining employee expectations, responding to dissatisfaction, and incorporating them [employees] in the ownership of the firm. Most also involve educating employees and managers to operate under a new philosophy of management."[230]

Organizations can successfully motivate their employees to participate actively in the workplace. Countless efforts to do so show that this is not an easy task.

However, evidence suggests that for those who succeed, the rewards are substantial. In a service context, employee behaviors are key to organizational success. Therefore, organizations must master the art of transferring power through the organization and must reexamine the traditional hierarchical mode. More important, employee initiatives to protect and preserve the organization are vital to ensuring long-term flexibility and service adaptability.

As discussed earlier, organizations can no longer rely on single great individuals or leaders to adapt to the ever-changing marketplace and the diversity of consumers' needs. House and Aditya[153] argue that there is no evidence that supports claims of stable and long-term effects of leaders on followers' self-esteem, motives, desires, preferences, or values. The leaders can, without a doubt, cause changes in followers' psychological states, but these states do not continue after the separation of the leader and his followers. Furthermore, there is little evidence that charismatic, transformational, or visionary leadership do indeed transform individuals, groups, large divisions of organizations, or total organizations, despite claims that they do so. *Therefore, a collective effort is needed in which every individual in the organization believes that his or her interest is best served by protecting and preserving the organization's interests and takes the initiative within the framework of the organization's goals to do so.*

> *You have to learn to treat people as a resource . . . you have to ask not what do they cost, but what is the yield—what can they produce?*
>
> —Peter Drucker

Distribution of leadership has emerged because of changes in the division of labor and changes in organizations' external environments. It occurs when the aggregate leadership of an organization is dispersed among some, many, or maybe all of the organizational members to enhance flexibility and competitive advantage. In this view, distributed leadership is the opposite of focused leadership, where only one individual is attributed the status of leader. Distribution of leadership allows for the possibility that all members of an organization can and may be leaders in some sense. In that respect, managers may be leaders but not necessarily by virtue of holding management positions. In fact, leadership has become a question of influence—not just authority.

In light of this development, how can the transition from traditional hierarchical ways of thinking and managing take place? The first step is to abandon the use of the word *leader*. The question is not who is leading whom, but rather, how can an organization exercise a leadership mind-set? Within this mind-set, each individual must

- Believe he or she has the ability, will, and desire to be at the *forefront* of whatever profession, job, or task he or she is responsible for
- Regard it as his or her job to do everything to make sure the organization excels in whatever it takes to help reach organizational goals

These goals may include achieving or maintaining a leadership position in a certain market or segment or achieving leading quality status in a certain industry. Whatever the goal, the driving force in all employees is the desire to excel in whatever they do as individuals, as a group, or as the entire organization. The challenge is to ensure that the leadership mind-set is collective and not individualistic in nature. No one person—a "leader"—can ensure a competitive advantage for his or her organization in today's service industry.

In an ever-changing environment where there is an absence of clear policies and "recipes" for behavior, each individual needs to rely on personal judgment in carrying out his or her job. Ideally, frontline employees would be able to decide on the specifics of their own tasks rather than have to be given step-by-step directions of exactly what to do or say in every situation. This kind of individual empowerment is the beginning phase in developing a leadership mind-set for the organization.

Thus the second step is to build a leadership culture that empowers. The objective is to go beyond traditional empowerment, progressing toward the situation in which employees assume an active role based on intrinsic motivation or internal justification for decision making, shared responsibilities, and integration for problem solving. The final stage is reached only when a person becomes a model for others through engaging fearlessly in the act of leadership, aiming to protect and promote the shared interests, goals, and ambitions of the group or organization.

Toward a Leadership Culture

Leadership research has, since the mid-1980s, increasingly been investigating the dynamics of corporate culture and its role in organizational change and effectiveness. Although there are varying definitions for *organizational culture* (for a quick overview, see Baker[19]), Schein[265] provided the following classic definition:

> A pattern of shared basic assumptions that the group learned as it solved its problems of external adaptation and internal integration, that has worked well enough to be considered valid, and, therefore, to be taught to new members as the correct way to perceive, think, and feel in relation to those problems.

Thus corporate culture becomes a process of communication by which organizational members make sense of their organization and their roles and duties. Cultural management has now become an important element of leadership. Leaders must know and understand their own organizational culture and know how to adapt or change the culture to meet the organization's needs as it changes and progresses.

Research on leadership behaviors and change by Baron[25] suggests that not only is there an increasing need for leadership in today's organizations, but different skills are also needed for effective cultural management, which is yet another reason for the cultivation of a collective leadership mind-set.[25, 134, 151] When employees have a shared vision and understanding through the corporate culture of "how things are done around here" and engage in the act of leadership to go above and beyond what is necessary to achieve organizational goals, an effective *service leadership culture* has been born.

Shared service leadership mind-sets can enable organizations to achieve extraordinary levels of commitment, dedication, and performance through collective leadership behaviors based on clear vision, frame alignment, role modeling, risk taking, and competitiveness. Typically, empowered people have a sense of self-determination, meaning, competency, and impact. They must feel personally connected to the organization, believe they are free to make decisions, and know their actions will have an impact on the organization. As Quinn and Spreitzer[249] argued, management can create a context that is empowering, but employees must choose to be empowered. Therefore, just as with empowerment, a collective leadership mind-set is "not something management does to employees, but rather a mind-set which employees have about their role in the organization."[12] In a sense, empowered people empower themselves.

The question is, then, how can organizations strategically and efficiently change in a culture where managers must influence rather than demand and where leadership roles are shared. Developing management roles in empowered organizations is a gradual process. It has been suggested that first one person follows another's lead and models his or her behaviors on that of the leader. He or she then begins to develop a real understanding of the privileges and responsibilities of empowerment and employs the appropriate behaviors. Finally, that person becomes a leader and mentors others.

Management Skills

Wilson and Wellins[323] identify tactical and strategic skills that can be applied in today's team-oriented organizations. Those skills are needed to cultivate the necessary conditions in which service leadership mind-sets and actions can flourish.

> From a tactical perspective, they specify communication skills, performance management, analysis and judgment, coaching, and championing continuous improvement and empowerment. Strategic skills essential for leading in high-involvement environments include leading through vision and values, building trust, facilitating learning, and building partnerships with other parts of the organization.

Management Roles

The manager's role becomes the creation of certain conditions for active employee participation and initiative. Quinn and Spreitzer[249] suggest the following four things that managers must continuously do:

1. Work to clarify the sense of strategic direction for their people, to set a clear strategic vision

2. Strive for participation and involvement, to foster openness and teamwork

3. Work to clarify expectations regarding the goals, tasks, and lines of authority, to provide a sense of discipline and control

4. Work to resolve the conflicts among their people, to give a sense of support and security

Furthermore, research has shown that employees initiate action and participate more actively when they are intrinsically motivated or have internal justifications for their actions. Managers need to help create a working environment where employees' behaviors are governed from within but guided by a clear corporate framework. As hierarchical structures become flatter, individuals take on more responsibility, have more influence, and consequently require more leadership qualities. Thus leadership involves the cooperative effort of an entire group of people who share a meaning that guides the group's behavior toward a common goal. This substantiates the theory of leadership as a process in which the combined efforts of managers and employees set the conditions that allow an organization to respond to the ever-changing service market.[12, 87]

Traditionally, leadership has been conceptualized as an individual-level skill, and leadership development should occur primarily through training of interpersonal skills and abilities.[22, 83] According to Fiedler[95] these approaches, however, ignore nearly a half century of research showing leadership to be a complex interaction between the designated leader and the social and organizational environment. Because leadership development is a continuous process, organizations should learn to develop leadership by improving everyone's ability to participate in the process of leadership. This requires more investment in leadership development across all organizational levels, as well as development of leadership capacity in all employees and across all organizational systems.

> *The final test of a leader is that he leaves behind him in other men the conviction to carry on.*
> —Walter Lippmann

Summary

Our social and corporate environments are constantly changing, thus creating the need for a new kind of leadership in today's organizations. The characteristics of the service process—for example, intangibility, variability, and interactivity—as well as dependence on the service providers call for a revised leadership model. Leadership is most needed in times of uncertainty and change, conditions that are very familiar to most service organizations. Service organizations have to be able to predict and understand changes in customer needs and then to deliver the right amount of service at the right time in the right way. To do this, organizations strongly depend on the active involvement of and feedback from their frontline employees.

Over the last 80 years, researchers have worked to identify the characteristics of a leader. They discovered that most people labeled as leaders are hardworking, emotionally stable, and self-confident. They also have a high level of self-control, have integrity, are power and results oriented, and have a hunger for learning. Research also reveals that most leaders who fail are less emotionally stable, more defensive, and often arrogant. They also tend to have less integrity and poorer communication skills.

No matter what personal characteristics a leader has, he or she is usually successful within a given set of circumstances. One who is successful in a given situation at a given time may fail in another situation with a different group of people. From an organizational standpoint, the fact that leadership characteristics are not transferable is reason enough not to give one person too much power. Therefore, leadership theories moved away from the traditional search for typical characteristics of great leaders toward power sharing within the organization.

Organizations have recognized that, when employees are involved and show initiative, the organization can compete more effectively. Therefore, in the 1990s, *empowerment* became the focus as organizations wrestled with how much employees should be involved and how much power they should be given. Many of these early efforts were not successful because of the lack of commitment to follow through on the power transfer. However, in an ideal situation, when employees are successfully empowered, the benefit is evident in better service quality, more productivity, employee satisfaction, and customer retention. A key way for empowerment to be effective is for the organization to choose and train good employees.

A paradigm shift has occurred in the way we have perceived leadership in the last few years. This shift allows us to apply leadership in a new way in service settings. Organizations can now foster a leadership mind-set among *all* organizational members and can weave it throughout the corporate culture. This new service leadership paradigm goes beyond empowerment. Collective leadership is not a promise of power transfer, which so often fails, but a shared understanding of the role of the entire population of an organization. The employees base their actions on the knowledge and skill of many, instead of relying on each person's individual abilities.

In addition to the need for organizations to empower their employees, it is essential for them to manage their corporate culture. Fortunately, this concept ties in perfectly with the cultivation of a collective leadership mind-set. When employees understand and share the organization's goals and are invested in the organization's corporate culture, then there is a true *service leadership culture.*

Cambridge Leadership Associates on the Dangers of Leadership

Ronald A. Heifetz and Marty Linsky are the principals of Cambridge Leadership Associates, a leadership consulting, development, and coaching practice. They are also on the faculty of Harvard University's John F. Kennedy School of Government and the authors of *Leadership on the Line: Staying Alive Through the Dangers of Leading* (2002). Over the past 25 years, Heifetz and Linsky have worked with thousands of managers and other professionals seeking to engage more effectively in the act of leadership.

Linsky[194] maintains that "people thinking and talking about leadership *spend too much time on the inspiration side and not enough on the perspiration side* and they fail to recognize how dangerous and difficult leadership truly can be."

According to these Harvard professors, "danger lurks" in the form of the resistance that exercising leadership inevitably generates. Resistance appears when we ask people to abandon the safety of what they know for a better but uncertain future. Leadership also involves challenging people to live up to their word, however, and to close the gap between what they say and how they actually behave. "It may mean pointing out the elephant sitting on the table at a meeting—the unspoken issue that everyone sees but no one wants to mention. It often requires helping groups make difficult choices and give up something they value on behalf of something they care about more."[137]

Heifetz and Linsky suggest that most of us, most of the time, pass up these daily opportunities to exercise leadership because it may be personally difficult and even professionally dangerous.

Why Is Leadership Dangerous?

Leadership is dangerous because it is not about rank or status. It is about taking or initiating action when needed. It means going outside the scope of our daily routines and comfort zones. We play many different roles in our lives, but in every single one of those roles, people have certain expectations of our performance and conduct. Heifetz and Linsky point out that "as long as you do just that—meet their expectations and stay within your scope of authority—you will receive praise and support."[137] Therefore, they state that if leadership were about giving good news to people, the job would be easy.

The fact of the matter is that you may appear dangerous to people when you question their values, beliefs, or habits of a lifetime. "You place yourself on the line when you tell people what they *need* to hear rather than what they *want* to hear. Although you may see with clarity and passion a promising future of progress and gain, other people will see with equal passion the losses you are asking them to sustain."[137]

Key Points

- Leadership often means challenging your people to live their values.

- Leadership often means challenging your own realm of authority.

- People will often go to extremes to silence the frustrating voices of reality.

- People do not resist change as such. People resist loss.

SOURCES: Heifetz and Linsky[137] and Linsky.[194]

Key Concepts

Directions: The following are key concepts presented in this chapter. Write a complete definition for each one.

Leadership

Great man theory

Collective leadership

Empowerment

Questions

1. Briefly describe the five major trends in the development of leadership theory.

2. Why should the act of leadership be seen as a process rather than the position of a person?

3. What is the difference between passive service adaptation and leadership in service?

4. What do Linsky and Heifetz observe about traditional leaders? How does this change the definition of leadership?

5. How is empowerment defined? Why has it been so challenging to implement?

6. What role have employees played within empowerment models as they have traditionally been implemented? What have been the results?

7. "Empowered people empower themselves." Interpret this statement in terms of employees' motivations to participate.

8. If you are a manager within an organization with empowered employees, what is your role? What can you do to maximize the quality of their performance?

9. What role does corporate culture play in the cultivation of a collective leadership mind-set?

10. Imagine you are designing a corporate training program for managers within your organization. What effect do you think a new collective leadership mind-set will have on your training program and its contents?

Advanced Activity

Ask someone you know to do something he or she otherwise would not do. You cannot say that this is a class exercise. Write a short report on your experience, summarizing the following: (a) what you did, (b) how the person reacted, (c) what obstacles you faced, and (d) if you were successful, what you think made the difference.

Search the Web

Choose three leading companies in the service industry.

   a. Examine their Web sites, including their annual reports, mission statements, and press releases.
   b. How do they convey their philosophy about service?
   c. Can you find any indications of how much they empower their employees?
   d. Write a report comparing these three companies' service messages.

Suggested Readings

Linsky, M., & Heifetz, R. (2002). *Leadership on the line: Staying alive through the dangers of leading.* Boston: Harvard Business School Press. Retrieved July 4, 2005, from http://www.cambridge-leadership.com/images/ Heifetz_LOTL.pdf

Manz, C. C., & Sims, H. P., Jr. (1991). Super leadership: Beyond the myth of heroic leadership. *Organizational Dynamics, 19*(4), 18–35.

Formulating Strategic Promises

A strategy is not just a notion of how to deal with an enemy or a set of competitors or a market, as it is treated in so much of the literature and in its popular usage. It also draws us into some of the most fundamental issues about organizations as instruments for collective perception and action.

—Mintzberg and Quinn[213]

Objectives

After completing this chapter, you should be able to

1. Understand the need for specific service strategies

2. Recognize different approaches to strategizing

3. Appreciate the historical context of strategic formulation

4. Identify the link between service leadership and organizational culture

Service Organizations Need Unique Strategies

A company cannot begin to even think about becoming a leader in delivering impeccable customer service without having a solid strategy in place. Service strategies are crucial for organizations looking for ways to outperform their competitors efficiently—especially in places where everyone has easy access to resources and technology—as well as for ways to generate a healthy profit.

> Treat a man as he is, and he will remain as he is. Treat a man as he can and should be, and he will become as he can and should be.
>
> —Goethe

In the service industry, having an appropriate service strategy is central to the development of the service promise to customers and the delivery of that promise. A successful company must first determine whether it is possible to satisfy the organization's desire to deliver quality service and, at the same time, produce a superior return on its stockholders' investments. Then it must implement the following key actions:

1. Identify the optimal market for its services and the optimal service for its market and ensure a proper match between the two.

2. Determine what changes are needed and create an arsenal to be used in the battle for market leadership.

3. Provide necessary value for customers to drive the organization's growth and success.

Because customers' needs and competitors' capabilities change constantly, developing an accurate and timely strategy is especially challenging in today's service industry.

Realizing the importance of service is one thing, but actually figuring out the best strategies and then knowing how to apply them in a competitive market is a completely different matter. Application of the appropriate strategy helps organizations deal with deciding *what* to do and *why* to do it in the service management process. It is highly inadvisable, if not impossible, to take the traditional corporate strategies that have been practiced for years and simply apply them to the service industry. This is true for the following three reasons:

- The unique nature of the intangible service process
- The speed with which customer service needs are changing
- The strength of competition throughout the service industry

More than 250 years ago, the famous German philosopher Immanuel Kant said that the greatest gift of men was their courage to use their own sense to guide their actions. However, that is a real challenge for most people in service leadership positions today. They have to decide what methods they can use to better understand and navigate the market environment in which they must operate. They have to decide what form of customer service to deliver, what to promise the customer, and how to deliver that promise. In other words, having the courage to use their own sense to guide their actions is extremely challenging when the primary task is to select the right actions and promote the best customer service behaviors.

From all that has been said so far, we can see that developing the service promise can be a daunting task. Every service organization must face the balancing act of providing quality service with the need to turn a healthy profit, as well as deciding how the primary direction of the organization is to be set. Should an organization rely on a single leader to guide, based on his or her vision of the future, for others to follow, or is it better to draw on the collective knowledge, perceptions, and initiative of all organization members to determine the company's direction? The way service organizations formulate timely and applicable strategies is critical for their success. Despite the importance of this topic, it has unfortunately been underrepresented in current service management literature. However, it forms the foundation of this chapter.

The Impact of Strategy

The objective of any business strategy is to earn superior returns on shareholders' capital—but why do some firms consistently outperform their competitors? Evidence suggests that organizations that have succeeded in creating profitable customer relationships have certain things in common; namely, they have developed a unique set of linked activities that provide integrated solutions to customers' problems.[122a, 222] In other words, they use strategy (consciously or unconsciously) to guide their maneuvers in the marketplace. A strategy is needed to help an organization (a) draw a route to desired outcomes; (b) focus its activities and energies, sense of purpose, and direction; (c) define its character, much as a personality defines an individual; and (d) provide consistency. Mintzberg argues that a genuine strategy is always needed when the actions or responses to those actions from the opponents are likely to seriously affect the intended outcome.[211, 213a]

> Keep on going, and the chances are that you will stumble on something, perhaps when you are least expecting it. I never heard of anyone ever stumbling on something sitting down.
>
> —Charles F. Kettering

Pettigrew and Fenton[236] point out that strategy development must start with a fundamental analysis of what it takes to win in the market, what creates customer value, what drives costs, and how profits are maximized. In an ever-changing and intensely competitive environment, these elements can be difficult to identify and even more difficult to operationalize. The challenges managers face in the quest for the optimal strategy are apparent in the words of Gustafsson and Johnson:[122b]

> Keep in mind that transactions, moments of truth, and relationships don't just go away as your organization evolves. As a service organization, you have to become effective at managing individual transactions, service encounters, and customer relationships as you simultaneously build relationships with partners within networks and alliances.

The Nature of Strategy

Although the application of strategy is relatively new to business, a very complex and fragmented world of strategic thoughts and research has developed over the years. Modern business strategic theory rests on the foundation of military history.

An understanding of past applications of strategy helps to enhance our own capability of strategic formulation in service settings. Therefore, the following is a brief overview of various aspects of the field of strategic management. Although it is not an exhaustive presentation of all theory and research in the field, it helps explain the development of strategies and highlights practical tools and applications for a better understanding of the concept of strategy in service.

Strategy: The Art of the Army General

Strategos is the "art of the army general."[94] In ancient Greece, the term referred to deadly encounters of war, but today it is also used to describe actions designed to ensure victory on the battlefields of business. Strategies have existed from the earliest days of human civilization. They were developed by armies of men seeking power, wealth, and adventure. Early stories and poems describe victories and defeats, providing a body of knowledge and wisdom for those yet to come. "As societies grew larger and conflicts more complex, generals, statesmen, and captains studied, codified, and tested essential strategic concepts until a coherent body of principles seemed to emerge."[213b] In these words, Mintzberg and Quinn describes the birth of strategic theory. He suggests that most basic principles of strategic thinking had developed long before the Christian era. Since that time, these same principles have only been adapted to more modern environments. The ideas and principles of military strategies (the business of battle) have now become central to the battle of business.

Since the early 1980s, strategizing has been well established as a legitimate field of business research and managerial practice.[282] If we get an overview of the fundamentals of strategic management, then we can build on that knowledge and enhance our probability of success. Although the reference to military history is fairly straightforward, the use of the term *strategy* in today's business and academic worlds has turned out to be quite complex. Mintzberg and Quinn have pointed out that no one definition takes precedence over another and each one adds to an understanding of strategy and its application.[213]

In service leadership terms, a strategy is a plan of action that will set an organization, product, or services apart from its competitors. By strategizing, one looks for ways to identify and develop a competitive advantage. Let's begin with a fundamental definition of the word *strategy* within a business setting:

> Strategy is a pattern or *plan* that *integrates* an organization's *major goals,* policies, and action sequences into a *cohesive* whole. A well-formulated strategy helps to *marshal* and *allocate* an organization's resources into a *unique* and *viable* posture based on its relative *internal competencies* and *shortcomings,* anticipated *changes* in the *environment,* and contingent moves by *intelligent opponents.*[247a]

Thus strategies not only determine and reveal organizational objectives, purposes, or goals; they also generate policies and plans for achieving those goals and define the range of business the company is to pursue. Effective strategies develop around a few key concepts and thrusts that give them cohesion, balance, and focus. At the same time, they must be able to deal with the unpredictable and the unknowable. Strategies have to form a structure or posture that is so strong and flexible that the company can achieve its goals, even in times of market unpredictability and economic uncertainty.[10a, 247b]

Strategic Approaches

If we look at the literature on strategies and strategic planning, we find a wide variety of perspectives. Approaches to strategic theory and practice can be classified as either *prescriptive* or *descriptive* and as either *static* or *dynamic.*

Prescriptive Strategies

A prescriptive approach is a top-down approach. The strategy is formulated at the top, usually by the chief executive officer or leader of an organization, and then passed down within the organization. The prescriptive strategy is an analytical process and is, in fact, regarded as a carefully laid out, highly rational plan of action. In other words, under the authority of its executive officer, an organization would formally examine its environment and develop a plan to guide its every step before any action is taken. Such an approach to formulating strategy can only be applied successfully in a stable, predictable environment. For this type of strategy to work, customer needs should be predictable and easily anticipated with few changes or surprises. The threat from rivals or competitors must be low. Service companies that rely on prescriptive strategies may suddenly find themselves in a dangerous position. Customer needs can and do often change rapidly, and competitors are increasingly vigilant, adaptable, and willing to exploit any opportunity they may see. Adding to the risk is the fact that the information a company uses for a prescriptive analysis may already be outdated by the time a plan has been formulated and put into action. Furthermore, overreliance on the CEO's judgment and vision may result in a fatal error because of his or her distance from the front line where the customer encounters take place. Unfortunately, only the CEO can prevent this from happening. A perfect recipe for disaster is to have a CEO (or any corporate leader and decision maker) who is "out to prove something" or make a name for him- or herself. This is particularly true if subordinates believe that pandering to the boss's ego is more important than expressing honest and independent opinions. Large egos and wisdom are usually incompatible. It is a rare, ego-driven CEO who will recognize the value of honest, informed input when it does not support his or her own opinions, prejudices, or preconceived ideas.

Descriptive Strategies

The opposite of the prescriptive approach to strategizing is the descriptive approach, which has been gaining influence in recent years. In a descriptive form, strategy is visionary but is believed to emerge or develop in a spontaneous manner from the bottom up.[313] Taking this approach to strategy enables organizations to monitor and listen continuously for any changes in the environment, using the eyes and ears of all employees to communicate information through the ranks of the organization. This allows the organization to expand its market position and competitive advantage through the input derived from the eyes and ears of its employees. Enhanced knowledge of customer behaviors, wants, and needs shortens company response time to any movement within the marketplace.

Descriptive strategies are dynamic. A new plan of action does not have to be developed before action is taken. Action can, in fact, precede strategy. Thus, rather than being prescribed or dictated by management, strategies can be observed and formulated as they evolve.

Static Strategies

A strategy is identified as static when the underlying premise of the strategy incorporates the beliefs that you can plan the future, that a strategy is long lasting, that an advantage is sustainable, and that business boundaries are fixed. This approach is applicable when time is not critical and organizations can develop the strategy first, then formulate its structure and implement the agreed-on actions. Emphasis is placed on adhering to rules and procedural actions. The strategy is based on past experiences and emphasizes a few big moves instead of incremental changes. Value is believed to be created through organizational efficiency and how well the organization's products and services fit its market.

Dynamic Strategies

A strategy can be called dynamic when it allows the organization to evolve from the past and experiment into the future, where business boundaries are constantly changing.[33a] In that way, the strategy can be surprising and improvisational and allows for continuous business redesign. Time is critical and competitive advantage is regarded as temporary. Often, the structure develops before the strategy, and time paces a mix of moves designed to promote the organization's growth. Value is the result of reinvention.

> *Leadership develops daily, not in a day.*
>
> —John C. Maxwel

Strategic Views Over Time

In their search for a competitive advantage and market superiority, organizations have used different strategic approaches over time. In many aspects, the way they approach their market reflects their market and economic environment. O'Keefe[222] has suggested that over the last 40 years, the following three views to strategic thinking in business can be identified: (a) the industry view, (b) the resource-based view, and (c) the relational view. The views have changed from linear thinking and a static way of looking at the corporate environment to a dynamic way of thinking about products, services, and the marketplace as organizations move through the 21st century.

In the 1960s, organizations believed their markets to be stable, and, indeed, many organizations were somewhat insulated from environmental threats, so their strategies could remain fairly static. The 1970s came and went, leaving organizations with an appreciation of the importance of flexibility to deal with changes in the market environment. At this time, managers saw the need for and the beginnings of nonlinear strategic thinking. Global planning and the "Golden Age" of strategic planning came in the 1980s, with process thinking, reengineering, and a growing appreciation for human capital as a resource. Information technologies in the 1990s paved the way for the introduction of the customer into the strategic process. Today, we see the participation of employees and customers in the strategic process, where strategies are concurrently developed and implemented.

The Industry View

The field of strategic development in business began to take shape in the 1960s with the writings of pioneers in the field such as Chandler[63] and Ansoff.[11] Chandler introduced the notion that strategy drives structure and outlined a rationalistic view of strategy. Ansoff's planning-oriented view saw strategy as a rule for making decisions to match the firm to its environment. He saw strategy as an opportunity for organizations to have a *defined scope* and a profitable *growth direction,* contrary to earlier writings of Levitt and March,[191] who argued for a much broader scope. In his famous analysis of the railroads in the United States, Levitt suggested that they could have sustained their business life by defining themselves not as railroad companies but as transportation companies. However, Ansoff believed that Levitt's approach was too broad and did not see how the existing skills, facilities, and experiences of a railroad company could help it to become a transportation company. In hindsight, we know that many U.S. railroads lost a large market share to the trucking industry because they did not view themselves broadly enough as transportation companies and thus did not include nonrail modes of transportation in their company description.

The focus of the industry view during the 1960s was linear. The assumption was that the environment was stable and relatively predictable and all decisions made at the top could be implemented successfully.[191] According to this view, formulation of the strategy was in the hands of management and could not, under any circumstances, be delegated downward. It was also believed that the desired outcome of any strategy was first and foremost the accomplishment of organizational goals.[33b, 62] The economic crises of the 1970s illustrated the importance of flexibility and nonlinear thinking and the need for effective communication in strategic thinking. Many companies burdened with a rigid planning process or, worse, no planning process at all, suffered devastating consequences at the hands of escalating oil prices, wars, governmental instability, and increasing global competition.[223] In the late 1980s, academics and practicing managers began to question the prevailing industry perspective and suggested that *internal organizational factors* had more impact on profitability than did *industry structure*. With this, new strategic theories began to take shape.

The Resource-Based View

In the resource-based view of strategy, an organization's sustainable competitive advantage is believed to be based on the resources or assets of the organization—particularly on core capabilities that are not easily bought, substituted, or copied. More often, these capabilities are the intangible assets of an organization that are both socially complex and deeply embedded in the organization itself. According to the resource-based view, the outcome of strategy and the key role of managers is to create and nurture these capabilities.

The concepts of the resource-based view can be traced back to the writings of Penrose in the late 1950s, but the conceptual transfer of the approach into strategic management literature took place in the mid-1980s and is generally credited to Wernerfelt.[33] Theoretical developments and popularization of these ideas became evident in the early 1990s with the work of Prahalad and Hamel[128, 245] and Barney.[23]

Many factors have created a new context for the development of organizational strategies. These include global and rapid changes in technology, increased competition, deregulation, and dramatic market changes. Prahalad and Hamel[128, 245] have described this transition as a "silent industrial revolution." They have argued that the highly competitive environment of today's service industry allows organizations to enjoy their current advantages only for a short period. A stable end stage is but an illusion, requiring organizations to continuously rethink their strategy and structures. This is a dramatic shift from the industry view that predominated during the lengthy stable periods and predictable changes of the 1950s and 1960s.

Relational View

No matter how big a change the resource-based view represents compared with the industry viewpoint, critics have argued that specific resources and strategies easily become redundant during times of continuous change. Under these conditions, organizations need to move away from dependence on existing resources and toward a dynamic approach of innovation and continuous renewal. As the second millennium arrived, advances in technology and communications allowed the strategic thinking of organizations to shift toward a combination of internal and external emphasis. That is, the strategic planning of an organization should focus simultaneously on both its inner resources and its environment. From this foundation, the concept of the *value-creation network* was born.[52, 222, 303]

Organizations' focus on strategy has shifted away from the industry- and resource-based perspectives toward the belief that the pathway to sustainable success lies within the organization and in its relationships with its stakeholders.[33c] The suggested advantages of cooperation are, according to Dyer and Singh,[88] knowledge sharing, use of complementary capabilities or resources, lower transaction costs, and an investment in relationships.

> *I have accepted fear as a part of life—specifically the fear of change . . . I have gone ahead despite the pounding in the heart that says: turn back.*
>
> —Erica Jong

Understanding Strategy

From the overview provided here, it becomes apparent that there is no single way of strategizing. Various factors affect the choice of strategy formulation and application of that strategy. Henry Mintzberg, one of today's leading scholars in the field, suggests that strategy can be understood in five different ways.[213c] Mintzberg's Five P's, as they are sometimes called, are important enough to be considered next. The Five P's are based on Mintzberg's argument that an organization's strategy can

1. Be a tool to *plan* its future course of action

2. Focus on a *ploy* against a rival or competing company

3. Emerge through a *pattern* of behaviors without any deliberate planning

4. Involve a careful selection of a *place* (or *position*) in a market believed to be poised for success

5. Be centered on building a unique company *perspective* or culture to enhance the organization's competitive advantage

Perhaps the most widely recognized definition of *strategy* is that of *strategy as a plan*. It suggests a *consciously intended course of action* or a guideline to deal with a situation. Strategy is therefore an attempt to establish a direction or a pathway to achieve organizational goals. For example, a service organization can formulate a plan of action based on a careful examination of its internal and external environments. Based on this analysis, the organization first determines a certain position (i.e., where it is or wants to be) in the market. Foreseeable changes in customer *needs,* competitors' *weaknesses,* or the organization's own *strengths* determine where and how the organization plays the field. The new or adapted position an organization identifies as optimal can call for an increased level of service quality or for lower levels of service, depending on overall corporate goals. Next, the organization identifies the appropriate service level that will allow it to operate and compete efficiently in its chosen position. Organizational structure, processes, and human resources are then modified or enabled to successfully carry out the plan.

Strategy as a ploy is a *specific act* designed to outsmart an adversary. Competition takes central stage, and all actions are under the pretext of threats or bluffs against the opponents. For example, a service organization can introduce and promote an enhanced service level to customers or can offer added value benefits with purchases. These strategies are carried out not to improve the company's service ratings but to warn a potential rival against entering that particular market segment. The threshold of entry for that competitor suddenly becomes higher and hence more difficult to overcome. New companies entering a certain market have also been known to use strategy as a ploy. In that case, they use their promotional material to downplay or criticize the competitors' services but say little about the quality of their own services. This buys them time to build a customer base and lure new customers away from their competitors. This is done not on their own merits but on the basis of their competitors' weaknesses in service delivery or service failures.

Strategy as a pattern refers to a *stream of actions* or a set of consistent behaviors. According to this definition, strategies do not have to be intended or planned; they can simply evolve, without prior planning or intention. This intangible concept of strategy is also *meaningless* unless accompanied by actual behaviors. In fact, companies may not realize they have a strategy, although it exhibits itself in their consistent behaviors. For example, a restaurant or a movie theater may ask or encourage customers to remove their own trash before they leave the premises. The company may not even recognize this as a strategy that not only serves its next customers but also allows it to lower labor costs and apply those savings to its marketing activities or to other means of acquiring a competitive edge.

Strategy as position refers to a *place* in an organization's environment *where resources are likely to be located.* Organizations use this form of strategy to find a position in the marketplace to meet, avoid, or bypass competitors. In military terms, positioning becomes "the site of battle." More specifically, positioning relates to how you deploy your soldiers and their weapons (artillery, tanks, etc.) after you have chosen the site of battle. For example, an organization may choose to provide a full range of services in a certain market segment but not in others. This can happen for a variety of reasons, such as a high concentration of competition, the cost of market penetration, and market demographics. The impetus behind the idea is for the organization to allocate its resources only where the likelihood of success is greater than it would be in other positions, thus maximizing its return on its investment. On the other hand, an organization can also choose to provide a certain range of services knowing that it will not be profitable by itself. Here, the organization simply chooses to support other services or markets. Often this approach requires that a company find a niche or a market segment that it can choose to service or not to service.

Strategy as perspective or a culture is *an integrated way of perceiving the world.* It is directed inward, as opposed to positioning, in which the focus is outwardly directed, toward the organization's market environment. Perspectives that are shared by organizational members are difficult to change and are normally deeply embedded in an organization's core. They can best be compared to what personality is to an individual. Thus perspectives affect the whole of the ideology and behaviors of an organization. An example of this approach is to use the company's culture to ensure service quality and organizational success. A company might have a corporate culture centered on a collective leadership mind-set that includes all the organization's individual members. It would then use this mind-set to outperform opponents in certain markets. In this case, although there is a collective mind-set, the company has to carefully reinforce—through its training and its management practices—the individual's power to continuously improve operations to achieve organizational goals. The concept of service leadership can be placed under the heading of this approach to strategizing.

> *Four steps to achievement: plan purposefully, prepare prayerfully, proceed positively, pursue persistently.*
>
> —William A. Ward

Service Leadership

According to a recent survey, only 8% of the Fortune 1000 executive directors rate their leadership capacity as excellent. About half rate their leadership capacity as fair or poor.[157] In addition, one fifth of large American companies were expected to lose at least 48% of their top talent to retirement from 2000 to 2005.[213a] The challenges are great, but the opportunities for those who master the science of leadership in the service sector are also tremendous.

Leadership should be integrated throughout an organization. Each person in the organization—regardless of his or her formal position—should perform some kind of leadership role. In addition, the corporation should always strive to be the leader within its own market segment. Major General Hugo Baron von Freytag once stated: "All men have some weak points and the more vigorous and brilliant a person may be, the more strongly these weak points stand out. It is highly desirable, even essential, therefore, for the more influential members of a general's staff not to be too much like the general."[157b] These words take on extra meaning in times of constant change, when organizations strive for a competitive advantage through a strategic application of service quality and the fulfillment of customers' needs.

As discussed in Chapter 3, employee empowerment has been introduced in recent years as a powerful tool to improve service performance. Empowerment, which gives employees the power to make work-related decisions, has its advantages and disadvantages. The main benefits are believed to be (a) enhanced responsiveness to customer needs, (b) better handling of service breakdowns, and (c) enhanced job satisfaction. It is also true that empowerment is associated with higher personnel selection costs, training costs, and labor costs.[46] We have all heard it said that there are three types of people—those who make things happen, those who watch things happen, and those who wonder what happened—regardless of the level of authority handed to them. Therefore, *careful personnel selection and training are crucial, but costly, elements in the empowerment process.*

The concept of service leadership takes the idea of empowerment further to overcome the disadvantages associated with power transfer and fully capitalizes on the investment in higher selection, labor, and training costs.

Employees must be encouraged to do more than just wait for things to happen, calling problems to the attention of management when they occur. They must c*rave authority* and *regard it as their responsibility to act proactively* in ways that will protect and preserve their organization and collectively shape their future working environment to ensure organizational success.

Leadership is in fact a complex interaction between all the members of an organization. In an organization in which all employees have the leadership mind-set, every employee knows that each meeting with a customer is an invaluable opportunity to provide outstanding service and win customer loyalty. When an organization has this culture, *every individual takes responsibility and pride* in helping the organization achieve or maintain its dominance in its own market. One way it does this is by maintaining alertness in regard to customer needs and communicating those needs to others throughout the organization. This enables the organization to streamline its strategies and processes accurately and achieve *continuous service adaptation.*

As companies' hierarchical or organizational structure becomes flatter and more flexible, employees are selected, trained, managed, encouraged, and rewarded for taking initiatives. Many decision-making responsibilities that have historically been held by managers are, today, gradually being turned over to employees. This does not mean, however, that people who traditionally were labeled managers or leaders in the traditional sense of hierarchical control are no longer needed. What we are witnessing is simply the evolution of the role of leadership within many organizations.

Leaders are now often integrated into employee teams. They have a new set of responsibilities to make the team as successful as possible. These include the following:

- Facilitating
- Coaching
- Managing relationships
- Creating a bridge between top management and the teams
- Obtaining support resources
- Helping to budget time and the availability of team members

Perhaps the most important task for these managers is to create an environment in which people are not afraid to take risks. The method used in doing so, however, is drastically different today than in the past.[123] Leaders can elicit the commitment of others, allowing them to expand their skills and thereby contribute more broadly to the organization through collaboration, openness, and the creation of shared meaning.[157]

> *Nurture your mind with great thoughts. To believe in the heroic makes heroes.*
>
> —Benjamin Disraeli

The Quest for Competitive Advantage in Service

Sustainable competitive advantages can be obtained through service leadership—in other words, to dare *not* to do what has always been done before, at the organizational level as well as at each employee's individual level of responsibility. It is essential for the organization striving for service leadership to *expect* and *foresee* changes and to use the power of the collective leadership mind-set to

- Break new ground
- Go further and faster to obtain organizational goals of growth, profits, and service quality
- Use unconventional methods and "go against the grain" if necessary

Standardized procedures and carefully laid out processes ensure speed and accuracy of the service. However, if an organization is going to use customer service as its primary weapon in the battle for market superiority, it must simultaneously accomplish two almost contradictory things: namely, *it must use proven methods of success* and *dare to be different.* It must position itself differently and successfully manage its human resources to foster initiative, encourage helping behaviors, and promote efforts for continuous improvement.[117] Not only is this consistent with the marketing theory and practice of the past two decades, it is also at the core of leadership science and human resources theory and research. In short, a service leadership mind-set inspires a person to dare to use his or her intelligence and initiative to break market, organizational, or personal barriers that are holding the organization back. In this way, the organization will exhibit what can be called *proactive service adaptation.*

The impetus of the concept of service leadership is that it demands courage, and maybe even heroic acts, at all organizational levels—from top management, middle management, and the service providers in the front line and second front line. These can now be discussed as follows:

- From an *organizational* perspective, service leadership demands the courage to differentiate and, when necessary, to break new ground.
- From a *management* perspective, service leadership demands that managers have the courage to lead and not to overmanage or control. First they must hire the best talent possible and foster a culture of collective leadership. Then they must be brave enough to empower their employees and to trust them to make good decisions and take appropriate action.
- From a *frontline staff* perspective, service leadership demands that they have the courage and the ambition to innovate, communicate, and participate in the development of the organization.

The organization's future and the adaptability required for it to survive are the business of every employee and every manager. The cumulative energy that is released in the process of collective service leadership empowers people, giving them the strength, authority, and confidence to go where they would not go otherwise.

The theoretical framework of service leadership presented in this book is based on the assumptions that the leadership mind-set of organizational members is powerful and that a leadership mind-set can be a driving force for achieving a sustainable competitive advantage. The concept of service leadership is defined as a culture that empowers the organization to strategize its promises, design its processes, and engage its people in a proactive quest for competitive advantage. Competitive advantage is based on the capacity of

> *There are no shortcuts to any place worth going.*
> —Beverly Sills

individuals and groups to shape the future of their organization and continuously evolve and adapt to the ever-changing market through a collective leadership mindset. This concept is based on the idea of a strong organizational culture in which the values and norms encourage all organizational members to use their initiative, knowledge, and expertise to help the organization realize its goals of profitability and customer satisfaction.

Service Strategies

What does all of this mean for service organizations looking for the path to continuous adaptation and seeking a competitive edge? Managers faced with this fragmented world of strategy are bound to ask themselves: What do I do? When and how do I do it? Is there a best way to strategize in service? Textbooks on the topic of customer service highlight the application of classical schools of planning and positioning and discuss models such as Porter's Elements of Industry Structure. The purpose is to analyze the organization's internal and external environments and plan appropriate actions to be implemented as a response to its environment or to influence the environment in some way. However, from the discussion in this chapter, it should be evident that it is important to examine alternative methods of approaching and managing strategic efforts in service organizations.

Like a road map, strategy pinpoints destinations and draws a line from one destination to the next. It also helps an organization focus its resources, energy, and activities, and it creates consistency in the organization's efforts to pursue its goals. For that purpose, classical approaches to strategizing can be useful. However, they only apply for some aspects of the service process, and for certain conditions, such as highly regulated environments, monopolistic markets, or markets with one or two dominating players. In other words, these classical approaches work best where the rate of change in customer needs and level of competitive rivalry is limited, either because of a regulatory environment (e.g., governmental rules or regulations or standardization regarding safety or health issues) or market conditions (e.g., a limited number of participants in the market or a low level of competition). In these situations, service organizations can apply design, planning, and positioning approaches without time constraints or the threat of immediate competitive innovations or breakthroughs. However, if an organization finds itself (a) relying primarily on its human capital for competitive advantage, (b) in a highly competitive market, or (c) with constant and rapid advances in service delivery, then the classical approaches to strategy simply cannot keep up. They can in fact mislead the organization and slow down its adaptation process. Like the Titanic, the organization is likely to hold its course long after it needs to turn. In those circumstances, the organization needs to take a dynamic approach to strategizing. The strategy can be designed to respond to a development in the market or to customer needs, or it can be proactive, to create market opportunities or prepare for possible changes that could occur at some time in the future with little warning.

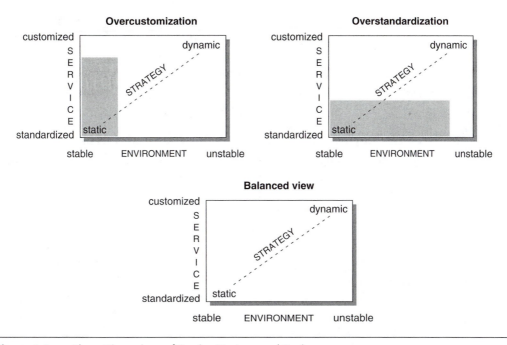

Figure 4.1   Three Dimensions of Service Strategy and Design

Figure 4.1 shows three cases representing the condition of the environment (stable or unstable), the nature of applicable strategic approaches, and the characteristics of service (standardized vs. customized). In short, stable environments allow for static and prescriptive approaches, whereas unstable environments require more dynamic approaches. The third element is the characteristics of the service itself. Standardized procedures, which are often designed to enhance the speed, safety, and accuracy of the service, could be compatible with static approaches to strategy. However, when the service requires judgment, sales behaviors, and insight into customer needs, static approaches could stifle the employees' service initiatives, which are needed to keep up with customers' needs and competitors' capabilities.

Like most things in life, reality is rarely black or white. Most organizations find themselves at both ends of the continuum to some extent. Some parts of the service process can be more stable than others, and the same thing can be said about certain markets in which the organization operates. To use a nautical example, the captain of a sailing ship does not redesign or rebuild his entire ship overnight when the winds change. Instead, he adjusts his sails, turns the rudder as needed, and urges his crew on. Some parts of his ship need to be highly adjustable or responsive—others should be fixed and immovable. The ship itself will change over time because of technological developments and innovations. Therefore, changes in customer needs over time may impose changes on the captain (the CEO), his ship (the organization), and the crew (employees). The tempo of that change governs the rate of changes required in the framework and structure of the ship or organization and the way in which it is operated.

Likewise, the nature of changes and their intensity greatly affect service developments. In dangerous waters, the entire crew is on watch, highly flexible, and ready to respond, doing everything in their power to preserve the ship and bring it home to port. The application of strategic thinking in this context suggests that the environment and type of service should determine the selected strategic approaches in service organizations. In fact, there is no one right way to strategize in service organizations. Under competitive conditions, when the service is complex and not standardized, dynamic approaches are most likely to create the conditions necessary for appropriate strategies to emerge. In such cases, the organization can use its past experiences to continuously adjust, or, in extreme cases, reinvent itself appropriately and fast enough to successfully wage its battles. Under more stable conditions, the approaches move further to the left on the continuum.

As expected, strategizing concepts have changed over time and will continue to do so. Strategies are highly individualized and need to be in line with each organization's environment and overall organizational objectives. The planning approaches to strategy formulation that are traditionally presented in books on service management often lack the flexibility needed to deal with the dynamic nature of the service industry. The theoretical framework for service leadership suggests an overall corporate strategy as a perspective or culture. It is governed by service-based values and norms that inspire and encourage employees to take the initiative and act responsibly to achieve success. Strategic decisions, such as the level of customization or standardization, emerge through the active participation of employees and customers and are largely determined by the environment in which the organization operates.

> *I long to accomplish a great and noble task, but it is my chief duty to accomplish small tasks as if they were great and noble.*
>
> —Helen Keller

Summary

Application of the appropriate strategy helps organizations decide *what* to do and *why* to do it in the service management process. Having an appropriate service strategy is central to the development and the delivery of the service promise to customers. Choosing the best service strategy and deciding how to apply it in a competitive market is a major challenge for any organization. A strategy is needed to help an organization (a) plan a route to desired outcomes; (b) focus its activities, energies, sense of purpose, and direction; (c) define its character; and (d) provide consistency in its policies and practices.

The unique nature of the intangible service process, the speed at which customers' needs change, and the competitive nature of the service environment make it impossible to apply traditional planning methods of strategizing in today's service industry.

Organizational strategizing can be either *prescriptive* (strategy is regarded as a rational, formal plan of action based on careful analysis by top management and imposed from the top down) or *descriptive* (strategy is more visionary and, ideally, develops from the bottom up through the ranks of the organization).

Strategies can be either *static* (based on the view that time is not critical, strategy is long lasting, competitive advantage is sustainable, and business boundaries are fixed) or *dynamic* (when time is critical, advantages are regarded as temporary, and business boundaries are constantly changing).

O'Keeffe identified three views of business strategy: (a) the industry view, (b) the resource-based view, and (c) the relational view. Today, strategy has shifted away from the earlier industry- and resource-based views. Corporations now realize the advantages of cooperation and knowledge sharing and are investing more and more in relationships with their stakeholders.

The classifications discussed here enhance our understanding of the global characteristics of strategies. They provide an insight into where and when a particular approach should be taken to develop a corporate or service strategy. However, they address neither the content nor the process of strategizing.

Mintzberg's Five P's provide the following five ways of viewing an organization's strategy: (a) as a *plan* to guide the organization, (b) as a *ploy* (defensive action) against competition, (c) as an unplanned *pattern* of behavior, (d) as a way to find a *place* (or *position*) in a given market, or (e) as a *perspective* or culture.

For individuals and organizations alike, this book emphasizes the necessity of developing leadership in today's service-driven economy. It is critical for the organization to assume a leadership role—and thus competitive advantage—in the marketplace and for each individual to become a leader within the organization. The advantages of empowering employees to make work-related decisions include (a) enhanced responsiveness to customer needs, (b) better handling of service breakdowns, and (c) increased job satisfaction. The main disadvantage is the increased labor costs associated with employee selection and training.

Leadership is a complex interaction between all members of an organization. In an organization in which all employees have a leadership mind-set, both employees as individuals and the organization as a whole know that they must serve every customer well, make improvements in customer service where possible, and win customer loyalty through everything they do. An important goal for many managers is to create an environment in which employees are not afraid to take risks. Employees are selected, trained, managed, and rewarded for taking initiatives; they are encouraged to use their knowledge and expertise to help the organization achieve its goals of profitability and customer satisfaction. In summary, a service leadership mind-set inspires employees to use their intelligence and initiative to break market, organizational, and personal barriers that are holding the organization back.

The concept of service leadership introduced in this book can be characterized by strategy considered as a perspective or culture. Service leadership is based on the idea of a strong organizational culture in which values and norms promote superior ambition and initiative from all organizational members. In a company in which the entire organization has a leadership mind-set, every employee-customer encounter is considered to be an invaluable opportunity to improve customer service and engender customer loyalty.

PRACTICAL INSIGHTS

The Masie Center on Leadership in the Age of Technology

Elliott Masie, who heads a think tank that focuses on how today's organizations can benefit from technology, emphasizes the opportunities organizations have to improve their performance through harnessing the power of new technological inventions. He argues that organizations can run the risk of squandering those opportunities as competitors figure out strategies for taking advantage of them. Therefore, he maintains, "there is only one particular ingredient that organizations cannot do without in this brave new world of technology—*leadership*."

According to Masie, the examples of the positive impact technology can have on business processes are numerous. Amazon.com, for example, has figured out how to use technology to closely track its customers' buying habits and suggest new products to them in a highly targeted way. That strategy has moved the company from employing technology in a merely transactional way to using it behaviorally to develop relationships with customers. "I see technology as an inspiring thing," Masie says. "Our role is to be the transition generation and to understand how we can make clear decisions on using it."

He also suggests that a fundamental problem for many organizations is the fact that they spend way too much time on content and not enough on context. In Masie's view, "what leaders want is real-time context that allows them to put information in a larger framework and make sense of it quickly, so that they can enhance their learning and readiness in a given situation." Technology, used in the right ways, can help cultivate that context, he says. Leaders need to think more strategically than ever about how to be "a learning organization with digital devices in our hands."

Employee Training Through Technology

A good example of a company that uses technology to enhance employee training and efficiency is McDonald's. An application of electronic learning tools in training has allowed them to deliver consistent training throughout their vast organization with far less manpower than before. Stores using the new training technology have reported substantial increases in sales, profitability, and employee retention, according to the Masie Center.

Elliott Masie has pointed out that for every success story involving technology, there are other examples of lost opportunities. For example, many organizations overuse PowerPoint technology. In fact, PowerPoint software has become the most widely used knowledge tool in many organizations. However, according to Masie, information in PowerPoint, no matter how critical it may be, is rarely placed in a central repository or backed up in some way. This failure places the organization at risk of losing important information. Furthermore, it can be applied as a "weapon of mass destruction" when used to overwhelm people with information. It can "knock important meetings and strategy sessions off course instead of serving as a valuable tool for driving home key points," Masie says.

Key Points

- Leadership often means challenging your people to live their values.

- Leadership often means challenging your own realm of authority.

- People will often go to extremes to silence the frustrating voices of reality.

- People do not resist change as such. People resist loss.

SOURCE: Masie.[201] For additional information on creative leadership techniques, see the articles at the Creative Leadership Center Web site (http://www.ccl.org).

Key Concepts

Directions: The following are key concepts presented in this chapter. Write a complete definition for each one.

Strategy

Prescriptive strategies

Descriptive strategies

Strategy as perspective

Questions

1. What is *service leadership,* and how is it different from *empowerment* in a service context?

2. What is *strategy* in service leadership terms?

3. Under what circumstances should the classical approaches to strategizing be avoided? Choose two large corporations that should avoid the classical approaches and explain why.

4. Why can prescriptive strategies be dangerous for service companies?

5. What advantages do descriptive strategies have over prescriptive strategies?

6. Why is a relational view of strategy development better for service organizations than either the industry view or the resource-based view?

7. All companies have a strategy, whether it is formally developed or not. Suppose your startup company has grown so fast and been so successful that you, as CEO, never really took the time to make a formal strategic plan. Under which of Mintzberg's Five P's are you operating? Under what conditions might this approach to strategic planning become a serious problem for your company?

8. You learn that a company that is quite a bit smaller than yours is about to introduce the "Tabbit," a new product that is almost identical to your company's very successful "Cabbit." The small company is planning to sell the Tabbit at 20% less than your Cabbit's market price. List several strategies that your company might apply at this time to counter the competitive threat.

9. Describe the role of managers within a service leadership organization.

10. In what ways does service leadership require an organization to dare to be different?

Advanced Activity

Select a local service company with which you are familiar. Use Mintzberg's five descriptions of what strategy is to write short statements for the service company highlighting how the company should work to achieve a competitive advantage. Then briefly describe how the company can use strategy as *plan, ploy, pattern, place,* and *perspective* to succeed.

Search the Web

Find two or three examples of corporate mission statements. Examine the statements in terms of content and choice of words. What role (if any) does service play in the corporate mission of the company? What role (if any) does leadership or leading position play in the statement? (a) Print out the statements and bring them to class. (b) Underline wording or sentences you find particularly interesting. (c) Write a short report, giving your analysis.

Suggested Readings

Mintzberg, H. (1987, Fall). The strategy concept II: Another look at why organizations need strategies. *California Management Review, 30*(1), 25–32.

Oliver, R. W. (2001). Real-time strategy: What is strategy, anyway? *Journal of Business Strategy, 22*(6), 7–10.

PART

two

Designing the Process

This section highlights practical tools and methods for designing services. The first two chapters in this section discuss design principles for service strategies and processes. The third covers the crucial area of service recovery—what a company must do to recover the customer when service is not delivered correctly the first time. The final chapter in this part discusses the use of metrics in all phases of the service design and delivery processes.

The Power of the Transformer

George Mikitarian

CEO, Parrish Medical Center

W e have all been there—inside a massive building with long hallways, strong medicinal smells, urgent beeping and paging, rushing interns (yet no one to answer questions), and blaring ambulance sirens. Whether as a patient or a visitor, chances are we did not want to be there, in the hospital, which is usually not "hospitable" at all. "My view of such a place was totally and favorably altered during our recent trip to Parrish Medical Center," reported John Julian, a first-time visitor.

One look at the photograph of Parrish Medical Center's (PMC's) main entrance and atrium and you can immediately tell that this is no ordinary hospital. Start with its carefully chosen name: *medical center*, not *hospital*. In November 2002, PMC opened its 371,000 sq. ft., $80 million facility in Titusville, Florida. Already, this modern and innovative medical center has been recognized by many individuals and a number of organizations as one of the finest healing environments in the country. PMC has earned high-quality rankings from the industry's leading quality watchdog groups, and its unique facility and excellent patient satisfaction scores have been reported in a number of publications.[116, 170, 262] Still, the atmosphere at PMC is very "un-hospital-like." Entering what is usually called a "lobby," visitors find themselves in an expansive, open atrium. The contrast to what one expects to find on entering a hospital is dramatic. *Building Florida*[286] reported that the medical center "is not only technologically advanced and efficient, but one that is patient-sensitive, provider-friendly, and if you didn't know better, appearing more like a five-star hotel."

Even the colors and shapes are unexpected and surprisingly relaxing. Stark white and harshly contrasting colors have been replaced with soothing pastel tones. Harsh angular features are absent—replaced with rounded, flowing curves, which characterize the walls, entrance hallways, and wide stairs. A central fountain, art displayed throughout, large plants, and multistoried vertical height are features that are immediately obvious to the visitor who, on arrival, feels that he or she has just entered a Disney Resort Hotel or another outstanding hotel. Moving through the corridors or riding the elevators, one slowly realizes just how soothing it is not to hear the customary intrusive messages being paged throughout the building, urgently summoning doctors or staff. Visitors and patients do not share the same elevators—another feature that benefits both parties. Again—so "un-hospital-like"! Indeed, Parrish Medical Center has transformed the concept of a hospital.

Parrish Medical Center's CEO, George Mikitarian, said, "People expect hospitals to provide quality, technologically advanced medical care; what makes the difference between choosing one hospital over another is service. How did we make them feel during their stay or visit? That's why PMC has dedicated resources to several amenities many would associate with a hotel, not a hospital. 'At Your Request' dining, the equivalent of hotel room service, was implemented shortly after they opened. Today, when asked, 'How would you rate the food that was delivered to you?', patients consistently rate us at or near the hundredth percentile, according to our research firm PRC. Other amenities provided to support the healing experience at PMC include full-service concierge, a full-time executive chef, aromatherapy, pet therapy, humor therapy, and massage therapy. Our concierge not only tends to the needs of visitors and patients, but also facilitates dry cleaning, car detailing services, dining reservations, and much more for busy staff."

PMC kept the customer—in this case, the patient and his or her family and friends—in mind when both tangible and intangible elements of service delivery were being designed. Prominent themes throughout the medical center are circular elements, representing the continuum of care, called the *Circle of Life* (see Figures IIa and IIb). The sweeping spiral stair in the four-story atrium pictured here [Diane, do you have this picture?] is the central feature of the *Circle of Life* theme, intended to imply hope and optimism, and the use of natural light throughout the facility is both soothing and spirit enriching.

With all of these innovative, hotel-like amenities, customer satisfaction still does not happen without the solid service strategy that is embedded throughout the corporate culture of PMC. "Our service strategy is to align our corporate culture with our vision to be America's finest healing environment. To be successful means that we must never waiver in our commitment to our values; we are consistent in our actions; and we are always present for patients, families, visitors, and each other," commented Mikitarian. PMC uses the "game plan" as the framework for consistent, standardized communication of the organization's annual business strategic goals and expectations at all levels of the organization. It is supported and directed by the medical center's board of directors but is incorporated and implemented through every employee of the organization. The game plan, discussed further in Chapter 6, focuses on five key areas that drive organizational success: (a) internal relationships (quality of work life), (b) service (patient satisfaction), (c) quality of care, (d) finances, and (e) growth.

The 2004 game plan goals for service include being ranked in the 93rd percentile nationwide in terms of patient satisfaction, which is linked to providing the highest quality care, using appropriate regulatory, industry-standard quality indicators as benchmarks. Each of the basic goals has key drivers and objectives. For example, the service goal of achieving a 93rd percentile in patient satisfaction has the following key drivers: (a) medical center staff's courtesy and friendliness, (b) pain management, and (c) nurses' promptness in responding to calls. Under the key driver of courtesy and friendliness, the specific objectives include

- Continue to develop "greeter" atrium services.
- Continue to develop scripting.
- Use developed Voluntary Hospitals of America protocols regarding friendliness and courtesy.
- Develop and implement employee customer service training.
- Expand criteria-based performance evaluation tool to include service.

Significantly, PMC has a parallel goal for its own personnel, to achieve employee, physician, and auxiliary satisfaction scores of 93%. CEO Mikitarian stresses that creating a service-oriented, patientcentric culture must begin with the people who are delivering the care. That is why PMC devotes considerable resources toward the development of its people, so everyone at PMC understands, and shares a deep dedication to, its vision and values.

PMC service goals include reaching out to the local community. Not only is PMC the community's medical center, it also wants to be viewed as a familiar facility that the local residents can enjoy. Mikitarian observed, "People don't often think of a hospital that way, but . . . we sought to create an environment that encourages people to visit the medical center often when they are healthy, to become familiar with us and thus lessen fears and anxiety. To accomplish this, year-round weekly live music concerts are held in the atrium. Beautiful art objects, crafted by local artisans, are hung throughout the facility, similar to an art gallery, which invites people to stroll about and look at the artwork. Numerous community celebrations and events are held in the atrium or conference center annually, again demonstrating how PMC has fostered familiarity and taken the fear out of coming to the hospital."

The following statement from PMC's Web site (https://www.parrishmed.com/about/index.php) summarizes its dedication to its service leadership mind-set:

> Providing care and comfort is Parrish Medical Center's highest mission and is reflected in our Vision and Mission statements. We pledge to our guests, and each other: the finest in personal service, courtesy and respect, and a satisfying experience. We strive to deliver personalized care and health-related services consistent with quality medical and ethical standards to improve the health status of those the hospital serves.

Developing the Service Strategy

Business success is less a function of grandiose predictions than it is a result of being able to respond rapidly to real changes as they occur. That's why strategy has to be dynamic and anticipatory.

—Hamel and Prahalad[127]

After completing this chapter, you should be able to

1. Understand how strategic formulation and implementation interact

2. Identify key characteristics of implementing strategy direction

3. Understand the importance of vision, mission, and goals for strategists

4. Realize managerial implications of service strategies

n the early 1990s, Valarie Zeithaml and her partners, A. Parasuraman and
Leonard Berry, pointed out the importance of leadership in service. They
focused on the role of *the leader* in the service industry and on those attributes
and characteristics of the leader that would enable the organization to better
achieve quality service. They maintained that managing in the traditional sense is
not enough in today's competitive service industry.

> *Every act of creation is first of all an act of destruction.*
> —Pablo Picasso

We have seen first hand how strong management commitment to service quality energizes and stimulates an
organization to improved service performance. We have
seen first hand how role ambiguity, poor teamwork, and
other negatives fester in a rudderless, leaderless environment, sapping an organization's service quality.[327]

This, they said, was why the direction and inspiration associated with effective
leadership were essential. Therefore they suggested that a service leader should be
someone who is able to build a *climate of excellence* to overcome any obstacles to
service quality. Such service leaders fundamentally believe that high service quality
pays off on the bottom line. According to Zeithaml et al.,[327] a service leader must
have the following four general characteristics:

1. *Service vision.* Service is seen as integral to the organization's future, not just
   a peripheral issue.

2. *High standards.* Legendary service is sought after, and it is good enough so
   that customers can differentiate one organization from others.

3. *In-the-field leadership style.* A hands-on approach is applied to obtain the
   desired level of service quality. The manager emphasizes two-way personal
   communication and is visible to the staff—observing and coaching, rewarding and correcting, questioning and listening. The leader's purpose is to have
   the best available knowledge of what is really going on in the field.

4. *Integrity.* Being fair and having personal integrity are characteristic of
   successful service leaders. This springs from the notion that it is actually
   impossible to cultivate a service-minded attitude in an organization where
   the managers do not practice what they preach.

Although Zeithaml et al.[327] state that service leaders come in all shapes and sizes,
their focus is on the job or position of a leader, not merely the act of leading itself,
as the latest theories of leadership suggest. There are those who can lead and those
who will follow—"the committed servers." Today, however, service leadership is not
just the interaction between those who lead and those who follow. There must be a
collective effort by everyone within the organization to build the kind of service
quality needed to set the organization apart from its competitors.

Looking at the concept from a different angle, a multidimensional meaning may
be perceived. First, service leadership can in fact be a *market passion,* created by a

competitive advantage that has been gained by outstanding service delivery that differentiated the organization enough to make it the leader in its particular market. However, service leadership can also refer to the *act of leadership*, which ultimately leads to successful service delivery, as discussed in previous chapters. Service leadership does not, by any means, refer only to managerial responsibilities or characteristics. Yet again, it is a question of *leadership* as opposed to *leaders*. The four characteristics of service leaders previously mentioned were identified before the days of contemporary collective leadership theory but long after the days of the Greek philosophy of the individual's potential for leadership. The four characteristics focus on the behavior of a leader. However, the characteristics can be argued to be central to any member of a service organization who truly believes in the power of differentiation through service, and who hence aspires to excellence in service. It may well be a top or middle manager who does so, but it can and should be equally true about the frontline staff members themselves.

Why is this difference in perspective on leadership important for service? The importance of leadership in the service sector is great due to the growth and dynamic nature of the industry itself and the rate at which changes in service delivery are occurring. It is important because the way an organization defines the act of leadership (the leader vs. a collective effort) fundamentally affects how service management is approached in that organization.

The need for leadership in service is beyond question. How it is defined determines

- The role of the management and staff
- The level of involvement in the organization
- The distinction between the formulation and the implementation of service strategy

Effective leadership has always been found to enhance teamwork, proactive behaviors, job satisfaction, and service quality, but now what is changing is *who* is in the driver's seat. Traditionally, only managers have taken the role of the leader, carefully directing and motivating their staff toward a desired goal. However, in our complex and fragmented world, such enormous tasks should no longer be entrusted to a single individual. Increasingly, the involvement of all organizational members is expected and their collective knowledge is being recognized as an intangible organizational asset. The same is true about the formulation and implementation of strategy in service organizations. If an organization subscribes to theories of collective leadership, then the level of involvement of its staff in strategic thinking and action is drastically different from an organization that maintains that all strategic thinking should be done *at* the top *by* the top.

> *How many things are looked upon as quite impossible until they have been actually effected.*
>
> —Pliny the Elder

The purpose of this chapter is to explore further the impact of applying leadership principles to strategic approaches in service. First, we examine the strategic planning process itself and clarify the basic terms of service vision, mission, objectives, and goals and how they relate to the organization as a whole. Second, we take a look at the formulation of strategy in relation to its implementation. Finally, we address the issue of the role of the strategist in the process at both the corporate and the division levels.

Strategic Plan Design

As discussed earlier, modern application of strategy in business draws on the ancient art of war. The battleground may be different, the stakes have changed, but in the end, the goal is basically the same—to conquer your opponents and protect your own interests. Today's battleground is the marketplace, so the organization's strategies are overall plans for how it will achieve a competitive advantage in that arena. Strategies, in both business and war, are mainly applied to planning and positioning resources so that an advantage can be achieved *before* the enemy or competitor is engaged. On the other hand, tactics—as opposed to broader strategies—involve maneuvering or shifting one's forces *during* a battle or service process. They are the individual activities that an organization plans to implement to carry out the organization's strategies. To be successful, of course, the organization must stay flexible enough to adapt its tactics as the situation develops within the marketplace.[135]

Strategy is about selection of goals and objectives, which is what makes every single strategy unique in nature. Jack Welch, former CEO of General Electric, said the following five simple questions brought strategic thinking to life for him:

- What is the detailed global position of your business and that of your competitors?
- What actions have your competitors taken in the past 2 years that have changed the competitive landscape?
- What have you done in the last 2 years to alter that landscape?
- What are you most afraid your competitor might do in the next 2 years to change that landscape?
- What are you going to do in the next 2 years to leapfrog over their moves?[317]

No matter how managers conceptualize strategizing, developing any strategy is a complex process. The stages between an organization's mission and the final implementation of the strategy have fuzzy boundaries. However, Figure 5.1 helps bring structure to the concept.

As shown in the figure, the first stage in the planning process is the *understanding* stage. For an organization to determine where it is currently located, it needs to analyze and understand its own current state and that of its environment. One of the most widely used tools for strategic planning is the strengths, weaknesses, opportunities, and threats (SWOT) analysis. Drawing on the data from the analysis, the corporate or business unit develops its strategies. Both offensive and defensive plans of action are rationalized by a belief in the organization's *internal* strengths, as well as by fear of *external* factors, such as competitors' capabilities or opportunities or threats in the market environment.

To build a foundation for the business or services being developed, a framework of purpose (the corporate or service mission) and philosophy is set by the development of organizational values. Once an organization knows who and where it is and what values should guide its business decisions, the development of general objectives for the future (vision) and specific goals for each of the objectives can be identified. Finally, once the objectives and goals have been determined, strategies and

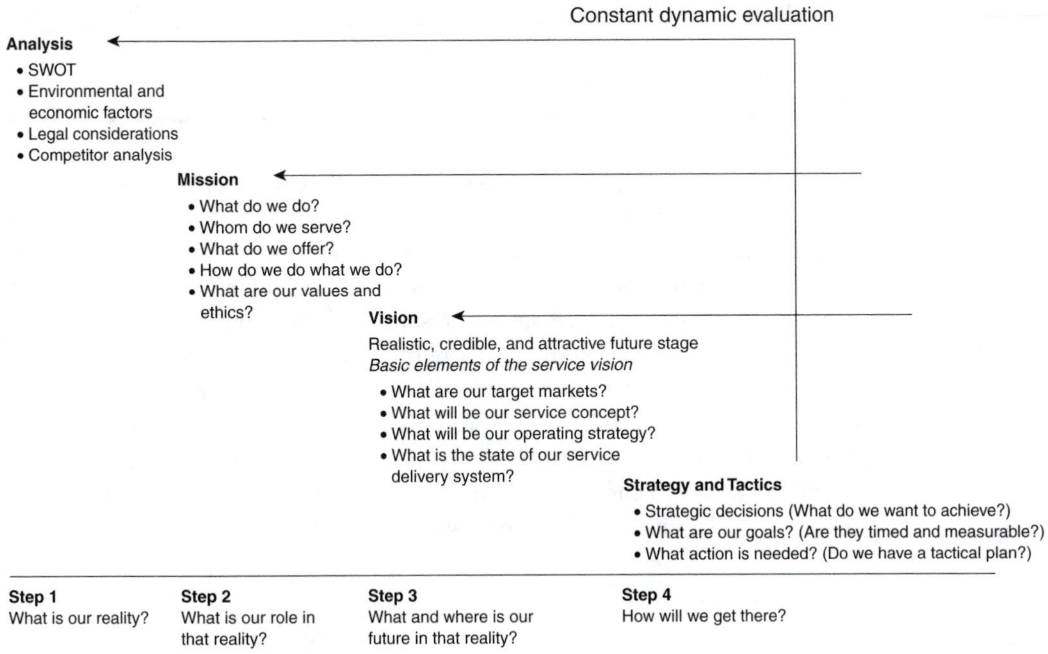

Constant dynamic evaluation

Analysis
- SWOT
- Environmental and economic factors
- Legal considerations
- Competitor analysis

Mission
- What do we do?
- Whom do we serve?
- What do we offer?
- How do we do what we do?
- What are our values and ethics?

Vision
Realistic, credible, and attractive future stage
Basic elements of the service vision
- What are our target markets?
- What will be our service concept?
- What will be our operating strategy?
- What is the state of our service delivery system?

Strategy and Tactics
- Strategic decisions (What do we want to achieve?)
- What are our goals? (Are they timed and measurable?)
- What action is needed? (Do we have a tactical plan?)

Step 1	**Step 2**	**Step 3**	**Step 4**
What is our reality?	What is our role in that reality?	What and where is our future in that reality?	How will we get there?

Figure 5.1   Stages of Strategic Planning

relative tactics on how the organization is going to get where it wants to go are for-mulated. As is discussed later, it is in this part that writers and scholars of strategic management differ in their opinions. At this stage, some argue for the need for a specific implementation program and action plans. Others believe implementation is an integral part of the formulation process itself and that through it, patterns of behavior and actions emerge. No matter which approach an organization takes, it needs to evaluate its progress throughout the process.

Shinkle, Gooding, and Smith[279] point out that managers often make the mistake of attempting to lay out their specific objectives and goals prior to understanding the purpose of their organization (its mission) and prior to having a concept of what the organization intends to be in the future (its vision). To successfully design a strategic plan of action, strategists (management or other participants in the process) need to have a clear understanding of the critical ingredients of such a plan. Let's take a look at these critical elements: (a) mission, (b) vision, (c) objec-tives and goals, and (d) strategies and tactics.

Mission

The importance of mission is often neglected and is in fact still underresearched in the field of management. However, two schools of thought can be identified in relation to organizational mission statements and their application. On the one hand, mission is referred to as a business strategy seeking answers to the question "What is our business?" On the other, mission is expressed in terms of philosophy and ethics.[59] The strategy school of thought regards the organizational mission primarily as a strategic tool that defines a company's business rationale and its target markets. However, mission can also be thought of as "cultural glue," governed by strong values and norms and enhancing collective understanding of events and unity within the organization.

In any event, a corporate mission statement should not be a shallow slogan but should highlight what the company really stands for. Whom do we serve, what do we offer, how do we do what we do, and so on. The mission statement often includes (a) an evaluation of the customers served and not served, (b) the field of competition or market, and (c) the products and services that define the limits of what is offered.[59] When an organization determines its purpose or mission, it is essential that it understand its customers and other stakeholders. Through that understanding, the company can determine its service offering. Ultimately, the organization can determine whether and how it plans to establish differentiation through its service.

Let's look at how the Actavis Group, an international generic pharmaceutical company, demonstrates its mission, as shown on its Web site.

Our Mission

Our MISSION is to create value in pharmaceuticals for employees, customers and shareholders.

Our Commitment

Actavis considers the interests of all its stakeholders, including employees, customers and suppliers, as well as the local communities and environments in which it operates, as being integral to its business operations.

The Executive Board takes responsibility for matters relating to corporate, social and ethical policies. The Group is committed to being honest and fair in its relationships with customers and suppliers and to being a good corporate citizen in the countries in which it operates.

In the mission statement, the company recognizes the importance of all stakeholders for the success of the company. Despite the highly competitive nature of the generic pharmaceutical industry, Actavis has experienced both internal and external growth of 15% to 20% over the past few years, returning record profits to its shareholders, and the company expects this level of growth to continue. The success of the company is based on its unique culture and dynamic workforce. With a combination of committed scientists, mainly from Northern Europe, strong local sales networks around the globe, and strategically located manufacturing and material sights to ensure high-quality, low-cost manufacturing, the company has been able to provide its customers with products and services that differentiate the company in its market. The products and services are developed in a culture of close cooperation among scientists, market analysts, and service providers. In addition, Actavis actively seeks input from customers and other stakeholders across cultures and market segments.

Vision: Who, What, How, and When in the Future Tense

Vision can be similar to the mission, or it can be something totally different. Leadership theory identifies the concept of vision in the following way:

> To choose a direction, a leader must first have developed a mental image of a possible and desirable future state of the organization. This image, which we call a vision, may be as vague as a dream or as precise as a goal or mission statement. The critical point is that a vision articulates a view of a realistic, credible, attractive future for the organization, a condition that is better in some important ways than what now exists.[59]

As is the case with corporate visions, the purpose of a service vision is to paint a picture of the future that motivates and energizes those who are going to get the organization there. For the vision to have practical application, the organization needs to specify its stakeholders, products, or services in the future as well as the company's future location, as determined by the location of potential future customers of the organization. Moreover, the organization's vision needs to address what will enable it to succeed in its future game plan and when its implementation is going to take place.

The service vision of Actavis can also be found on its Web site (http://www .actavis.com/investors/corporatefactsheet.htm): "Our vision is to become a leading company in the sales, development and manufacturing of quality generic pharmaceuticals in the international market."[1]

Here the company does not specify the stakeholders (as it did in the mission statement), but it highlights its products and services, its value chain, and the future location of its customers. However, the Actavis Management Board does not publicly release its game plan regarding what factors will enable the organization to succeed in its future. Such information is kept confidential and is embedded in the short- and long-term tactical plans of the organization.

In 1986, James L. Heskett made an important contribution to the discussion of service strategy formulation when he introduced the concept of strategic service vision in his book *Managing in the Service Economy*.[140] As illustrated in Figure 5.2, he identified seven elements (four are basic, three are integrative) of a strategic service vision. The four basic elements include the target market segments, service concept, operating strategy, and service delivery system. The three integrative elements consist of positioning, value-cost leveraging, and strategy-system integration. The strategic formulation starts with an evaluation of each of the seven elements. Heskett's model includes questions to guide practitioners through the process of service strategy formulation.

The four basic elements of Heskett's strategic service vision model involve a careful analysis of the organization's customers, its services, and its operational efficiency. In addition, these basic elements include an evaluation of the service delivery system and its capacity to deliver the service promise made to customers.

To formulate an effective service strategy, every organization needs to know and understand its customers, their needs, and their circumstances. Thus the first of the

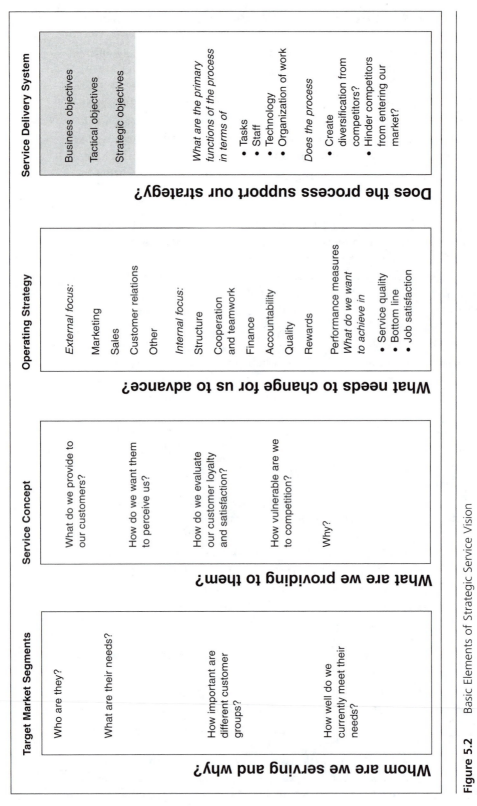

Figure 5.2 Basic Elements of Strategic Service Vision

SOURCE: Adapted from Heskett, J. L., *Managing in the service economy*, copyright © 1986, Harvard Business School Publishing Corporation. All rights reserved.

100

four basic elements, the *target market*, deals with identifying the market segments or groups of people the organization sets out to serve. After segmenting the market and pinpointing which customer segments are most likely to be profitable and applicable to its services, the organization must analyze the benefits or value created for the organization's stakeholders (employees, customers, and shareholders). The second basic element is the *definition of an organization's primary business*. This definition should be broad enough to allow for possible extensions to the definition because of such factors as technological advances or changes in consumer needs or wants. If the definition is too narrow, the organization may be at risk from organizations in related industries. However, if the definition is too broad, a business may try to stretch outside its core competencies.

The third step in the process is the *development of an operational strategy* to enhance the efficiency of service delivery. The purpose is to develop a set of strategies for important elements in the organization's day-to-day operations, such as marketing, human resources, finance, and operations. Important steps include identifying where investments should be made, in which areas the most effort should be spent, and the extent of changes that need to be carried out with respect to the impact on service quality and productivity. The goal is either to maintain or to enhance the organization's competitive advantages.

After analyzing benefits for stakeholders, defining the organization's business, and developing the organizational strategy, the final basic element concentrates on *delivery of the service*. The elements of the service delivery system—its capacity and important features, such as people, technology, workplace layout, and procedures—are needed to help ensure quality, differentiate the service from the competition's service, and provide barriers to entry for potential rivals.

Heskett's three integrative elements of strategic service visions (positioning, value-cost leveraging, and an integration of the organization's strategy and its systems) help the four basic elements fit together to provide a consistent service strategy.[125]

Objectives and Goals

General strategic objectives are formulated on the basis of the gap between the current mission and the future vision of the organization. The purpose is to close the gap in the time determined to be appropriate relative to the organization's capability to act, its resources to act, and the *tolerance* of the environment demanding those changes. The objectives are relatively few in number and should be stated in general terms, allowing for flexible and creative ways of identifying appropriate tactics needed to see them through (see Figure 5.3).

The fact is that goals and strategies are interrelated concepts. As Hatch[135] noted,

From the rational perspective, goals give organizations the direction they need to perform effectively. From the emergent perspective, they help the organization to adapt to changing circumstances, and in the symbolic view, goals give organizations the appearance that they know what they are doing.

Strategic Plan 200___
[Name of division/department]

[Pinpoint here the department's role in the company (department's mission statement)]

[Pinpoint here what the department is going to do next year to support and fulfill its mission and realize the company's vision. Specify overall divisional objectives for financial performance, customer care, process improvements and talent development, i.e. objectives and tasks]

[state tasks or tactics here]

Finance
We aim to . . .
[state objective here]

☐ Action ONE
(write short
description of task)   NN MM/YY

☐ Action TWO
(write short
description of task)   NN MM/YY

☐ Action THREE
(write short
description of task)   NN MM/YY

Customers
We aim to . . .
[state objective here]

☐ Action FOUR
(write short
description of task)   NN MM/YY

☐ Action FIVE
(write short
description of task)   NN MM/YY

☐ Action SIX
(write short
description of task)   NN MM/YY

Internal Processes
We aim to . . .
[state objective here]

☐ Action SEVEN
(write short
description of task)   NN MM/YY

☐ Action EIGHT
(write short
description of task)   NN MM/YY

☐ Action NINE
(write short
description of task)   NN MM/YY

People
We aim to . . .
[state objective here]

☐ Action TEN
(write short
description of task)   NN MM/YY

☐ Action ELEVEN
(write short
description of task)   NN MM/YY

☐ Action TWELVE
(write short
description of task)   NN MM/YY

NN = owner of task   **Monthly and quarterly follow-up [mark as shown]**

☐ Not started   ☐ On track   ☐ Completed

Figure 5.3   Strategic and Tactical Plan

To further define the objective, goals are assigned to each objective. The goals are specific in nature and usually have a shorter term focus. They define tasks, ownerships, and deadlines. There are two types of goals—official goals and operative goals. *Official goals* are broad and general in nature and are intended to provide general guidelines and set expectations. Goals of this type need to be passed down the organizational ladder until every member of the organization has been delegated a share of the overall organizational responsibilities. Second, there are *operative goals*, which focus attention on the issues that require effort on the part of specific units and particular employees. Therefore, operative goals define the direction that specific units and individuals should take. They can also be used as criteria for evaluating performance.[135]

Strategies and Tactics

Finally, we come to the strategic part of the overall strategy. Many managers do not really decide what their real objectives and goals are before they begin strategizing. It is hard to decide whether the goals come before the strategy or the strategy is determined before setting the goals.

An understanding of environment provides insight into *what might be done*. Actions of competitors determine *what must be done*, but the resources of the organization limit *what can be done*.[279] Knowledge of the environment gives the management team a sense of urgency and puts them under pressure to act. Often, this pressure to act causes the management team to skip or jump over critical steps needed for their strategies to be comprehensive and in line with the organization's overall direction. On the other hand, objectives, goals, and action plans are tangible, measurable concepts that are welcomed by a rationalistic management team. They can be developed step by step, using systematic, widely accepted, and easily comprehended methods within the organization. The process, objectives, and goals reflect the evolution of control and predictability for the future. What makes the transition into strategic work difficult is that it needs to be creative—it often requires skills and capabilities far different from those of organized goal setting. It requires insight, in-depth knowledge of the business and industry, and the ability to see patterns where others fail to do so.[212]

Traditionally, strategy development has been considered to be the responsibility of the top management, who would set goals and delegate their decisions downward through the different levels of the organization. Today, however, this traditional view of an authoritative, top-down management is changing and becoming more democratic and participative. In these situations, management only specifies broad guidelines, leaving strategy development (the how) and goal setting (the what) up to individual divisions and employees.

The size of an organization will have a major impact on its strategic efforts. In larger organizations, strategies may be formulated at each level of the operation. Multiple strategies are often coordinated with and integrated into the overall corporate strategy. Some firms, however, prefer to use a hands-off policy, allowing separate business units to operate more or less independently.[135]

An organization may have many different strategies. Typical strategies include marketing, sales, technology, finance, operations, supply, human resources management, purchasing, and service strategies. To ensure harmony and noncompetitive interaction between different strategies, each needs to be considered together with the others, as a part of the whole.[279]

In addition, there are different levels of strategy. *Business-level* strategies involve issues that define how an organization intends to compete in its market. Typical business-level strategies might include the following activities: building new plants, expanding into new territories, achieving product or service differentiation, implementing quality enhancement programs, and launching cost-reduction programs. At a higher level, the so-called *corporate strategies* are found. They deal with large-scale decision making that determines the scope of the corporation's activities and its future direction. This level of strategizing decides in what business activities the corporation should engage. In general, this level determines how the organization segments its market and how different parts of the organization can address different opportunities with maximum overall results. Typical of the corporate level of strategy formulation are decisions to acquire other firms, engage in joint ventures, diversify, and reorganize. If the environment presents more threats than opportunities, then strategic decisions will be made at the corporate level to divest, downsize, and concentrate on existing lines of business.[135]

The purpose of strategy is to provide clear direction for organizational members. Since an organization cannot focus on many strategies simultaneously, it is essential for it to limit the number of strategies without compromising the completeness of the plan itself. Research suggests that ideally, an organization should focus on one vision, one mission, three to five objectives, one to five goals for each objective, and three to seven strategies. However, it can have as many action plans as required.

Strategic Intent

Companies that have risen to global leadership over the past 20 years invariably began with ambitions that were out of all proportion to their resources and capabilities. But they created an obsession with winning at all levels of the organization and then sustained that obsession over the 1 to 20 year quest for global leadership.[279]

Hamel and Prahalad[127] term this obsession *strategic intent*.

To analyze it, we must ask the following key questions: Is strategic intent merely a blind and uncontrollable hunger for winning? At any cost? Is it simply the old warrior gone wild in the battle for business success? The answer to these questions is no. Hamel and Prahalad[127] suggest that ambition alone is not sufficient. Many companies may have the hunger but fail to win because they do not proactively *develop* the required strategies and then *implement* them well. To consistently succeed, organizations must

- Focus all their management efforts toward achieving victory in the marketplace
- Motivate their employees through instilling in them the values of the corporation
- Encourage individual and team involvement and contributions
- Be flexible enough to revise operational definitions and procedures as required

This last point is particularly important because successful competitiveness ultimately depends on how fast a company exploits new advantages rather than relying on past performance or a stockpile of perceived advantages.

It is virtually impossible to separate corporate strategies from the culture and structure of an organization because they are a product of complex interactions between organizational members and the environment in which they live and work, the competition they face, and the motivation they have to strive for victory in the marketplace. Indeed, a secret ingredient to succeeding is to make sure that all members of the organization understand how the organization's challenges relate to their own jobs and, conversely, how the performance of their jobs affects them personally as well as the organization as a whole. Creating that kind of personal responsibility enhances the organization's ability to wage its everyday battles. To reach the energy level required to carry this out, top management is required to

- Create a sense of urgency
- Develop a competitive focus at every level through widespread use of bench-marking against only the "best in class" at every level
- Provide employees with the skills they need to work effectively
- Give the organization time to digest one challenge before launching another
- Establish milestones and review mechanisms[127]

Implementation

Leadership is essential to the accomplishment of any strategy. In fact, strategies are decisions an organization makes on how it should go about its business. Although an organization reaches a decision, action does not necessarily follow. Mintzberg and Quinn[213] have pointed out that "ineffective implementation can make an otherwise sound decision ineffective."

The old riddle of the four frogs sitting on a lily pad is very applicable here. The four frogs are sitting on the lily pad minding their own business. One decides to jump. How many are left? Three? None? Does the lily pad tip over? Do the others follow the one that decided to jump? The least obvious answer may be "all of them remained on the lily pad!" Just because one frog *decides* to jump does not mean he *carried out* the decision. We automatically expect decisions to be implemented. However, our experience tells us that even the best New Year's resolutions are not always kept; thus, we stay overweight, the kitchen is still unpainted, and we still have not visited our elderly aunt. In spite of our painfully obvious failures to implement decisions we make every day, we still expect the most complex business decisions—whether about incremental or radical changes or about transformations of processes and behaviors—to take place when it comes to strategizing in an organizational setting.

Crafting Strategies

Obviously, before anything can be implemented, the strategies must be formulated, so let's take a closer look at that process. Strategists often begin the strategizing process by using SWOT analysis, as presented earlier, in Figure 5.1. Those who apply this method believe that thoughts and actions come in a neat, chronological order. However, to most of us, life is seldom that well organized. It is generally messy and complicated, and we often learn through trial and error. Problems are in the habit of popping up when we least expect them, and the resulting actions and reactions to them often provoke unexpected responses. Then again, this is what makes life interesting. Mintzberg's and Quinn's alternative method of strategizing rests on that assumption. He calls the method "crafting" strategies. It highlights the process in which effective strategies develop in harmony, not contradiction, with the contemporary business environment.

> Craft evokes traditional skill, dedication, and perfection through the mastery of detail. What springs to mind is not so much thinking and reason as involvement, a feeling of intimacy and harmony with the materials at hand, developed through long experience and commitment. Formulation and implementation merge into a fluid process of learning through which creative strategies evolve.[213]

Mintzberg and Quinn point out that crafted strategies have the following characteristics:

- They are based on past patterns.
- They emerge without any formal intention or deliberate act.
- They consist of broad guidelines.
- They often take place in a quantum leap.[213]

First of all, although strategies are plans for the future, they are simultaneously suggestive of patterns from the past. An actual plan can be a strategy even though it has not deliberately and rationally been identified before the fact. Often, effective organizations turn action into patterns of behavior that later become a form of strategy that the organization applies consciously or subconsciously.

Second, strategies can emerge. Most of the literature has depicted strategizing as a deliberate process. However, strategies can emerge without any formal intention or deliberate act on behalf of management. "Strategies can *form* as well as be *formulated*. A realized strategy can emerge in response to an evolving situation, or it can be brought about deliberately, through a process of formulation followed by implementation."[213]

To tap into the resources found in the knowledge of customer needs and organizational strengths or weaknesses found throughout an organization, many organizations apply a bottom-up process in their strategic efforts. Such strategies have been labeled *emergent strategies*. According to Hatch, this view moves beyond participation of selected individual organizational members and encompasses the impact of all organizational members—by whatever method—on the strategy process.

Third, strategies develop in all kinds of strange ways, and experience tells us that there is no single right way to make a strategy. To enhance flexibility and to draw on the experience of those closest to the action, only broad guidelines from management, called "umbrella strategies," are set in many organizations today. These umbrella strategies are based on careful observation of what is actually happening in the organization and are constantly reevaluated. Meanwhile, managers leave the figuring out of *how to achieve the strategy* to other organizational members.

This kind of general plan evolves through trial and error, which allows strategies to "emerge en route." In this way, emerging strategies can foster learning. This is contrary to planned strategies, in which learning does not take place after the decisions have been made and the formal implementation phase begins. Then the order of the day is to do as instructed and not to construct.

When strategies fail, managers often blame the strategist, who they feel has simply not been "smart enough" to see the future, or they blame those who have failed to implement strategies correctly. This is an oversimplification. In fact, strategists and management often get much better results by "allowing their strategies to develop gradually through the organization's action and experiences. Smart strategists appreciate that they cannot always be smart enough to think through everything in advance."[213] Some have gone beyond the point of talking about emergent strategies and state that in many cases formulation never really takes place. In that case, the organization's "strategy" is based solely on successful action, which might have been either chanced on by pure luck or inferred from prior action.[135]

Fourth, Mintzberg and Quinn[213] suggest that organizational changes often happen in "quantum leaps," not through slow, incremental adaptation. This is especially true when structures are well established and those doing the strategizing have a vested interest in keeping the current structure in place. Finally, these researchers assert that to manage strategy is to craft thought and action, control and learning, stability and change. Therefore, they argue that, contrary to the popular view of the strategist as a planner or visionary, the strategist should first and foremost be seen as a *pattern recognizer* or a *learner* who manages a process in which visions of the future and strategies to enable that future can both emerge or be deliberately formulated. To manage in this context, according to Mintzberg and Quinn, is to create an organizational environment or climate in which a wide variety of strategies can grow. They further point out that more complex organizations may require "building flexible structures, hiring creative people, defining broad umbrella strategies, and watching for the patterns that emerge."

As noted earlier, in many cases, plans are formulated by senior management and then carried out by other people. Hatch[135] argues that strategy researchers tend to focus on top managers and, regrettably, ignore the interests and concerns of other organizational members; in doing this, researchers "silence their voices." In recent years, however, those voices have been getting stronger. Their power is increasing as the world gets more complicated and the organization needs fast, accurate, and timely input for its decision making and actions. Traditionally, the focus of strategic planning research has been to identify and develop guidelines for managers so they can find the right strategy for every occasion, just as researchers have attempted to find the right traits, attitudes, and behaviors for leaders, to enhance leadership development. As always, the world is not simply black and white. Just as the quest for traits and behaviors in leadership has often involved tilting at windmills, finding the single perfect strategy also suffers the same fate.

Contrary to the view that strategies emerge, the idea of *rational approaches* to strategizing views strategy development as a process of designing an organization as you would design any tool or machine; therefore, the logic behind such attempts is completely rational. In this approach, the organization looks for ways to allocate its resources and plan its actions in a very intentional way. It tries to achieve competitive advantage by equating its strategic plans with its decision-making process, and it tries to make sure these are strategically connected to the organizational goals and values.[135] This sets the tone for how strategizing is approached by those who prefer the controlled and systematic way of making sense of their environment. These people carry out a systematic analysis of a given situation (market, competitor, and customers) and of their own organization's strengths and weaknesses.

Rational planning aids in focusing efforts and energies toward a common goal, but at the same time, it encourages separation between strategy formulation and implementation. In many, if not most, organizations, this separation takes place through a hierarchical division of labor—that is, top managers or formal planning teams formulate strategy and others (middle management on down) are responsible for implementing it. Therefore, top management can concentrate on identifying and analyzing the external threats and opportunities and on devising strategies for maximizing performance on the basis of the organization's core competencies. Meanwhile, those at the operations level of the organization handle the day-to-day activities involved in achieving the organization's strategic objectives.

> If the only tool you have is a hammer, you treat everything like a nail.
>
> —Abraham Maslow

The Strategic Plan

Regardless of whether strategies are deliberately developed or simply emerge, most companies cannot afford to just meander along and hope they stumble on the right plan. As discussed in the beginning of this chapter, this is why an organization needs direction and a common understanding of the pace in which its *vision* of the future is to be realized as well as of the means of getting there (*strategies* and the *tactical plans* to realize those strategies). To create the level of energy necessary to take the organization forward, all employees need to understand the organization's mission or purpose. They need to have a vision of the future so they can understand and visualize where the organization is going. They also need something to guide their behaviors so they will know what enables or restricts their actions in getting there. Typically, those boundaries are set by organizational objectives, goals, values, and norms.

How do we make sense of all of this? The terminology can be confusing, so misunderstandings commonly occur when an organization attempts to communicate its strategy and the related tactics. This is where strategic plans come into play. In the quest to make sense of our world, many companies become overly dependent on strategic planning, resulting in a lack of flexibility and slow response to changes in customer needs or in the company's environment. However, an organization needs a frame of reference through which it can understand how to channel its resources, and it must have energy to optimize its ability to compete in the marketplace. Rational models of strategy implementation operate on the assumption that strategic decisions are consciously made and need to be implemented as planned. This assumption forms the basis of a strategy implementation process, which includes resource allocation, controls, and human resources (HR) systems to support the direction taken, to evaluate and reward performance, and to provide feedback to managers on the progress.[135]

As noted, the line between strategic formulation and implementation can be somewhat vague. Today's service environment embraces the idea of emergent strategies, and the concept of service leadership thrives on it. However, the strategic plan can still have a purpose—when applied sensibly. At the core of the matter is the fact that companies need to

1. Define the direction in which to go

2. Make sure everyone knows and supports the direction

3. Ensure that all actions support moving in the right direction[279]

On paper, developing the strategic plan sounds like a straightforward and logical task. However, determining and achieving all three points has turned out to be a daunting task for most organizations. A strategic plan provides a frame of reference that can be successfully applied in service. Now let's take a look at what a good strategic plan should encompass.

Strategic plans are broad in scope and multidimensional in nature and have both an internal and an external focus. A complete plan would include the following basic elements:

1. A vision of desired future results

2. A set of strategies and tactics needed to realize them

3. An implementation approach

In fact, a strategic plan answers four fundamental questions: (a) Where are we now? (b) Where do we want to go from here? (c) How are we going to get there? and finally, (d) Are we making any progress in reaching our goals?

In their book *Transforming Strategy Into Success,* Shinkle, Gooding, and Smith[279] identify the following 10 points of successful strategic management:

1. Create a vision.

2. Develop management commitment and align everyone's actions to reach the vision.

3. Establish a cross-functional approach to running the business.

4. Establish clear strategic plans with measurable goals and specific initiatives and actions.

5. Ensure that responsibilities are assigned and understood.

6. Provide leadership, empowerment, and coaching.

7. Use an open communication process to create an awareness and understanding of the business.

8. Establish a management process to ensure that progress is being made in following the plan.

9. Create a high-responsibility, participative, "no fear" environment that encourages teamwork.

10. Recognize and reward results and valiant attempts (i.e., reward people for doing the right things).

Accordingly, a strategic plan starts by considering the environment and its impact. The plan itself must include how the organization will determine what its current and potential customers want and do not want, what its competition's present offerings and policies are, and what the competition may do in the future. The plan must also address the possible impact of current and possible new government regulations and laws, in addition to possible scientific and technological developments. In light of these factors, self-assessment is used to determine "Where are we now?" and to decide "Where do we want to be in the future?" and "Why do we want to be there?"

The beginning and the end of the plan both involve discovering ways to leverage opportunities and close performance gaps in line with the organizational culture and its members. In general terms, strategy formulation involves the following:

- Considering various alternative actions intended to balance the organization's capabilities and the needs of its environment
- Establishing criteria for selection of alternatives
- Comparing and choosing among the alternatives[135]

The organization must solidly analyze its capabilities and strengths, as well as the market environment, to understand the key elements or success factors it needs to win in the marketplace.

Key success factors specify the true assets of an organization. Usually they are few in number and clearly distinguish one organization from another. They are the backbone of any strategy. If an organization attempts to strategize without a real understanding of what makes the company great or sets it apart from others, the likelihood of a successful application of strategy is slim. The challenge in identifying the key success factors is to determine a distinction between them and other important factors that are nice to have or even critical to have but are not as rare, are less difficult to duplicate, or are less able to create true added value for the organization. Oddly enough, many organizations have not identified what their few determining key factors are; hence, they are missing a critical piece of information in their decision-making process. Furthermore, key success factors can change over time as the organization matures and the environment changes.

One size does not fit all. Different organizations have different competencies or key success factors. They operate in various markets and environments. The needs of their stakeholders are unique. Therefore they may have different objectives that call for different strategies and tactics if they are to realize their vision of the future. To compensate for the rigid nature of strategic planning, such plans should be treated as dynamic plans and updated and adjusted whenever appropriate.[260]

Evaluation

How do we know whether the strategies we formulate and implement are effective? In practice, we can evaluate them on the basis of how the business is performing. We need to look beyond the short-term performance of the organization and evaluate performance on key factors and trends important to successful operation in a given market or industry. Rumelt[260] suggested that the following three basic questions be asked in such an evaluation:

- Are the objectives of the business appropriate?
- Are the major policies and plans appropriate?
- Do the results obtained confirm or refute critical assumptions on which the strategy rests?

On a divisional level, the most practical and common measure of effectiveness can include market share and profit margins. However, corporate strategies are often evaluated on the basis of the effectiveness of investment capital or on overall financial return.[135] Other evaluation methods are discussed in Chapter 8.

> *Imagination is more important than knowledge.*
> —Albert Einstein

The Role of the Strategist

How much should organizational members in general participate in the strategic work of their organization? Some studies have indicated that levels of participation and involvement can affect the implementation of any strategic decision made. Psychological studies have shown that when they have not been involved in establishing their goals, people in general are less motivated to achieve them.[135] The participation of various levels of management and key personnel can be used to enhance the quality of both the strategic process and decision making, as well as to ensure buy-in and more comprehensive implementation of decisions made in the process. A recent study of 600 managers found that participation positively affects peoples' perception of the process. They believe it to be less top-down, more rational, more focused by a shared vision, and more adaptive to organizational and individual needs, without having been slowed down by internal politics or culture.[71]

Management Roles

What, then, is the role of the manager in all of this, if participation and involvement are believed to have become a necessity? Should managers be hands-on or completely hands-off when it comes to divisional direction and decision making? Raynor and Bower[252] pointed out that in the 1990s, conventional wisdom held that corporate leaders should leave divisions alone, so long as they delivered on their objectives and goals. However, these researchers also have pointed out that this is changing. They maintain that in uncertain markets, CEOs need to provide strategic guidance more quickly and more often than before. Technology, communication, and transportation, as well as globalization itself, are working against strategists in the sense that planning to go from Point A to Point B in a logical and systematic manner is becoming practically impossible. The environment itself seems to be fostering the approach of emergent strategies. Raynor and Bower state:

> We have found that responding effectively in uncertain markets often requires more—not less—direction from the center. Our research into contemporary diversified companies suggests that, in industries undergoing rapid and difficult-to-predict change, corporate headquarters must play an active role in defining the scope of division-level strategy.

Many organizations are currently moving away from independent business units, adopting an approach where there is more overlap and sharing of responsibilities between units. Such structures are more complex, and senior management often shares responsibilities with operating units. Management's job here is to help guide the interdependencies between units. In their book *Parenting in Complex Structures*, Goold and Campbell[113] highlight the implications of the overlap and sharing of responsibilities when the distinction between corporate and local business units is blurred and the value created by corporate executives becomes less and less obvious. In the eyes of the local managers, corporate executives destroy some value by increasing overhead costs, slowing down decisions, and making some ill-judged interventions, and many do not add enough value to compensate for this. To justify their existence, corporate executives need to add clear value for organizational activities. That value shapes the responsibilities as well as the influence and power of the management team. Determination of this value is critical for any valid corporate strategy.

Traditionally, corporate functions have had the tendency to expand and diversify rather than to decrease. In the eyes of the local managers who get flooded with various requests from headquarters, this can have the appearance of interruption rather than value creation. However, the role of the corporate management team should be synergistic—creating value that is greater than the sum of the parts.

One of the latest trends in international business, explained in *Profit From the Core* by Zook and Allen,[329] emphasizes the risks of diversification. The key concept is that the best way for an organization to be more profitable and continue to grow is for it to focus on its core competencies or capabilities, with all managers throughout the organization contributing directly to those core competencies. In essence, "Identify what you do uniquely well, consolidate it as the stable foundation of a growth strategy, and then look for new growth opportunities in adjacent markets."[307]

Traditionally, divisional managers have been concerned with operating issues, and corporate leaders have been concerned with strategic issues and major investments. However, new research indicates potential ambiguity and confusion in such arrangements. Regardless of whether corporate's role in the process is to add value through its expertise or through assisting managers in other ways, responsibilities need to be discussed and clearly defined to keep focus, communication, and the chain of command clear and to keep expectations realistic. In this context, Goold and Campbell[113] maintain that there is a delicate balance between acting as policymaker and as police officer. Rigid corporate guidelines and policies applied to the execution of strategies hinder flexibility and proactive participation from those closest to the front lines. Such negative reinforcement has proven to undercut motivation and promote a lack of accountability among those who are expected to deliver on a day-to-day basis.

> In creating strategic flexibility, a corporate office must balance the immediate need for divisional autonomy with the potential need for future cooperation. Without this balance, divisions may act in ways that advance their current competitiveness but undermine opportunities to collaborate in the future.[252]

Complete freedom to act to serve one's own purpose in isolation from the whole can be as destructive as too many constraints. Raynor and Bower[252] point out that something that can make perfect sense in isolation could in fact undermine activities that the larger organization is pursuing or wants to pursue in the future. Divisional and local managers need to trust corporate intentions and rely on their overview and insights when it comes to judgments affecting the larger picture.

The moral of the story is, if you want to support a dynamic strategy, have a lean but powerful corporate office. Corporate executives should assist the CEO by keeping the CEO informed and by demonstrating sound judgment, not just by maintaining formally defined corporate roles. Furthermore, corporate and division executives need to spend time on strategy, apart from time that must be spent on operational issues.

In conclusion, the discussion in this chapter of strategy formulation and implementation should, as M. J. Hatch[135] puts it,

> encourage us, on the one hand, not to take ourselves and our organizations so seriously, and, on the other hand, to take our responsibility for our outcomes more seriously than we ever have before—in short, to consider alternative identities with which we might reform our actions, ourselves, and our organizations.

> *We shape our environments, then our environments shape us.*
> —Winston Churchill

You can plan to provide direction and a frame of mind in which organizational members may thrive, but you need the involvement and participation of the people associated with the emergent strategies to survive the service game. If fact, you must plan to change—but not plan in detail how you will implement those plans.

Summary

The distinction between leaders and acts of leadership affects how any organization approaches its strategic work; for example, does it use planning or crafting to develop its strategies? This distinction also affects the level of involvement organizational members have in the process. Traditionally, senior management has been responsible for setting strategies for others to implement. The emerging trends of collective leadership and the more demanding service environment have paved the way for a more dynamic approach to strategizing that goes beyond limited involvement to full participation as strategies emerge en route.

Managers now understand the need for more flexibility, but they also realize that this approach hinders the effect of the traditional planning approach to strategizing. During the strategy formulation process and its implementation, organizational members need to know and understand the organization's mission (what we do) and vision (where we are going). To bridge the mission and the vision, organizations set the pace by identifying general objectives designed to close that gap. Specific goals can then be attached to each objective along with applicable actions.

The traditional division between strategy formulation and implementation is disappearing; strategies can emerge either deliberately or through patterns of behavior. Hence the strategist needs to change from a planner to a *pattern recognizer* or learner who draws on the experience of others and successes and failures in the industry. Consequently, the role of corporate executives is also changing, with an approach that demands that each manager or executive add value to the core competencies of the organization.

Victoria's Secret on Customer Intelligence

Express, Lerner New York, and Limited stores include more than 2700 specialty shops. Limited Brands, the parent company, also owns controlling interest in Intimate Brands, Inc., the leading retailer of intimate apparel, beauty, and personal care products sold through more than 2400 stores under the brands of Victoria's Secret, Bath & Body Works, and White Barn Candle Co.

In 2004, the Limited, Inc., and Intimate Brands, Inc., began pilot studies using customer relationship management (CRM) software (from SAS Institute Inc.) to explore the potential return on market investment. The software segments the company's customer database to determine which customers are most likely to respond to a particular marketing campaign or activity. According to the results of the pilot test, the most successful channel was a direct-mail campaign for a new Victoria's Secret fragrance line called Dream Angels.

After analyzing their existing customer base, Victoria's Secret used SAS software to select more than 100,000 clients to receive a special direct mailing for the fragrances. The mailing, which invited these customers to visit a Victoria's Secret store to sample the scents, proved successful in moving catalog-only clients to the retail counter. "Our analysis has shown that customers buying Victoria's Secret products through all three channels—retail stores, the Web and catalogs—spend three to five times more than customers who buy through only one channel," said Bill Lepler, vice president of CRM at the Limited, Inc. "Based on this valuable analysis, The Limited and Intimate Brands can better understand our customers' behaviors and tailor marketing campaigns for all our brands."

The Key to Successful CRM Lies in Applying Powerful Analytics

According to Lepler, the key to successful CRM lies in applying powerful analytics to a single, customer-centric database—one that gives a comprehensive view of all customer interactions." This method allowed his company to identify the right customers for specific marketing campaigns, which resulted in multichannel shopping. "At Victoria's Secret, it's imperative to have a 360-degree view of our customers' activities across all channels, because a single-channel view can't give us full insight into customer needs," said Lepler. In the pilot test for Victoria's Secret's e-commerce Web site, a potential 400% return on investment was reported by the company and their partners from the SAS Institute. "SAS is scalable, which is very important when you're looking at whether a campaign that you've piloted on a hundred thousand customers will run against an enterprise database of over 25 million buyers."

Key Points

- CRM technology helps to identify the right customers for specific marketing campaigns.
- Customer intelligence enhances understanding of customer behavior.
- Technology can be used to enhance customer service.
- Better understanding of customer behavior is profitable.

SOURCE: "SAS customer intelligence."[263]

Key Concepts

Directions: The following are key concepts presented in this chapter. Write a complete definition for each one.

Service vision

Strategic plan

Mission

Crafting strategies

Questions

1. What is the difference between *leadership* and *leaders* within the service industry?

2. How is an organization's *mission* different from its *vision*? Give a real or hypothetical example of a company's mission and vision.

3. What is SWOT analysis? How does a company use it?

4. Heskett proposed four elements of a successful service strategy. What are these four elements?

5. What are *emergent strategies*? How do managers control their direction?

6. Describe the process of rational strategizing. What are one advantage and one disadvantage of this approach?

7. Shinkle, Gooding, and Smith identify 10 elements of successful strategy management. Condense these 10 elements into four statements.

8. What are an organization's key success factors? What is their role in the organization's strategy development?

9. What are the benefits of a participative style of strategy development?

10. What is the role of the CEO and other corporate executives within the new model of participative strategy development?

Advanced Activity

Formulate a strategic service vision for a company of your choice. It can be an actual company, or it can be one that you would like to start one day. Follow the steps in Figure 5.2 to formulate the vision. Write it up and present it to your class.

Search the Web

Find two or three examples of *service mission statements*. Examine the statements in terms of content and choice of words. What is the service promise made to customers? Does the statement say how the company is going to fulfill the promise? If and to what extent are employees mentioned in the statements? (a) Print out the statements and bring them to the class. (b) Underline wording or sentences you find particularly interesting. (c) Write a short report containing your findings.

Suggested Readings

Hamel, G., & Prahalad, C. K. (1989, May-June). Strategic intent. *Harvard Business Review,* 67(3), 63–76.

Mintzberg, H. (1999, Spring). Reflecting on strategy process. *Sloan Management Review,* 40(3), 21–30.

Designing the
Service Process

There is no such thing as a service industry. There are only industries whose service components are greater or less than those of other industries. Everybody is in service.

—T. Levitt[192]

Objectives

After completing this chapter, you should be able to

1. Understand the concept of service design

2. Know how to link strategy and service delivery

3. Identify the elements of the delivery process

4. Identify various methods for mapping a service process

5. Know basic steps in new service development

The Importance of Service Design

No matter what economic measure is used, there is no doubt about the importance of the service sector to the economy. Service design is far too important to be left to chance. It affects quality, cost, and organizational image. In fact, service is often the lifeline of an organization and therefore must be prepared for as much as possible before customers are encountered.

> Life can only be understood backward, but it must be lived forward.
>
> —Søren Kierkegaard

Quality improvements or new market developments provide the primary motivations for organizations to design their services. An organization may choose to redesign or simply adapt existing services to better fit customers' needs, to deliver the service better, or to enhance customers' perceptions of the service. On the other hand, an organization may choose to design a new service for existing customers or embark on a mission to design totally new services for markets never served before.

Stewart[292] identifies the following four primary foundations for service improvement efforts: culture based, design based, variation based, and failure based. *Culture-based improvements,* one of the earliest strategies to improve service, focus on customer interaction. The purpose is to create a service-driven culture powerful enough to ensure the flexibility and willingness of employees to engage in behaviors designed to enhance customers' satisfaction with the interaction. In the final analysis, it is the employees who usually determine whether customers are satisfied. Therefore, the overall success of the company depends on the employees becoming full members of the service culture. Drawing on customer needs, perceptions, and satisfaction parameters, *design-based improvements* aim to enhance service performance through a careful design of the service encounter and processes. *Variation-based improvements* rely on statistical process control (SPC)—a method well known to manufacturing. The nature of service limits the application of this method in service because of the lack of numerical data other than time, demand, and satisfaction scores. The final theme focuses on *failure-based improvements.* Methods of failure prevention, analysis, and recovery are at the heart of those efforts.

According to Pine and Gilmore,[240, 241] we have moved beyond the service economy to what they describe as the experience economy, in which service providers are actors, customers are guests, and the company is the stage. The goal is not just to deliver a one-time service but to deliver an experience that taps into the emotions and causes the "guest" to favorably remember the company's product or service in the context of a memorable experience. Disney World provides the quintessential experience, beginning with the fact that their employees are called "cast members." Rather than just selling amusement park rides and Mickey Mouse ears, Disney sells an entire experience, in which guests are immersed in sensations that are remembered for a very long time.

It is easier for some companies than others to adopt this experiential approach to their service delivery. Service organizations such as entertainment companies and high-end facilities in the hotel industry could easily provide customers with memorable experiences. This philosophy is much more challenging for those in organizations such as manufacturing plants, which sell business to business (BtoB), and retail stores that sell such mundane products as groceries or hardware.

Pine and Gilmore[240, 241] have even gone beyond the concept of *experience* to that of *transformation*, in which the consumer is actually changed by the event. They point out that, although it is not feasible for all service organizations to provide transformations, certainly a competitive advantage ultimately will lie in how successfully an individual, a group, or an organization delivers a favorable customer experience or transformation. A carefully designed service process, perfectly aligned with organizational strategies, is essential for that task. In fact, service failures frequently result from problems with the development, design, and specification of the service. An editorial in the *Journal of Operations Management*[312] even goes so far as to suggest that there is ample evidence that a well-designed service system is a representation of the quality of life in many societies. That may very well be true.

Service design is an important topic, both for the academic community and for the service industry itself. Managers and researchers are challenged by many compelling questions, such as

- How can customer needs and service offerings best be aligned through the service design process?
- What should the chain of events be in the design process?
- How do time and level of risk affect strategic decisions in the design process?
- Should an organization strive to adapt continuously to the changing needs of customers, or can it to some extent overcome the rate of change by proactively designing its services and, hence, shape the future needs of its customers?

These are all important questions, because in our new economy, it is no longer enough to carefully formulate strategies. Today, organizations also must be able to implement them swiftly and efficiently. They must in fact be able to adapt to their environment and customer needs while simultaneously striving to gain some control of the chain of events by shaping their market proactively. Service design, which is a direct descendent of organizational and service strategies, is a tool for both of these challenges. The organization's service goals and strategy determine the organization's intentions regarding the *service process: the flow, timing,* and *impressions.* The purpose of this chapter is to provide insight into the design of a service process that bridges from the formulation of an appropriate strategy to the delivery of the service promise. The chapter also highlights practical tools to use in mapping and delivering the service process, such as blueprinting, service mapping, sequential incident analysis, and benchmarking. The final section discusses methods for new service development.

Framework for Service Design

As discussed in the previous chapter, before an organization can begin to formulate any strategies, it has to establish its overall goals. The first questions that have to be answered are *What are we going to deliver?* and *What promise are we going to make to our customers?* To answer those questions, the organization also has to address the following:

- How will we treat our customers?
- What tasks are needed to deliver the service promise?
- What series of events will make up the service process?
- What tangibles need to be considered as a part of the service?

Thus developing the service strategy requires an examination and often documentation of the total series of tasks that make up the service process.

Once an organization has answered the fundamental question *What are we going to deliver and to whom?*, the formulation of the service promise can begin. The next question becomes *How, when, and where are we going to deliver the promise?* Now we enter the world of service design.

The rigor of the design depends on the organization's strategy or promise to its customers, but the basic principles in the design process remain the same. The design needs to highlight those unique features of the organization that have created or will create its competitive advantage. In other words, if the organization promises flexibility, then flexibility needs to be built into the service provision. If the promise states that speed and accuracy are most important, then more discipline and control are needed in the design. In addition, as discussed in Chapter 4, the environment itself has an impact on the design. If the environment is stable, then more of the process can be standardized. Therefore both the stability of the environment and the level of competition affect the selection of processes to be standardized and those that will be more dependent on the employees' actions.

The basic steps in designing a service are more or less the same regardless of the service promise or the organization's environment. Before the design process begins, the organization must understand the customer, the competition, and the market environment. In addition, it must get to know its own key success factors— what it has to offer that will make customers come to this company instead of going to the competition. All of these elements are needed for effective strategizing.

Once a strategy has been formulated, the process of deciding how to implement that strategy through the service processes can begin. The *basic* steps in the service design process are the following:

1. *Align* the overall organizational goals, service strategy, and service processes.

2. *Involve* employees and customers in the design.

3. *Map* various methods for visualizing the service process.

4. *Prepare* training for employees and changes in tangible artifacts or goods.

5. *Test* the system for weaknesses and revise as needed.

6. *Launch* by actively marketing the services in all target markets.

7. *Improve* by constantly evaluating the systems and services.

The extent of each step varies depending on the situation. Step 1, *strategy-design alignment,* needs to be carefully considered in any market environment. A typical question at this step would be *What strategy is the service design supposed to support?* The overall design must support the strategy that the organization intends to implement. Often a service process is designed in a vacuum, detached from the rest of the service system, resulting in service gaps and or service failures. The second step, employee and customer *involvement,* is important, but the degree to which their involvement is needed can vary depending on the situation. Typical questions at this step would be *What do employees and customers need? What are their roles in the process?* In a stable or highly regulated or inflexible environment, their impact can be less frequent and have less input on the service design. However, in an unstable environment—one that is highly flexible or unregulated—organizations are highly dependent on employee and customer input into the process, both in the initial design phase and throughout the lifetime of the service. Only with their participation can the organization collect information and build training and competence levels into the process. This allows service delivery to be appropriately aligned with customer needs and employee requirements.

Mapping is the third step. Various tools and methods have been developed for mapping the service process to make it more visible and easier to communicate. We will look at a number of these methods in this chapter. These methods are most appropriate when standardized practices can be adopted as a part of the service. Typical questions would be *What are the tasks to be performed? How are the tasks sequenced and timed?* A visual map of the process is then produced based on the answers. In a highly unstable environment, where service strategies emerge rather than result from a formal strategic formulation, such maps cannot be produced in a timely manner. In other words, where the service is so flexible that it constantly changes, organizations have no time to produce maps of the process. This creates a wealth of challenges for managing the process. These challenges include resource allocation, employee skill requirements, training of new employees, and cooperation between service divisions. As discussed in Chapter 3, under conditions of constant change, the entire organizational culture is entrusted with the management of the service process.

To implement a strategy and the accompanying processes successfully, the company must carefully consider the *task* itself, the *tangible* items and artifacts associated with the service, and the *treatment* given to customers. *Preparation,* the fourth step in the service design process, is essential before a new service or adjustments to existing services can be launched. Typical questions to be answered are *What preparations do employees need to carry out their tasks successfully? What tangible things must be developed or need to be changed?* The preparations could range from simply giving information through employee training to making changes in the layout and design of facilities and tangible items visible to the customers or in goods accompanying the service. The extent of the preparation is dependent on the time allowed for the formal design process. If the emerging strategy is embedded in the corporate culture, then the organization can rely on its usual methods to support its culture and employee initiatives. Of course, these methods sometimes need to be supplemented with formal training and skill building for specific tasks. The organization also highly values input from employees and customers when it is making decisions about the tangible aspects of the service. In an unstable and highly flexible environment, employees and customers may be the only ones in a position to point out important elements in a timely manner.

A service design must be a dynamic phenomenon. Thus the company must actively monitor the process. Before adjusting the service or creating a new one, the organization should use *tests* to detect design flaws and allow for adjustments before the service is provided to the public.

The following typical questions should be asked at this time: *Does the service meet the requirements of our strategy and the particular customer needs that we intend to meet? Are we ready? Have we ensured continuous evaluation of the service and feedback from customers?* An organization that employs a strong service culture strategy asks these questions constantly as a part of everyday operations. In a more regulatory environment, the process is more formal and can take time. In contrast, in a vibrant and highly competitive environment, organizations must be ready to act very quickly. Only after these design steps have been completed is the service *launched* into the market. As indicated earlier, both how formally the service is created or adjusted and how long it takes to do so depend on the situation and the strategy of each individual situation.

Finally, *continuous improvement* must be built into the process. Arthur M. Blank is one of the founders of Home Depot, the home improvement giant with more than 1700 stores in North America. His favorite T-shirt confirms his philosophy, "There is no finish line," thereby emphasizing that the philosophy of continuous improvement must be infused throughout the corporate culture—everyone must be tasked with designing, delivering, and constantly improving exceptional customer service.[16]

Let's take a look at how Parrish Medical Center (PMC) of Brevard County, Florida, handles its service design process.* PMC's strategic plan, which is referred to as the "game plan," identifies goals and key drivers in each of its five areas of focus (*service, people, quality, finances*, and *growth*). These five areas of focus are called PMC's *pillars of success*, a best practice they learned from Baptist Health Systems in Pensacola, Florida, and modified to fit their needs. The medical center's board, medical staff, auxiliary, and administrative leadership participate in an annual retreat to identify and set the goals for the game plan. The *people* and *service* pillars refer to patient and employee satisfaction. PMC's goal for these two pillars is to achieve a ranking of 93% or better.

To accomplish these goals, PMC formed seven culture teams, representing more than 150 staff members, volunteers, and physicians. PMC's leaders set the vision, and, together with the culture teams, they are vigorously working to move PMC along its path to becoming the "culture of choice." For example, when department heads and senior leaders make their "rounds" within the departments, they use questions as key drivers for employee satisfaction. Their purpose is to get to know employees, to determine if every employee has what he or she needs to get the job done, to be accessible and visible to employees, and to share information and answer questions informally.

The seven culture teams are focused on developing systems and processes for retention and recruitment, reward and recognition, education (curriculum),

---

*(All PMC information comes from interviews with CEO George Mikitarian and marketing director Natalie Sellers on January 10, 2005, and from e-mail communication with Natalie Sellers on November 15 and December 8, 2004, and January 18 and 27, 2005).

scripting, "bright ideas," orientation ("onboarding"), and rounding. By focusing resources on these seven areas, PMC intends to create an exceptional workforce, an exceptional work environment, and an exceptional (and sustainable) service experience for its patients.

PMC's strategy involves an inclusive process in which all stakeholders are involved. Staff, physicians, volunteers, and board members were all involved in identifying and defining PMC's values. The identified values—integrity, compassion, excellence, loyalty, safety, and stewardship—are not just words that are printed on a plaque or attached to the back of an employee badge never to be heard of again. PMC has made a conscious effort to recognize and celebrate its values through *storytelling*, a powerful communication tool. Every week, PMC holds weekly departmental "huddles,"—short, 10-minute stand-up meetings devoted to vision and values. During these huddles, stories are shared about how PMC employees, volunteers, and physicians are living their values.

> *Everything flows; nothing stays still.*
> —Heraclitus

PMC's culture transformation was part of its overall building strategy, described in Leadership Insights at the beginning of this section. To help explain its reasoning, PMC uses the following quote from Winston Churchill: "First we shape our buildings; thereafter they shape us." The belief is that the healing environment that was created at PMC will have an effect on the people working within the environment. However, PMC also understands that the environment is just one piece of a much larger service puzzle. Values, beliefs, and vision (the cultural onion) all are integral when one desires service excellence.

Designing the Service

Service design is a systematic way of describing tasks and the series of events that make up a service process. This design is used to execute organizational and service strategies. Service design should involve "developing a holistic view of the service while managing the details of the service."[41] Although the importance of delivering the service efficiently and accurately to customers is beyond dispute, few organizations have managed to design their services comprehensively enough to move beyond a consistent corporate image and appearance and standardized greetings of " . . . and how may I help you?"[169]

In some cases, standardized design principles from manufacturing can be useful in the service sector. In fact, the tangible nature of their products makes the service provided by many manufacturers straightforward and direct. Some of the customer benefits of the services that manufacturers offer include speed and accuracy of service delivery. This is especially true when it comes to replacing a defective product or honoring a warranty.

However, customers are human beings, which makes them complex phenomena—difficult to predict and understand. In addition, services are intangible and heterogeneous by nature, which means they cannot be examined beforehand or "tried on for size" or produced so that they are exactly the same over and over again. How can such an elusive phenomenon be described so that one can understand and communicate its components? The need to communicate the individual tasks or events that make up the service process is evident from both the employee's and the customer's points of view. The employee needs to be informed about how to perform the service as well as when and how to market the service. Marketing, of course, requires that unique features of the service are highlighted, customers' expectations are set, and the service is clearly differentiated from that of the competitors. The organization must absolutely understand the service process in its entirety, if it is to make available the resources needed for each task in the process, maximize operational efficiency, and ensure service quality.

When designing the service process, organizations must understand that *people* are at the core of service delivery—either as providers of services (from the organizational side) or as receivers of services (from the customer's point of view). In fact, Bateson[32] suggests that the service encounter may even be viewed as a tridimensional phenomenon, which includes (a) the customer, (b) the employee, and (c) the service organization. The creation of a positive service encounter is in their mutual interest. However, trying to apply the traditional manufacturing approach to service design often does not work because of the characteristics of service, such as perishability, inseparability of production and consumption, and the heterogenetic nature of service.

It is essential for organizations to move beyond a product-focused approach to service design and incorporate the interpersonal nature of the service encounter into the process. A key element here is an organization's human resources policies and practices, discussed more thoroughly in Chapter 11, "Implementing Human Resources Policies for Service Organizations." At PMC, George Mikitarian, PMC's CEO, believes that the philosophy of employing the right people must begin from the inside. He stresses that the organization must create an environment in which people want to come to work and to stay. To accomplish this, he has set PMC "on the journey to become the 'organizational culture of choice,' not just the employer of choice." He firmly believes that satisfied employees are better able to satisfy customers. Professional Research Consultants, Inc. regularly measure both employee and patient satisfaction for PMC. Mikitarian believes that if the goals of the first two pillars of success in PMC's game plan—people and service—are met, the others will fall into place. So far, their plan is working, because their employee satisfaction level is at the 96th percentile and their patient satisfaction level (staff courtesy and friendliness) is at the 93rd percentile. These percentages were determined by counting only the responses of "excellent" on the surveys—responses of "good" and "very good" are simply not considered to be good enough for PMC's goals.

How does an organization get to this level of satisfaction in both its employees and its customers? Klaus[183] suggests that the organization must pay attention to the "three T's" of service design: the *task*, the *tangible items,* and the *treatment* of the customers.[65, 66, 292] Let's examine each of these in turn.

The Task

When designing the service, the organization must first determine the *tasks* required to perform the service. What tasks are needed to deliver the promise to customers? How does the organization coordinate the flow and timing of events? What impression does an organization want to leave with its customers? Usually tasks are embedded in time, with a clear beginning and ending. It is through a task or series of tasks that value is delivered to the customers. Tasks may require some input or information from the customer, but they generally include procedures, scripts, processes, and decisions made for the benefit of the customer. Due to the interactive nature of service encounters, evaluation of the tasks can be somewhat subjective and is, to some extent, more difficult than the evaluation of goods or other tangible artifacts. Service measurements and methodology are the topics of Chapter 8, Designing Service Metrics."

When creating and arranging the series of tasks, it is necessary to consider three concepts that are very important for understanding the employee-customer encounter and are therefore crucial for a successful design. These key concepts are the *flow of the service experience, the flow of time,* and *the customers' perceptions* of the experience after the fact.[76] The following three questions address these concepts:

- What happens while the service is being delivered?
- How long does it *seem* to take?
- What did the customer think about it later?

The flow of the service experience is important for customer satisfaction and, ultimately, for customer loyalty. Customers summarize their perception of the sequence of events, and that summary affects both their decision to return and how they approach the next interaction with the organization. The summary alone does not explain the whole story, however. Behavioral research[14, 172, 253, 311] has suggested that our summaries are based mostly on (a) the trend (i.e., does the experience improve as we go along), (b) the highs and lows, and (c) the ending. Naturally, customers prefer a happy ending. Duration is not usually as important as the rate at which the service is improved. It is important to note that an unpleasant experience at the end of the service encounter can have drastic effects.

Flow of time plays an important role in the design of the service concept. Customers' perception of time is highly subjective and varies from individual to individual and from one situation to another. However, several common elements have been identified by cognitive scientists that are useful to service design: For instance, as most of us know, time seems to pass quickly when we are engaged in a task, but the clock almost seems to stop when we are forced to pay close attention to the passing of time. The classic example is being put on hold for an excessive duration of time during a telephone call to customer service. Furthermore, the greater the number of events in a sequence, the longer the process seems to have taken after the fact. "It is what you are doing, not how long you do it that sticks in people's minds."[76]

Parrish Medical Center admits that one of its remaining challenges in the area of customer service is dealing with making time go faster for its patients. It is a challenge on which PMC is actively working. One of its strategies is to give outpatients a small beeper, like the ones used in some restaurants for waiting customers, so they can be beeped when it is their turn. This way, the person can go to the café or gift shop to help pass the time instead of being stuck in a waiting room with little more to do than count the minutes. If someone is already sick or in pain, the passage of time can be doubly grueling. In PMC's emergency department, there is a plan to implement strategies to deal better with pain management and general comfort for patients who are waiting. For example, the department is considering having a small area where sick people can lie down while they are waiting to see a doctor, again to make the passage of time less stressful.

Customers' perception of the service after the fact, or so-called *counterfactual reasoning,* is the process of rationalizing the chain of events if something unexpectedly good or bad happens.[258] Customers seem to need to find a cause for what happens in the process after they have gone through it. For example, after a service failure, the customer feels better if he or she is given a plausible explanation of why the particular failure took place. It enhances understanding and establishes a sense of security that such an event is unlikely to occur again. Left without an explanation, the customer might feel confused and angry and would be hesitant about repeating the experience.

The Tangibles

The second element that needs to be taken into consideration when designing services is the tangibles that accompany the service. Tangibles are things or artifacts that meet the customers as they move through the process and affect their interpretation of the message being sent by the organization. They can include supplementary goods that facilitate service, manuals, company layout, or even the atmosphere where the service is being offered. Think about walking into a local retail store, dry cleaner, hospital, or your city hall. No matter what your experiences have been with each of these institutions, when you think about these places, you associate the tangible properties with your knowledge of them.

Tangibles can have a great impact on how customers experience and evaluate their service encounter. Because tangibles can usually be touched, smelled, or felt, their management and evaluation is easier and more objective than that of intangible, service-related tasks alone. As described in the Leadership Insights at the beginning of this section, Parrish Medical Center has implemented a wide variety of tangibles to improve each customer's service encounter.

The Treatment

The third and final element to be considered is the treatment of the customers. Treatment is represented through verbal and nonverbal messages evident in employees' attitudes, personalization of the service encounter, and the level of know-how available to customers. "Humans have a subconscious capability for such things as understanding threats and friendly ovations. These capabilities are based on interpretation of body language, facial expression, verbal intonation, and other subconsciously detected and evaluated cues."[76] Although a customer's perception of how he or she is treated is highly subjective, its impact on the customer's perceived quality of the service encounter is nevertheless enormous.

Every organization is continuously challenged to deliver high-quality person-to-person service. In addition to selecting the right service providers, careful training is a key strategy. As part of this training, many service organizations use scripting, both to help their employees deliver messages in the best way and to standardize the corporate message. For example, scripting can be used to help employees express what the company *can* do instead of what it *cannot* do. Therefore, instead of having employees say, "We do not accept Discover credit cards here," the company script would say, "We are happy to accept your VISA, MasterCard, or American Express card here."

Natalie Sellers, PMC's marketing communication manager, is responsible for writing most of PMC's scripts. At PMC, the human resources department has a critical frontline function. They were one of the first departments to adopt scripting. Their script includes standard language to use, such as "Always give a warm greeting. Say 'Welcome,' 'Hello,' 'Good Afternoon.' Do *not* use slang or informal words like 'hi' or 'hey.'" Through scripting, PMC teaches employees about the fundamentals, such as always acknowledging the other person; introducing yourself; explaining your role, skill, or function and what will happen next; and always ending the conversation positively with a "thank you" or "it was my pleasure." As Sellers says,

> We believe our service success lies in our ability to hire, inspire, and lead employees who share a passion for our values and vision. Without them, scripting and other service initiatives will fail. Our employees, volunteers and medical staff are integral to our service philosophy, which is to create healing experiences for everyone who enters the medical center. Because every healing experience is unique and deeply personal to the people we have the privilege to serve, scripts are used as a foundation for staff to build upon. It takes a fully engaged employee to effectively deliver the message within the scripts. People will sense right away if you are insincere.

Mapping the Service Process

Once all of the elements of the service concept have been considered—the tasks identified and sequenced, the tangibles put in place, and steps taken to ensure the proper treatment of the customers—then the actual design of the service process can begin. A number of tested methods have been used in service process design. Some of those methods are somewhat limited by the fact that they do not sufficiently incorporate the customers' perspective into the design. However, some principles of design are useful to have in mind before mapping the process.

Principles of the Service Process

Chase and Haynes[65] have suggested that five basic principles underlie the service process. First, make sure the service finishes strong. Although the beginning of a service is important to lure the customer to continue, research has shown that an escalation of satisfaction through the process with a strong finish has a greater impact on customer perception of the encounter than if the service had been evenly distributed throughout the process. Second, on a similar note, all undesirable experiences should be eliminated early in the service encounter. This means that the organization providing the service should focus on trying to minimize the risk of failure at the very beginning of each and every process as well as on making absolutely sure that the service process will have a strong finish. Third, attempts to segment pleasurable experiences may be useful in enhancing their perceived duration after the fact. Fourth, engaging customers in the process by allowing them to exercise some control over the encounter enhances customer satisfaction and commitment. Fifth, and finally, the organization should avoid unnecessary deviation from norms and rituals in the process. An unexpected change may disturb some customers. In those cases, unexpected changes can create uncertainty and frustrations, which are often blamed for service failures.[258]

More detailed principles for service design have been developed by Haksever, Render, Russell, and Murdick.[125] They suggest 12 steps, beginning with strategic issues and moving into supportive systems such as delivery and human resources requirements, process engineering, and data collection. Haksever et al. emphasize flexibility and both employee and customer participation in the design phase. The 12 steps are as follows:

1. Know your customer.
2. Determine which of the customer's needs will be satisfied (service concept).
3. Develop a service strategy and position the service for competitive advantage.
4. Design the service, delivery system, human resources (HR) requirements, and tangibles simultaneously.
5. Design service processes from both the customers' and the employees' perspectives.
6. Minimize handoffs (i.e., passing the customer over to other service representatives).
7. Design back-room operations to support front-room operations.
8. Incorporate data collection in the process design (data needs).
9. Determine the extent of customer contact and participation, specifically, level of customer involvement, which is determined by the nature of the service or level of automation.
10. Build flexibility and robustness into the system (possibility of responding to unplanned events).
11. Design employee and customer loyalty into the system.
12. Improve continuously.

All of these steps are important to keep in mind, but however the design is developed, management must be sure that it is objective, precise, and based on concrete facts.

Methods for Service Process Design

If an organization wants to match service specifications to customers' expectations, it has to be able to "describe critical service process characteristics objectively and to depict them so that employees, customers, and managers alike know what the service is, can see their role in its delivery, and understand all of the steps and flows involved in the service process."[326] Stuart[299] suggests that there may be only a very limited number of practical tools that could in fact be used by the managers faced with the challenge of service design. The well-known product-line approach to service,[192] the service-driven service company,[267] and the service profit chain[142] are paradigms intended to enhance efficiency and provide a better fit to customer needs. Various practical tools also exist to support effective service design and are ways to map or visualize the process. They include *blueprinting*,[281] *service mapping*,[181] *value analysis*,[319] *sequential incident analysis*,[289, 290] *benchmarking*,[280] and *quality function deployment*.[3]

Blueprinting

Blueprinting is a form of process flowcharting. The chart describes graphically what tasks are included in a process and the sequence in which they are performed. Such flow charts were originally developed at the time of the industrial revolution to organize production activities in manufacturing.[169] Figure 6.1 shows a blueprint or flowchart of PMC's testing flow for its outpatients.

The term blueprinting was introduced to the *service* literature by Shostack in the 1980s and has evolved into a more sophisticated technique. Indeed, it has become one of the most widely used tools in the design of services. Blueprints are methods of describing or documenting a service process and are very task oriented. However, in most cases, the tasks are not created or described from the customer's perspective. In spite of this drawback, blueprints can be a good starting point for other design and improvement tools.[96, 180, 280]

Service Mapping

Service mapping is a more customer-based approach than blueprinting. Service maps are management tools used to identify the chronology of tasks. Although still task oriented, they provide a more comprehensive picture of activities that need to be performed by first- and second-line employees as well as by customers. In fact, PMC's flow chart, shown in Figure 6.1, is closer to a service map than a simple blueprint. Figure 6.2 shows an example of a typical service map.

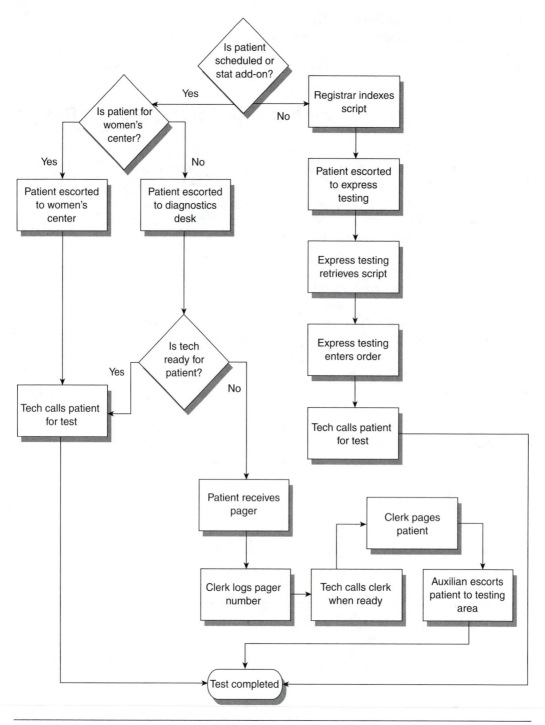

Figure 6.1   Outpatient Diagnostic Testing Flow

SOURCE: Printed with the permission of Parrish Medical Center © 2005.

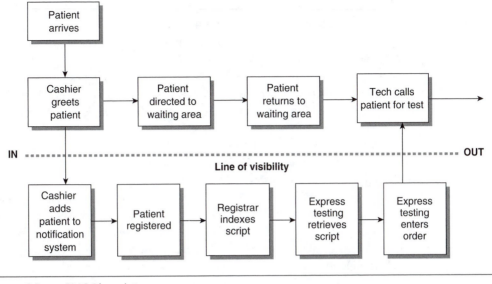

Figure 6.2   PMC Blueprint

Value Analysis or Value Engineering

Originally developed in the 1940s, value analysis or value engineering attempts to streamline the service process as much as possible. The aim is to provide the optimal quality and value for the smallest amount of resources, such as time, people, and materials. Value analysis is recommended after a blueprint or a service map of a process has been drawn.

Sequential Incident Analysis

This method documents both critical and noncritical incidents from the perspective of the customer. After a blueprint has been prepared, customers are interviewed about their perceptions of the transaction. Thus the method combines both the benefits of blueprinting and critical-incident techniques. The drawback to this approach is that it may miss the finer aspects of the service, which are often omitted in the reports given by the customers. Their account of the transaction is subjective and biased by those incidents they remember or find worthy of note.[289, 290]

Benchmarking

A useful tool for raising organizational service standards and for enhancing learning and understanding of how service could be performed is benchmarking. According to Camp, "It searches for the best-in-class practice in any industry to use as a source of learning and target for the process to be improved."[125a] The method was created by Xerox Corporation in the 1970s as part of a quality program, and today it is a widely accepted approach in service design and service management.

During its service design process, PMC used benchmarking as the basis for its game plan, using only the very best hospitals in the nation to benchmark against. In addition, to establish and maintain its uniqueness—and therefore its competitive edge—it benchmarked a lot of its service philosophy against the famous Ritz-Carlton Hotel. Several members of the PMC staff have made several site visits to the Ritz-Carlton to learn from it. The success of PMC's entire service leadership culture is demonstrated by the fact that it is now used as a benchmark by other health-care facilities. PMC is justifiably proud of this accomplishment and considers it to be a service to the health-care industry. However, its administrators recognize that as others learn more about the elements of their success and implement similar concepts—and indeed improve on them along the way—PMC's competitive advantage will be lost. This again underlines the need for continuous change within all organizations.

Quality Function Deployment

One of the most sensible tools from manufacturing, now frequently applied in service design, is Professor Yoji Akao's "House of Quality" or quality function deployment (QFD). The main purpose of this method is to integrate customer input into the design. As seen in Figure 6.3, customer needs, task identification, evaluation criteria, and comparison with competitors are integral parts of the method.

The first step in the application of the method is to identify the customer needs for a particular service. Those needs form the basis of the customer requirements in the model. Grocery shoppers may, for example, have little time to shop for groceries and may prefer low prices but still want to be able to choose from a number of different brands. This sets the tone for the operating requirements of the grocery store chain. They need to have their stores conveniently located, with easy access to parking. The store's layout and checkout counters need to enhance speed and accessibility. The stores need to keep the prices as low as they can but still offer the right amount of choices for their customers. Based on these criteria, the stores can evaluate their performance internally as well as in comparison with their competitors.

The future struggles against being mastered.

—Latin proverb

New Service Development

The development of new services is very important as a driver of competitive advantage for any service organization. What usually motivates a new service

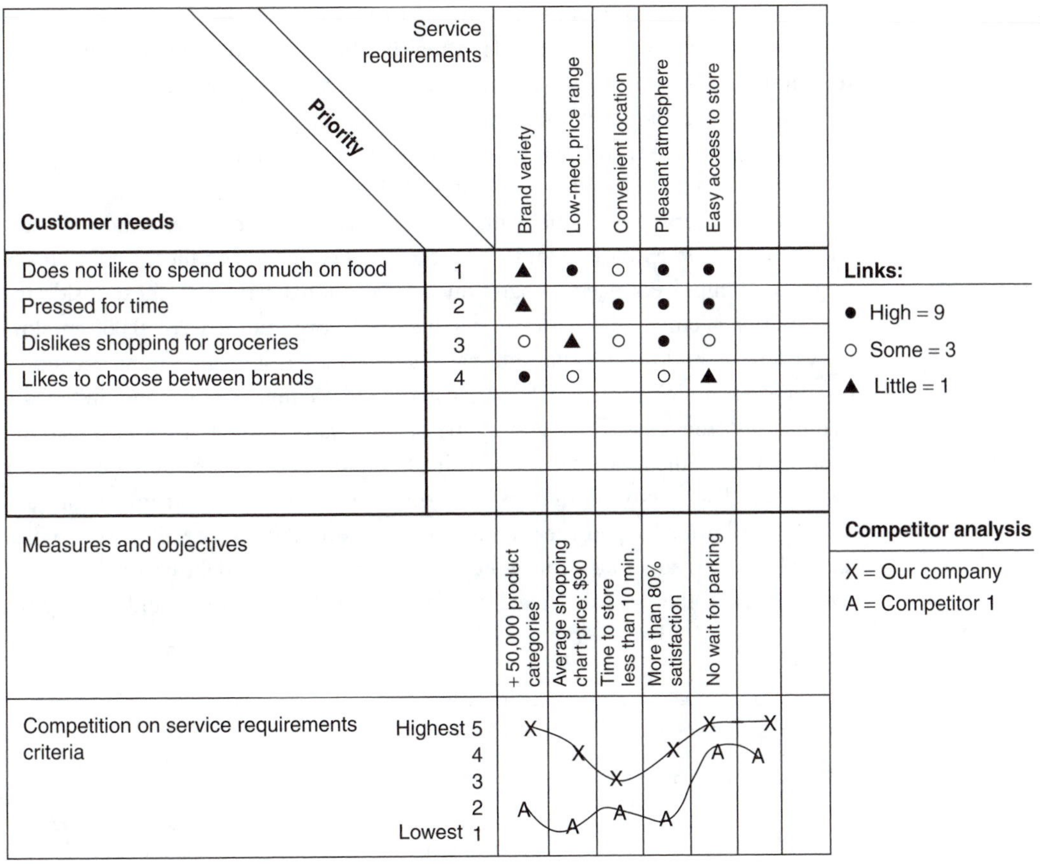

Customer needs	Priority	Brand variety	Low-med. price range	Convenient location	Pleasant atmosphere	Easy access to store			Links:
Does not like to spend too much on food	1	▲	●	○	●	●			● High = 9
Pressed for time	2	▲		●	●	●			○ Some = 3
Dislikes shopping for groceries	3	○	▲	○	●	○			▲ Little = 1
Likes to choose between brands	4	●	○		○	▲			

Measures and objectives: +50,000 product categories; Average shopping chart price: $90; Time to store less than 10 min.; More than 80% satisfaction; No wait for parking

Competitor analysis
X = Our company
A = Competitor 1

Competition on service requirements criteria — Highest 5, 4, 3, 2, Lowest 1

Figure 6.3   House of Quality

SOURCE: Adapted from Schonberger and Knod.[272]

development or design are (a) financial goals—profit, market share, or revenue; (b) competitive action; (c) globalization; (d) technology; (e) regulation or deregulation—companies can enter into markets not open to them before or vice versa; (f) elimination of professional association restrictions; (g) growth of franchising; and (h) balancing supply and demand.[125]

The benefits of service innovations can be huge. According to a recent study, service organizations report that almost a quarter of their revenues (24.1%) have come from new service for the last 5 years as have roughly one fifth (21.7%) of their profits.[206] Service innovations in fact enhance both the profitability of current service offerings and customer loyalty. Service organizations can, therefore, choose to grow by focusing on increasing their market share among current customers, by attracting new customers, or by developing new markets for their current offerings. Service innovations actually enhance organizational growth through changes in the service for current customers and the possibility of diversification, which means the company may be able to attract new customers.[11]

Smart organizations realize the value of service innovations, and they encourage and reward their employees for it. They may be able to develop innovative practices, techniques, or systems that result in major service quality improvements. These improvements could help the organization reduce paperwork, reduce costs, or deliver exceptional service to their customers in an innovative way.

Rewarding employees for innovative behaviors—toward both external and internal customers—is essential within a service leadership culture. Although many companies reward employees for the way they treat customers on the front line, many forget that employees need recognition for exceptional service to those inside the organization. Siemens, the giant German high-tech corporation, has 430,000 employees worldwide and realizes that internal customers are just as important as external ones. For example, Siemens UK, which has 18,000 employees, has just initiated a "Think Customer" award program. One of the awards was the Internal Customer Award. In 2004, the award went to a pair of employees who work in the company's metal shop. Their innovations saved time on a major classified government contract. Their contribution helped the engineering team do its job more effectively, which allowed the company to complete the project within its very tight deadline and at a reduced cost. Other awards were given for "Going the extra mile" and "Saving the day."[214] More information about employee rewards is given in Chapter 11.

New service category	Description
Radical innovations	
Major innovation	New services for markets as yet undefined; innovations usually driven by information and computer-based technologies
Start-up business	New services in a market that is already served by existing services
New service for the market presently served	New service offerings to existing customers of an organization (although the services may be available from other companies)
Incremental innovations	
Service-line extensions	Augmentations of the existing service line, such as adding new menu items, new routes, or new courses
Service improvements	Changes in future of services that currently are being offered
Style changes	Modest forms of visible changes that have an impact on customer perceptions, emotions, and attitudes. Style changes do not change the service fundamentally, only its appearance.

Figure 6.4   Incremental and Radical Innovations in Service

SOURCE: Mentor, L. J., Tatikonda, M. V., & Sampson, S. E. (2002). New service development: Areas for exploitation and exploration, *Journal of Operations Management*, p20. Reprinted with permission from Elsevier.

Organizations must involve their customers when they are trying to innovate and develop new services. New service development has been defined in a number of ways. As Figure 6.4 shows, service innovations can be either radical or incremental in nature.

There is no doubt that a well-designed strategy for a new service makes the entire effort more efficient and more effective. However, until recently, the generally accepted principle behind new service development was that new services "just happened" rather than being formally developed.[189] In comparison with tangible goods and products, new services are often underdesigned and inefficiently developed. In spite of their crucial importance for achieving a competitive advantage, relatively few service companies have made the necessary marketing and organizational changes needed to cultivate profitable service innovations.[266] The fact of the matter is that new services that prove to be successful rarely develop by accident. They need to be carefully planned and developed if efficiency and quality are to be achieved. When it comes to innovation, there are lessons to be learned from the consumer goods industry.

The following five ways of redesigning service have been suggested for the purpose of increasing customers' benefits or reducing costs: self-service, direct service, preservice, bundled service, and physical service.[41] *Self-service* is a method of engaging the customer in the process in such a way that he or she gains some control over time of and access to the service. For example, many airlines now allow ticket holders to check in online or at a kiosk, thereby avoiding a long wait in the check-in line at the airport. One reason companies like self-service so much is the cost-saving aspect. According to Forrester Research, the average cost for a customer inquiry is $1.17 for self-service, compared with $7.80 for an online chat, $9.99 for e-mail, and $33.00 for telephone.[294] *Direct service* brings the service to the customer, not vice versa. Some service-oriented automobile detailing companies go to the customer's home or office so he or she is not inconvenienced at all while they service the car.

Preservice aims to improve the initial contact of the customer, with the purpose of changing the experience as the customer moves through the process. A number of physicians and medical facilities implement preservice by mailing new patients all of the forms to be filled out before their appointments. Then the patients can complete the forms when it is convenient and save time on the day of the appointment. British Airways (BA) is taking a rather unusual approach to preservice. It has gotten a lot of attention for initiating sleeper service with flat beds in business class for the overnight U.S.-to-U.K. flights. This service is especially useful for businesspeople who want to sleep so they can be ready for work on arrival. To help them maximize their sleep time, BA has begun to offer a full preflight meal in its BA lounge at JFK Airport. Then, soon after takeoff, the lights are dimmed and these fortunate passengers can go to bed and sleep for a longer period.[227]

Bundled service is designed to enhance customer value by grouping services together. Added value is created through convenience and cost reduction. Siemens employs a "One Stop Shop" where its customers can get more than one

Siemens product, system, or service. If a company is building a factory, it can come to Siemens as a single source for a variety of needs. According to Helmut Macht,

> Building Technologies' solutions and products ideally meet customers' varied expectations with regard to convenience, security and enhanced efficiency. As a part of the Siemens Company, Building Technologies can offer total solutions extending far beyond building services—for example, the combination

> of building and industrial automation, the coordination of electronic and IT security, optimum equipment for medical facilities or airport security and logistics—for customers throughout the world.[320]

Physical service is focused on changing tangible items or artifacts in the service surroundings in the hope of having a positive impact on customers' experiences. For example, Melbourne Square Mall in Florida has recently renovated its public areas. Attractive groupings of benches and comfortable sofas have been placed throughout the mall so that tired shoppers can rest or people can simply enjoy sitting in nice surroundings, thereby enhancing their experiences at the mall.

New Service Development Models

Several models have been designed for the development of new services. Many of them depend largely on the product development format created by the consulting company of Booz, Allen, and Hamilton.[44] Their model incorporates first developing a new product and idea generation strategy at the corporate level, then going step-by-step through screening and evaluation, business analysis, development, testing, and, finally, commercialization. Later models go further and describe in more detail the evaluation stages of new services. They also take to a greater extent the complexity of service design, and they identify more steps to be taken before launching a new service into the marketplace. Furthermore, they incorporate the key influencing elements, both from within the organization (employees' perspective) and from its external environment (customer and market perspective).

Scheuing and Johnson[266] have designed the "normative model" of new service development, which goes beyond mere modification of existing manufacturing models. Their model includes 15 steps and can be categorized into the following four stages: direction, design, testing, and introduction, as shown in Figure 6.5.

Direction. The first stage establishes the *direction* in which the management team intends to take the organization. The key question being asked is *What business are we in?* This stage includes the first three of the 15 individual steps; these are the formulation of new service objectives and strategy, idea generation, and idea screening.

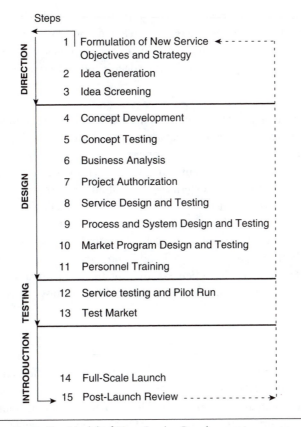

Figure 6.5   Normative Model of New Service Development

SOURCE: From Scheuing, E. E., & Johnson, E. M., A proposed model for new service development, in *Journal of Service Marketing*, 3(2).

Design. Once the direction is clear, the *design* can begin. Steps 4 through 11 involve design and adjustments of the new service. Furthermore, they also give attention to support systems such as marketing and delivery. In *concept development* (Step 4), the surviving ideas are expanded into developed concepts, with input from both customers and frontline service personnel. In this case, the concept is a description of a potential new service. It includes reasons for the new service offering and an outline of its features and benefits for customers. Step 5 is *concept testing,* which is a research technique designed to evaluate whether a prospective user understands the idea of the proposed service, reacts favorably to it, and feels it offers benefits that answer unmet needs.

A thorough business analysis is prepared at Step 6 for those proposals of new service that have made it that far through the process. Each proposal is carefully analyzed to determine its business implications. The purpose is to prepare recommendations for which innovations should be implemented. Once the recommendations are made, a complete market assessment is carried out, and a budget is drawn up for the proposed new service's development and introduction. In Step 7, top management commits resources to the implementation with *project authorization*. Possible marketing programs are created and tested, and prospective users are asked to provide feedback to an introductory marketing campaign during this phase. Then all employees must be trained on the details and delivery methods to be used with the new service.

Testing. Before a service is launched onto the market, the concept undergoes *testing* (Steps 8-13) to estimate the potential acceptance of the service. A pilot run of the service is generally used to assess customers' reactions to the new service. Then, using those reactions, the company can refine the service before it is launched. *Test marketing* helps a company to determine the salability of the new service and allows it to explore alternatives, such as different pricing or marketing options (Step 13).

Introduction. The final phase of the model is the *introduction* (Steps 14 and 15). The service has been designed and tested and is now ready to be introduced in the desired market segment. It is then essential for the company to conduct a *post-launch review* (Step 15) to determine whether additional adjustments are called for.

Risk

The normative model includes 15 steps. Each of those steps offers an opportunity to assess the likelihood of success and take preventive measures to reduce potential risks associated with the development and introduction of new or adjusted services. Throughout the process, the participation of both the providers and receivers of the service is crucial. This mutual participation allows for a more accurate assessment of potential perceptions of the service and necessary preparations that need to be made prior to the service launch.

One possible risk is the service culture itself. There is a strong link between the service culture and the service process,[269, 270] as well as between the service process and service quality.[121, 301] Hence there should be a relationship between service culture and the design of new services. However, suggested changes or modifications to the service may not match the current service culture, and thus various closely held beliefs and values within the organization may be challenged. To avoid unnecessary risk, the organization must closely consider the current organizational culture and the readiness of the organization to handle change throughout the design process. According to Stuart,[299] when new or modified service designs fail to fit with the existing service culture, the new service can fail, and customer dissatisfaction is a sure result.

An additional risk may result from attempts to describe the new or revised service to the members of the organization. Words alone may not be enough to communicate the abstract nature of intangibles such as service processes and service designs. Shostack[280] has pointed out four reasons for the inadequacy of words when trying to describe a service design concept. Using words alone to describe services runs the risk of oversimplification, incompleteness, subjectivity, and biased interpretations. *Oversimplification* is a risk because the service systems usually are too large or complex for words to capture. *Incompleteness* occurs because people omit details in the process with which they are not familiar or find inconsequential. They often form these judgments based on their personal experiences, which make them *subjective* in their analysis and *bias their interpretation* of terms and definitions frequently used to describe services. Even simple and common words such as "fast" and "empathy" have different meanings for different people. Zeithaml and Bitner[326] have pointed out that all of these risks become even more apparent when organizations attempt to design new services. The same is true when offering services to new customers or new market sectors. If words are not enough, how then how can we deal with the more complex, intangible service concepts?

Service is designed to maximize customer satisfaction during delivery of the service and after the service has been performed. Toward that end, service encounters can be designed much like a manufacturing process but with the full realization of the complex principles underlying human behavior and interactions. However, Zaltman[325] stresses that new research has clearly demonstrated that most managers do not fully understand their customers or their customers' ways of thinking. Leading theorists are realizing that input from a variety of sciences—including neurolinguistics and the social and behavioral sciences—could provide key insights into more accurate measures of what customers really want and how they feel about the services and about the organizations that deliver them. Some of this research clearly questions the validity of traditional qualitative research measures, such as focus groups.

All of the research in the area of service design gives organizations an increased ability to more accurately design new or revised services, which would ultimately improve their bottom line.

> *The ability to win over and over is through knowledge, courage, and a clear vision.*
>
> —Anonymous

Summary

Service design is a crucial process for practicing managers in the service industry. On a daily basis, managers are challenged by compelling questions regarding service design and development. One of the greatest challenges is that service organizations must simultaneously be able to (a) adapt to their environment and meet their customers' needs and (b) proactively strive to shape their market.

There are a number of reasons that companies decide to renovate their existing services or design new ones. These reasons may stem from a desire to create a service-driven culture or to enhance service performance. Organizations intent on renovation may also make changes because of statistical input on customer satisfaction, or they may be trying to recover from or prevent service failures.

In developing the service concept, the organization must clearly formulate the tasks and the sequence of those tasks. It must also design the tangibles that will accompany the service, as well as determine how the customer will be treated during the delivery of the service. The service concept determines the service process: the timing and flow of the process, in addition to customer impressions as they receive the service. An organization can use various methods of process documentation—such as *blueprinting, service mapping, sequential incident analysis,* and *benchmarking*—to help in the process design phase.

One of the most important elements of service design is alignment of the design with organizational strategies. Six basic steps need to be taken.

1. *Align* the strategy and design of the service concept and service processes.

2. *Involve* employees and customers in the design process.

3. *Map* the process, because a mere written description has proven to be inadequate for such complex phenomena.

4. *Prepare* people and tangibles for the change or adjustment being planned.

5. *Improve* the design by testing and building in continuous improvement.

6. *Launch* the service onto the market, then collect customer feedback to ensure and enhance quality.

The rigor of the design depends on the particular strategy or promise to customers.

The development of *new services* is very important as a driver of competitive advantage for any service organization. Models of new service development draw on models from product manufacturing. Models specifically designed for new service development include up to 15 steps, which can be grouped as (a) direction, (b) design, (c) testing, and (d) introduction of the new service. Service innovations and their developmental process are very important to every service organization, because a large amount of the organization's growth comes from new service generation, and a large portion of its profits depends on new services being introduced to the market.

PRACTICAL INSIGHTS

Redefining Leadership
From a Corporate Perspective

David Adams

Many companies and brands share an ambition to be leaders within their marketplace. Leadership, for the majority, means being the largest player. For majority brands, it is something that can be achieved and quantified, typically in the form of a market share. Still, is leadership really a destination that can be reached? Is it a question of size, or is true leadership a question of attitude and behavior? Equating leadership with size is one of the most dangerous things an organization can do. It is the number 1 killer of successful companies and brands—just look at Ford, and IBM from the "Big Blue" days.

The reason for this misguided thinking is simple: Ford and IBM's success was created by a *leadership attitude* . . . they got there by setting the agenda, challenging thinking and taking initiative . . . but the day they *became* the leader, they forgot what made them successful and started behaving like the big, fat cat—basking in the glory of their achievements. The door was thus opened to new leaders in the form of Toyota and Dell.

Unfortunately, there are too few examples of companies who continue to step up to the leadership role after becoming market leaders. One of the notable exceptions is the home furnishings retailer IKEA, under the inspired leadership of Ingvar Kamprad. In 2004, IKEA reported impressive growth and profits. Many companies would have taken the opportunity to congratulate themselves on being the dominant global player in their market.

Instead, Ingvar Kamprad, only too aware of the dangers of being crowned leader, immediately created a crisis in the form of a challenge to IKEA's leadership. Success, he said, had taken focus away from production costs, and IKEA would risk losing its leadership position to the Far East unless this issue was addressed as a matter of urgency—true leadership behavior.

So what makes a good corporate leader? There is no recipe for success, but many years of experience show that there are certain traits that often separate the good from the bad.

- The good leader believes that leadership is about attitude and behavior, not about size.
- The good leader sets the agenda.
- The good leader defines a path that others want to follow.
- The good leader is proud of results but never satisfied.
- The good leader invests resources where they can make the greatest difference.
- The good leader recognizes that actions speak louder than words.
- The good leader acts with authority but not with arrogance.
- The good leader creates the right environment for productivity and innovation to flourish in.
- The good leader never stands still but is always seeking to set new standards.

And in today's global environment, where there is ever-increasing focus on corporate social responsibility,

- The good leader strives to find the right balance between profit and principles.

Experience tells us that customers love a leader, because a leader's size is not important when it comes to being perceived as the leader from the customers' perspective. From a corporate perspective, there is a real need to redefine what makes a good leader.

Key Concepts

Directions: The following are key concepts presented in this chapter. Write a complete definition for each one.

Service design

Culture-based improvements

Strategy-design alignment

"Three T's" of service design

Questions

1. Why can it be problematic to apply standardized design principles from manufacturing to service? Choose a local service-oriented organization and explain why this organization would not be able to use standardized design principles.

2. Think about a local restaurant in your area. Describe how this restaurant implements the "three T's" of service design.

3. What are benchmarking and service mapping? When should an organization use each of these techniques?

4. Think of a recent experience you have had with a service organization that took longer than you expected. Describe how you evaluated the flow of the experience, the flow of time, and your total perception of the experience. What could the organization have done to improve this service encounter?

5. What is scripting? How and when can an organization successfully use scripting? When is scripting not appropriate?

6. What are the five basic principles, according to Chase and Haynes, underlying the service process? Why is each so important?

7. What role can employees play in service innovations? How can an organization encourage employees' participation?

8. Five ways in which service can be redesigned are suggested in this chapter. Choose two of these redesign methods, then choose a local business and explain how each of these redesigns could be implemented. You may use the same business for both or choose a different business for each redesign method.

9. In the normative model of new service development, in which steps does management play a key role? In which steps do customers get involved? Why are customers' and managers' roles so important?

10. How can an organization's culture actually present a risk to the new or redesigned service's implementation?

Advanced Activity

Pick a typical service company, such as a hotel, restaurant, car rental, or other organization. Use the "House of Quality" model in Figure 6.3 to (a) identify the needs of the company's customers and list what service requirements those needs demand, (b) identify measures for each of the service requirements, (c) rate the company against its major competitor on those measures, and (d) try to estimate the impact of each service requirement on customer needs to establish their priority. Bring the completed model to class and discuss your findings.

Search the Web

Find examples of two or more of the following service design tools:

Blueprinting

Service mapping

Value analysis

Sequential incident analysis

Benchmarking

Quality function deployment

What are the noticeable differences? What are the similarities? Which of these methods do you think has the most practical value to you? Print out your examples to bring to class. Write a short report comparing and contrasting the methods you choose. Be prepared to discuss your findings.

Suggested Readings

Berry, L. L., & Lamp, S. K. (2000). Teaching an old service new tricks: The promise of service redesign. *Journal of Service Research, 2*(3), 265–275.
Cook, L. S., Bowen, D. E., Chase, R. B., Dasu, S., Stewart, D. M., & Tansik, D. A. (2002). Human issues in service design. *Journal of Operations Management, 20,* 159–174.

Strategizing for Service Recovery

It is not a question of if *service failures will occur, but* when *they will occur.*

—Judith Strother

Objectives

After completing this chapter, you should be able to

1. Identify frequent causes of service failures

2. Understand the importance of planning for failure recovery systems

3. Understand the role of frontline staff and managers in service recovery

4. Know what steps organizations can take to prevent and recover from service failures

T he quotation from Marshall Field, founder of the famous Chicago department store, emphasizes the best of all attitudes toward customer complaints: Managers and service providers should welcome them as learning experiences and opportunities to excel.

It is essential to realize that, even in the best of times, service failures are *inevitable*. Even with the best of total quality management (TQM) and "zero defect" policies, every company *will* have both internal and external service failures. These failures can have a serious impact on an organization's reputation and profitability; however, they do not have to lead to dissatisfied customers who defect from the company.

> *Those who buy, support me. Those who come to flatter, please me. Those who complain, teach me how I may please others so they will buy. The only ones who hurt me are those who are displeased but do not complain. They refuse me permission to correct my errors and thus improve my service.*
>
> —Marshall Field

There are several unique reasons for failures within the service industry. We know that service processes cannot be controlled to the same extent as manufacturing or production processes due to the high dependence on the human element in service. Therefore, the outcomes are somewhat unpredictable, causing each service encounter to be quite different from all others. This is not surprising because of the number of variables from both sides of the service encounter. Although we usually focus on the attitude and behavior of the service provider, even more uncontrollable are the moods and attitudes of the customer.

In addition to the human element, a major reason for service failures is the conditions under which services are delivered. Service is produced and delivered simultaneously, which prevents the kind of quality inspections so frequently used in manufacturing prior to delivery of goods and products. Another factor is the fact that the service is provided in the customer's presence, making all attempts to hide mistakes extremely difficult. As a result, organizations have a lot riding on learning how to handle these inevitable failures when they occur and how to minimize the damage they can do to the organization. According to customer studies, effective recovery from service failure is one of the most important attributes of service.[326]

Dissatisfaction is usually the result of broken promises or failure to meet customers' expectations. Unfortunately, many companies overpromise through their marketing efforts, and this raises customer expectations to unreasonable levels. Yet these same companies underinvest in getting the business basics right, thus setting themselves up for service failures. This can result in diminished customer loyalty, negative word-of-mouth references, damage to the organizational image, and, finally, customer defection. Depending on how failures are handled, they can also have a negative impact on employees' job satisfaction, their loyalty to the company, and even their intention to stay.[145, 228, 254, 255]

The purpose of this chapter is to discuss both the theory and practice of service recovery and cover the following topics:

- The need for risk management and service recovery planning
- Data and research findings on the impact of service failures on organizations

---

This text takes a management perspective, but see Lucas[197] and Odgers[221] for tips on how frontline service providers can deal with difficult customers.

- Practical methods and implementation of service recovery strategies
- Tactical service recovery actions
- The impact of successful service recovery on employees' job satisfaction

The Cost of Failure

It is a well-established fact that when people experience bad service, they usually tell others about it. The following data from Technical Assistance Research Programs[238] provides a sobering reminder of just how critical the results of bad service can be:

- The average customer with an unresolved complaint will tell 9 to 10 people.
- Thirteen percent of customers with an unresolved complaint will tell more than 20 people.
- As many as 90% of complainers will return to your business if their complaint is resolved. That number increases to 95% if the problem is resolved quickly.
- For every complaint received, the average company has 26 unhappy customers who never complain. Thus, for the organization that receives five complaints a week, there are as many as 130 dissatisfied "former customers" who do not talk to the company but are out there telling their side of the story to others.

As these statistics demonstrate, the costs of frequent and simple service failures are often underestimated by employees and their managers. A vivid, real-life example of a typical such case is often used as a part of the new employee training program for one of Europe's largest retail grocery chains.

The example begins with a customer who went to one of the company's grocery stores to return a box of apples because the apples had been badly damaged by worms. Fortunately, this kind of incident is very rare in this store, but it was considered a severe failure because the company prides itself on quality service and fresh produce.

A complicating factor in this particular exchange was the frame of mind of the store employee who handled the complaint. Just a few minutes before coming to work, he had had a serious argument with his girlfriend, and he was emotionally unstable when this customer came in to complain. Instead of leaving his personal problems at home, he let them influence his behavior on the job. To make a long story short, when the customer complained about the bad apples, the employee insulted the customer and handled the complaint in a rude and inappropriate manner—he did not even offer the customer compensation or a refund for the damaged goods. The customer left in a rage, vowing never to return to the store. To make matters worse, that same night this particular customer was hosting a party for 12 women from her club where she had planned to serve a special dessert made from the fresh apples she had bought from the store.

The company decided to use this case as an example to enhance new employee training, so they made special efforts to follow up on this case. They interviewed the angry customer who had complained and found out that, in a matter of 24 hours, 64 people had been told about the poor treatment she had received:

a. The customer told her family of 4 and her 12 friends who came over that evening. This meant that 16 people knew about the service failure almost immediately.
b. Each of these 16 people told an average of 3 people, which brought the number up to 64.

Based on further follow-up interviews, the company estimated that out of the 65 people who knew about the incident, one third did not return to the store for a matter of weeks—in some cases, for months. Actual calculations of lost revenues as a result of this one case of unprofessional employee behavior (following a simple argument with a girlfriend) indicate that the store may have lost more than $1500 the first week and more than $6000 the first month. Had none of these customers returned that year, the estimated loss would be more than $72,000. Over a period of 5 years, that amount would have been well over $300,000—an expensive argument indeed for one small grocery store!

> Service recovery has attracted increasing attention in recent years as a result of the premise that service failures are inevitable, but dissatisfied customers are not.
>
> —S. Michael[208]

Service Recovery Defined

The term *service recovery* was first used in a British Airways service quality campaign in the late 1980s and was first defined as "an attempt by an organization to offset the negative impact of a failure or breakdown."[328] Later, service recovery was defined more generally as "the actions a service provider takes in response to service failure."[208] Since then, the term has taken on a more proactive meaning, as a method of *seeking out* and *dealing with* service failures.[167] In fact, service recovery is a management philosophy that holds customer satisfaction as a primary concern. "This mind-set can change the rules of the game for service companies. It shifts the emphasis from the cost of pleasing a customer to the value of doing so, and it entrusts frontline employees with using their judgment."[133]

Service recovery is, therefore, not only about complaint management. Although one part of service recovery is to deal with and even seek out customer complaints, its focus is more strategic in nature. This means that service recovery must be part of the overall organizational plan, focusing on service failures in general and the organization's reaction to them by attempting to solve problems before complaints occur and before complaints lead to customer dissatisfaction. Both complaint management and service recovery are critical customer retention strategies. Collecting, storing, and distributing information and data on critical incident and other relevant information regarding service failures allow managers and employees to improve the way they present and handle complaints through an improved service system. Research has found that successful service recoveries not only affect customers' satisfaction but also employees' satisfaction and loyalty.

Planning for Service Recovery

Changes needed to create a successful recovery system are particularly difficult for service organizations committed to quality standards. Such companies have spent time and effort to adopt a philosophy of *zero defects* and *getting it right the first time*, through standardization of service processes and strict policies to control employee behavior. Product-based service delivery processes have proven in the past to deliver consistency and high service standards. They are not bulletproof, however. "The fact is that no matter how rigorous the procedures and employee training or how advanced the technology, zero defects is an unattainable goal."[133] Therefore it is essential for organizations to plan for the inevitable.

The essential message of this chapter is that service failures *will* occur and every organization *must* plan for this eventuality. We know that when a service failure occurs, if a service provider makes a spur-of-the-moment decision on how to handle it rather than using a carefully planned and implemented tactic, even if the short-term result is fairly positive, the long-term losses can be staggering. However, little is written about the formal planning phase of the service process that deals with service recovery. Organizations may have a crisis management plan in place, but it is usually limited to handling major disasters and mainly deals with the way an organization's public relations efforts are managed during a crisis; therefore, strategies within those plans usually deal with communication efforts aimed at various stakeholders and publics. General guidelines include these: Put the public first, take responsibility, be honest, and provide a constant flow of information. Fewer organizations prepare a risk management plan or engage in risk communication. This strategy deals with assessing areas that are likely to become problematic and communicating with the public about them regularly to help frame public perceptions before a negative event happens (see Seitel[274] and Wilcox, Cameron, Ault, & Agee[321] for good discussions of these topics).

Some of the basic principles of this important area of risk and crisis management apply well to service recovery.

A corporate disaster is defined as an extraordinary situation characterized by surprise, significant destruction or adverse consequences, a strong threat to important values, and a short decision-response time. Although there is a low probability of a major disaster occurring, when it does, it is an unexpected but very high impact event. It also has the potential to escalate in intensity, fall under close media or government scrutiny, interfere with normal business operations, jeopardize an organization's positive public image, and damage an organization's bottom line.

The primary goal of a crisis response plan is to ensure that the corporation is prepared to protect or repair the organization's image in the wake of the event.[297, 298] The most effective way to do this is to modify the public perceptions of the responsibility for the crisis or the public's impression of the organization itself.[77, 78]

Every corporate crisis involves some level of service failure for both internal and external customers. As we have seen from the European grocery store example, as well as the sobering statistics about how quickly word spreads about even the smallest service failure, an organization cannot limit its crisis or risk management plans to cover only large or disastrous events. Its specialized strategic plan should be able to incorporate a continuum of service recovery strategies—from the smallest to the largest—depending on the severity of the service failure to the customer.

Let's take a look at the airline industry to see how this would apply. Airlines must plan for crashes—the most serious kind of crisis for them. However, it is the day-to-day service failures that plague airlines with much greater frequency and also need to be carefully planned for. These service failures include a variety of events, such as a rude service provider angering a customer at the ticket counter, lost luggage, and major flight delays. The Practical Insights section at the end of this chapter gives a wonderful example of how one airline handled its service failure and experienced the service recovery paradox, discussed later in this chapter.

The entire range of possible negative events must be included in every organization's overall plans, with a service recovery strategy as well as specific tactics for each kind or level of service failure. Employees must be thoroughly trained to implement the strategies and tactics successfully. In addition, the metrics an organization uses (discussed further in Chapter 8) need to reflect the success of the service recovery plan along with all of the other elements of customer satisfaction that are typically measured.

Getting It Right the First Time

The hope of every service organization, manager, employee, and customer is for service encounters to go as planned and expectations to at least be met. Of course, customer expectations can be either high or low. In fact, Phillips[238] feels that because so much customer service is poor, customer expectations are usually low. This gives the organization an even greater opportunity to demonstrate superior customer service—or, when things go wrong, to welcome customer complaints as an opportunity to resolve them.

Although the primary aim is to get it right the first time, mistakes will inevitably happen. So, as discussed earlier, service organizations need to be prepared with service recovery strategies in place. Although in some rare cases a service recovery can be so successful that customers actually become more loyal than they would have been before the incident occurred (the service paradox), all evidence suggests that trying to avoid a service failure in the first place is the better way to ensure success.

The quality movement has, for the last few decades, emphasized the importance of getting it right the first time. Processes, procedures, and control systems have been put in place to ensure success. In fact, the International Standardization Organization has defined a service as a part of the total production concept. Edvardsson[90] suggests 13 propositions of service quality, to "get it right the first time," all based on international service research. To get it right the first time, the organization must do the following:

1. Engage in the act of leadership, meaning that top management must aggressively promote service quality in words and actions.

2. Put service quality at the center of organizational activities, reflected in management's tasks at all levels, and make it highly visible in the organizational culture.

3. Maintain a strong focus on the customers.

4. Ensure that quality improvement is everybody's responsibility, making sure that each employee has the knowledge, resources, and authority needed to provide the right quality.

5. Focus on new service development and service design as part of the organization's normal processes.

6. Make continuous improvement and reengineering an integral part of the organization's philosophy—moving from a focus on structure to a focus on processes.

7. Have quality improvement drive productivity and profitability.

8. Benchmark: Compare one's own organization with others to help guide service strategies.

9. Always implement service guarantees.

10. Use complaint management to monitor customer dissatisfaction.

11. Actively use employee commitment and customer involvement.

12. Systematically measure quality from the perspective of customers, employees, and owners.

13. Reward quality improvement based on facts.

Rick Sidorowicz, editor and publisher of the online *CEO Refresher* and "minister of culture of high performance retail,"[283] boils all of this down into one basic operating principle: *Customer obsession.* In a truly customer-obsessed organization, service recovery takes on a critically important role that becomes everyone's responsibility. Thus service recovery brings organizational values right down to the front line. In contrast, for an organization that just pays lip service to service recovery, Sidorowicz paints the following scenario: "Let's just give everyone a mediocre script to perform, build in a few buffers to attempt to placate the complainers, and keep our fingers crossed and hope we stay out of trouble." Imagine customers' reactions when calling such an organization to complain. In addition to the frustration they feel about the service failure, now the negative experience is intensified as they try to

> deal with customer care hotlines—the silly music and repetitive smiley face voices—while [they] wait on hold, stew, and then fume! I suggest that the customer that has had a negative (and very memorable) experience with you and attempts to contact you will tell *hundreds* of others about you, and that may be a conservative number!

Getting it right the first time would prevent this kind of disaster.

Evidence suggests that the relationship an organization has with its customers can have an impact on customers' tolerance for service failures and the way in which they react to them. In some instances, a good employee-customer relationship can act as a buffer or mediator for dissatisfaction, reducing the damage to customers' commitment and trust. Berry[39] has suggested that regular communication, name recognition, and regular contact with the same service personnel can indeed enhance customer tolerance for failures. However, not all research evidence is conclusive on this matter, so additional research regarding the impact of relationships on service failure tolerance is needed.[112, 179]

> *A man who has committed a mistake and doesn't correct it is committing another mistake.*
>
> —Confucius

The Recovery Process

Although companies try to prevent as well as prepare for service failures, sometimes the inevitable happens and customers' expectations are not met. Too often, the system and the employees are unprepared to deal with the situation. The fact is that most customers are left disappointed after a service failure. Research evidence even suggests that as many as half of all efforts to respond to customer complaints actually reinforce the negative customer reaction.[133] As a result, companies *must* figure out how to get it right the first time, as well as how to make it right when something goes wrong.

There is no doubt that service recovery can have a significant impact on organizational success, but there is relatively little empirical evidence on how to go about securing effective recovery efforts. One thing is clear, though: Frontline personnel play a crucial role in recovery efforts and recovery success. After all, they are the first ones to deal with a dissatisfied customer. Therefore, the most effective service recovery occurs when the frontline staff can immediately solve the customer's problem.

A model developed by Tax and Brown[302] gives a good overview of the steps needed for a successful recovery system and its implications for customers' loyalty, employee satisfaction, and the profitability of service organizations. As shown in Figure 7.1, there are four major steps: (a) identifying service failures, (b) resolving customers' problems, (c) communicating and classifying service failures, and (d) integrating data and improving overall service. The model incorporates the opportunity for service organizations to learn from failures and emphasizes a proactive approach to both service recovery and service failure prevention. Resolving customers' problems quickly and agreeably has a positive impact on both customer and employee satisfaction (of course, the reverse is also true). Furthermore, drawing on the lessons learned from the Service-Profit Chain developed by Heskett, Jones, Loveman, Sasser, and Schlesinger[141] (as discussed in Chapter 10 of this book), satisfaction has an impact on loyalty and ultimately on the bottom line through profitability.

Methods of Service Recovery

There are a number of ways organizations can try to prevent as many service failures as possible and recover effectively from those that do occur. As discussed

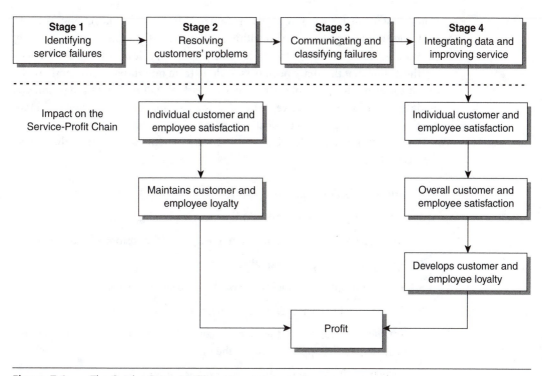

Figure 7.1   The Service Recovery Process

SOURCE: From Tax, S. S., & Brown, S. W., Recovering and learning from service failure, *in MIT Sloan Management Review*, Fall 1998, reprinted with permission of Tribune Media Services.

earlier, such strategies and actions can reverse what could otherwise prove to be very costly losses. We now have compelling evidence that customer loyalty is inextricably linked to profitability in service industries, so organizations should "shift their focus away from *offensive* strategies aimed at seeking new customers and toward *defensive* strategies aimed at satisfying and keeping current customers."[302] Despite data that clearly supports the importance of such practices, organizations have a long way to go in embracing and implementing this management philosophy in their strategic planning efforts, as well as in their day-to-day operations.

What, then, is the best way to handle service failures? Organizations have a number of tactical actions they can initiate when faced with a customer complaint. In each case, wherever possible, the complaint should be handled by the first person the customer encounters. Being passed along from one employee to another greatly increases a customer's sense of frustration, making the chance of a satisfactory recovery even more challenging.

Parrish Medical Center tries to prevent this kind of customer frustration by empowering its entire frontline staff (in person or on the phone) to deal with and resolve as many problems as possible. When these staff members cannot directly solve a problem or answer a question, they are instructed (and scripted) to tell the customer that they will get back to them with an answer or solution within a specific time frame that is reasonable for that particular complaint. For example, a frontline staff member may say to a customer, "Mr. Smith, I will get an answer to your question and get back to you within 30 minutes." When this technique is used, customers receive an answer from the same person they dealt with, thereby avoiding the feeling that they have been passed along from one employee to another. The caveat for using this particular strategy is the risk of failure. Before the promise is made, the employee must be very sure that the information is obtainable and that the time chosen is reasonable. Most important, *the promise must be kept.*

According to Bell and Zemke,[34] the following ingredients are key to the service recovery effort:

1. *Acknowledge* the problem or failure.
2. *Explain* the reasons for the failure wherever possible.
3. *Empathize,* with a sincere expression of feeling for the customer's inconvenience.
4. *Apologize* where appropriate.
5. *Solve* the problem as quickly as possible—speed is crucial.
6. *Compensate* the customer appropriately.
7. *Provide* extra value—in the form of coupons or extra services—to demonstrate regret and appreciation for the business.
8. *Follow up* with a phone call, letter, or other communication.

The appropriate elements of the recovery process depend on the customer's level of dissatisfaction, often triggered by the behavior of the service provider. A study of 700 critical incidents showed that it may not necessarily be the failure itself that leads to the dissatisfaction but the way in which it is handled.[42] As you can see in Table 7.1, some responses to problems appear to be more effective than others. Kelley and Davis[179] also point out that responses such as discounts, management intervention, and product replacement can be particularly effective, whereas apologies and refunds are less effective.

Recent studies have confirmed that the majority of customers are dissatisfied with the way companies resolve their complaints. In a study by Hart, Heskett, and Sasser,[133] more than half of the participating customers in their study were dissatisfied with how their complaints were handled, and only 38% reported that they were satisfied. Indeed, much depends on the attitudes and behaviors of frontline staff. A large empirical study suggests that 42.9% of encounters that left customers dissatisfied were the result of employees' unwillingness to respond properly to a service failure.[45] Ironically, it is very likely that the lack of a service recovery system or an inappropriate response to a complaint is the cause of the dissatisfaction—not the failure itself. Table 7.1 indicates which action is likely to satisfy customers who have experienced service failure. To achieve 100% customer satisfaction, the company needs to correct the problem immediately. Providing an apology to the customer and a written confirmation of the problem resolution has also been shown to give good results (see Table 7.1 for a detailed list of actions). However, a study by Armistead and Clark[15] revealed that only 5% of the organizations in their sample would go so far as to apologize to their customers for a mistake. Indeed,

Table 7.1   Actions to Satisfy Customers

Required Action	%
Put it right. If possible, put it right immediately.	100
Apologize to customer	88
Provide written confirmation to customer	38
Send letter to third party	38
Give assurance it will not happen again	34
Refund any charges incurred	32
Provide written apology to customer	20
Acknowledge mistake	14
Explain why errors occurred	8
Exhibit a helpful attitude	6
Act professionally	4
Apologize to third party	4
Research and investigate error	4
Be polite and courteous	4
Listen and be understanding	4
Provide compensation	4

SOURCE: From Hart, Heskett, & Sasser, 1999, Action to Satisfy Customer Service Industry Journal. Reprinted with the permission of the Taylor & Francis Group.

NOTE: Percentages indicate percentage of customers in the study satisfied with the response.

much depends on the attitudes and behaviors of frontline staff. A large empirical study[45] suggests that 42.9% of encounters that left customers dissatisfied were the result of employees' unwillingness to respond properly to a service failure.

Taking the customer beyond mere satisfaction to a delighted state requires more drastic measures. To achieve that result, more than half of the respondents in one study[169] said the corporation should follow up with a telephone call or a letter to the customer to confirm that he or she was now satisfied. Other suggested actions are listed in Figure 7.2.

The situation gets grimmer after an attempt to put something right has gone wrong. In the same survey,[169] more than one third of the respondents reported that they would threaten to or actually would take their business elsewhere. In this case, compensation seems to be crucial, with 76% saying they would expect immediate compensation with an apology. More than half of the customers stated that they would require a formal letter of apology with a managerial signature. In addition, 46% of customers said they would require a written explanation of why the problem happened and reassurance that it would not happen again.

The Service Paradox

Perception is everything. The organizational resources and efforts needed to restore customers' confidence and satisfaction vary depending on their perception of the severity of the failure, based on its impact on their financial or personal well-being. Effective service recovery strategies can even go so far as to restore satisfaction to a level that is higher than among those customers who have not experienced failures.

	Satisfy	Delight
Single deviation scenario First attempt to recover	Put it right Quickly Modest apology Written confirmation Deal with third party Refund costs incurred Assure it will not happen again	Put it right Quickly Modest apology Written confirmation Deal with third party Refund costs incurred Assure it will not happen again Follow-up call or letter Apologize by letter
Double deviation scenario Second attempt to recover	Staff to "put themselves out" Put it right better and faster Involve higher authority Provide compensation Managerial apology Written assurance Written explanation	Not possible

Figure 7.2   Satisfying and Delighting Customers

SOURCE: From Johnston, R., & Fern, A. (1999), Service Recovery Strategies for Single and Double Deviation Scenarios in *The Service Industries Journal*, 19, p. 80. Reprinted with permission from Taylor & Francis, Ltd. www.tandf.co.uk/journals.

This phenomenon is referred to as the *recovery paradox.*[203] The following example illustrates this paradox. Ms. Ramirez of Miami, Florida, had planned a very special dinner for her mother's birthday. She had invited 10 friends and family members to a very nice restaurant to celebrate and had made the reservations more than a week prior to the event. However, when the group arrived at the restaurant, the maitre d' told them there was no record of a reservation. However, he insisted they wait in the bar, where they were given drinks on the house. He immediately went to the manager, who opened a private dining room and had a table set up for them. Within 20 minutes, they were seated for dinner. After the meal, the manager himself came out with complementary desserts for the entire group. As a result of this sterling service recovery, the restaurant has become a favorite of the entire group of people who experienced it. In addition, they have told many others about how well they were treated, and this has resulted in even more business for the restaurant. This shows how an enlightened manager made a service failure into an opportunity to turn dissatisfied customers into delighted customers, in addition to gaining a new group of customers.

> Men are all alike in their promises. It is only in their deeds that they differ.
>
> —Molière

In conclusion, the costs of service failures are significant to the organization, both in actual costs—lost revenue from current customers and lost revenue from all those potential customers who hear about service failures from friends and family—and in damage to the company's reputation. It should be obvious that any organization must do whatever it takes to make it right for their dissatisfied customers.

The Application of Recovery Strategies

Frontline service personnel and their managers spend a great deal of their time in efforts to correct service encounters gone wrong. As mentioned earlier, however, instead of seeing service failure as a problem, they can in fact create satisfied customers. Service failures, if properly handled, can be regarded as a wonderful opportunity to learn from and improve the service processes and entire service systems, thereby affecting the long-term success of an organization. Unfortunately, very few organizations document or categorize complaints and failures systematically and hence miss the opportunity to learn from their mistakes and pass on that learning through the organization.[169]

At the organizational level, how can a company strategize to avoid problems where possible and recover from them when they happen? Hart, Heskett, and Sasser[133] recommend seven steps for an organization to take to build an effective and proactive recovery system. They suggest that organizations should (a) measure the costs of effective service recovery, (b) break customer silence and listen closely for complaints, (c) anticipate needs for recovery, (d) act fast, (e) train employees, (f) empower the front line, and (g) close the customer feedback loop. Let's take a look at each of these steps.

Measuring the Cost

Organizations and customers alike bear the cost associated with failure. Costs can occur in a variety of forms, including time, money, materials, damage to image, frustration, and customer defection. Unfortunately, too few service organizations collect and store information regarding the cost of service failures. The benefit of collecting the data is that if a manager can measure it, then he or she is more likely to manage it better in the future. Numbers definitely get management's attention. In the area of service recovery, managers often underestimate the amount of profit the company loses when a customer leaves unhappy. As a result, they do not adequately plan to avoid such losses through effective service recovery strategies. They concentrate more on attracting new customers, who might actually represent unprofitable business, and they fail to implement steps to retain more valuable existing customers. As discussed later in Chapter 10, the best 20% of customers often generate the vast majority of the company's total economic profit[275]—a solid enough reason to engender customer loyalty by avoiding service failures whenever possible and making a highly satisfactory recovery when failures do occur!

Another measurement involves recording the mistakes. To enhance learning from past mistakes and to have a chance to take action to prevent them from constantly recurring, organizations can use customer and product databases. In addition, when a company uses databases along with call centers and Web sites, it can better achieve its goal of fair treatment for all customers. When companies fail to use databases, it is very difficult for them to learn from their service mistakes.

Breaking the Silence

Most customers do not voice their dissatisfaction or unhappiness with services they receive. In actuality, it has been found that only 5% to 10% of all dissatisfied customers are likely to speak up. For the remaining 90% to 95% of dissatisfied customers, you may never get a chance to correct their problem.

Why are so many customers reluctant to complain? The following are some of the most common reasons:

- They do not believe that the organization will be responsive.
- They do not want to confront the person who was responsible for the failure.
- They would simply rather take their business elsewhere than face a confrontation.
- They do not know their rights and what the company is obligated to do.
- They worry about the amount of time and effort it takes to lodge a complaint and get the issue resolved.

The organization must make it as easy as possible for customers to provide feedback, thus enhancing the chance of recovery from that "silent majority." In fact, the customer service manager for Quill Corporation, the nation's largest independent office products dealer, has a simple motto: "A customer who is willing to complain is at least twice as loyal as one who remains silent."[238]

It is absolutely crucial for an organization to actively encourage their customers to air their dissatisfaction in any way they can. A number of resources can be used to accomplish this, including 800 numbers, hotlines, and on-the-spot surveys. No matter how important such activities may be, a good recovery system is also proactive in the sense that it engages in active problem seeking—looking for trouble in the making. Friendly, inviting, and proactive staff attitudes can be crucial, both in encouraging customers to speak up and in spotting potential problems in their earliest stages before they escalate. Asking customers simple, but direct, questions about how the service is and showing an interest in their well-being has been found to give excellent results.

Anticipate Needs for Recovery

As discussed in the section on planning for service recovery, all organizations must plan for the inevitable service failure. Some services and areas are more problem-prone than others. Managers know this and know where trouble usually starts to brew. To narrow their search for problems, they can focus carefully on these areas and schedule and coordinate people, equipment, and other resources with that in mind.

Act Fast

Problems have a tendency to escalate quickly. The faster a company can respond to a potential problem, the better it is for all parties concerned. As discussed earlier, unhappy customers will tell many people of their bad experiences. Without a quick and satisfactory service recovery, the damage to the company can be much more significant than the loss of a single customer. Therefore, it is crucial for a company to identify and resolve any and all problems and customer complaints as quickly as possible.

Train Employees

Because 65% of customer complaints are first brought to the attention of frontline staff, a recovery system must focus on this initial point of contact. It is here that the most damage can be done (for example, by a rude or indifferent employee), but it is also here that the most substantial recoveries can be effected by a well-trained employee with a good attitude. Therefore, service recovery training, especially for frontline personnel, is an important element in any attempt to build a successful recovery system. Service providers need to be trained thoroughly to handle each dissatisfied customer with care. To help achieve this, recovery training should focus on enhancing employees' confidence in their own decision making and developing their understanding of potential customers' reactions to a problem.

Employees must know what to do and what is expected of them if the organization is going to achieve service excellence. Therefore, the organization must develop guidelines for service recovery that focus on achieving fairness and complete customer satisfaction. Guidelines might include such tools as scripts for employees, what to do when a recovery is needed, how to treat customers under such conditions, and what the employees' limitations are within specific transactions. Such guidelines not only set the standard for performance but also serve as an important element in reinforcing and communicating the organization's customer-oriented culture and commitment to service quality.

Empower the Front Line

As mentioned earlier, the front line is the first line of defense when it comes to recovery strategies. Customers want and expect their problems to be handled quickly, professionally, and hassle free. Delays can cost them time and money, not to mention personal inconvenience and emotional stress. Therefore, frontline service providers must be able to handle most customer problems that arise. To be able to do that efficiently—from both the customer's perspective and the organization's point of view—employee authority and responsibility must be an integral part of the job. Employees must clearly understand the set of resources they can use and the decisions they are allowed to make. The organization must motivate and give incentives to its service providers to be proactive and take the initiative to do whatever is necessary to satisfactorily meet their customers' needs and resolve their customers' problems.

Close the Loop

Most customers just want to be treated fairly. People do not like to complain, and most avoid confrontation whenever possible. However, in the case of a customer who decides to complain, he or she feels much better about the decision knowing that it might lead to an improvement for others. When customers actually see that the problem-complaint-resolution loop has been closed, they feel as if they are contributing to the efforts of the company's quality-control team. Therefore, it is important to tell each customer what happened after his or her complaint and what measures have been taken, if any, to prevent this from happening again. If the company can do nothing in a particular situation, the company should explain courteously why action is not possible.

Customers have clear expectations when it comes to the handling of their complaints. Unfortunately, most customers believe that the treatment they receive is unfair. They often feel they do not get satisfactory compensation for the harm done or at least recognition of their cost, whether the cost is in time, money, or inconvenience.

What can an organization do to enhance customers' perceptions of fair treatment? Research findings suggest that fair procedures begin with accepting responsibility or blame for the failure. Second, the problem must be handled quickly and, preferably, by the first contact person. Also, customers are more likely to perceive their treatment to be fair when given options—not prescribed solutions—so the solution seems to take their personal circumstances into account. A more rigorous approach is needed if a service recovery attempt has failed than in the initial attempt to correct what has gone wrong.[34] Also, making a customer "delighted" takes a little more effort than merely satisfying him or her, as shown earlier in Figure 7.2.

Appropriate Levels of Service Recovery

As shown in Figure 7.3, the appropriate level of customization and employee empowerment goes hand in hand with the severity of the service failure.

The response to a service failure can frequently be standardized if the mistake has a low impact on customer satisfaction or if the problem can be easily corrected. A typical example is a restaurant order that was filled incorrectly. Let's say the customer ordered a baked potato with his steak and got French fries instead. It can be annoying and inconvenient, but this kind of mistake does not have a dramatic impact on the safety or health of the customer. However, the customer expects fair treatment, and speed of recovery is of the utmost importance. In this kind of case, a standardized response is appropriate. The employee does not have to use his or her own judgment to create a solution to the problem on an individual basis. Instead, the server should implement the standard procedure learned in training: For example, remove the incorrect dinner and replace it quickly and cheerfully with exactly what the customer ordered.

If the severity of the service failure is more complex, and especially if it has a greater financial, psychological, or physical impact on the customer, then the employee may need to go beyond basic training and use personal judgment and imagination to solve the problem. He or she may draw on standard response

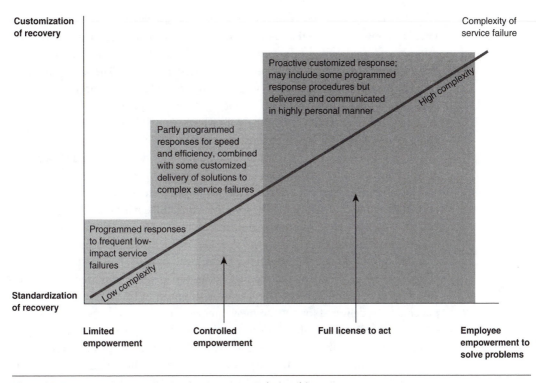

Figure 7.3   Empowerment–Service Recovery Relationship

procedures for part of the solution, to achieve a quick resolution. However, to ensure that the customer's needs have been met in spite of the service breakdown, a customized approach is often needed to supplement the standardized part.

For example, assume that Bankston, Inc., a large stock brokerage firm, has installed a new information technology (IT) system and needs to train most of its employees on the new system. Bankston has contracted with Acme Training Company to conduct a 4-day introductory training for its staff on how to use the new system. After the 4 days of training, direct feedback from the employees showed that they felt the training was poorly handled, and they were dissatisfied. In addition, individual performance texts showed that the employees were unable to complete the required tasks using the new system, so the training program was definitely a service failure.

Think about an appropriate service recovery strategy for this situation. Would Bankston be satisfied with just a refund of the training costs? No, because its employees would still not have the skills they need to perform their jobs using the new system. Would offering another 4-day training session without charge be a good solution? Probably not. It would be very difficult and costly for any company to take its employees away from their jobs for another 4 days to repeat the training—and the company, in this case Bankston, would have no reason to believe that the results of the repeated training session would be any better.

Is there any way Acme can recover from this serious service failure? Acme employees need to exercise initiative and creativity to analyze what can be done to recover from the failure and to secure future business from Bankston. In this case, a combination of several different tactics may be offered with customized delivery options—all designed in close cooperation with the customer so that the customer feels involved with the solution and predisposed to accept it. The standardized part would be to use off-the-shelf training packages as compensation, instead of a refund. The customized part could be the way it is delivered. Acme could agree to send its top trainers to coach the staff one-on-one or in small groups as their job schedule permits until the staff and administration feel confident that the skills have been well learned. Because Acme is going to great lengths to satisfy the customer and guarantee the results of the retraining, there is a much greater chance that the business relationship would be repaired and perhaps even strengthened as a result of the recovery paradox.

The greatest amount of employee empowerment and service customization is needed when the complexity and the severity of the problem are critical. Under these circumstances, the employee needs to be able to think totally out of the box—that is, creatively and unhindered by standardized quick fixes. Let's look at another real-life example that illustrates this situation. A European-based cargo carrier was faced with a critical problem when their biggest customer, which exported millions of euros worth of products every year, needed a shipment of brand-new promotional material to be delivered for an extremely important event—a Europeanwide broadcast of a presentation by the CEO, where the promotional material being shipped was to be featured. By mistake, the carrier left two containers of the promotional material behind. As soon as the cargo carrier discovered the mistake—knowing it involved a time-critical event for a treasured customer—it hired a private jet to transport the goods to their final destination. After having loaded the containers into the jet, everyone breathed a sigh of relief—not knowing that the customs officers in the country where the shipment was headed had long gone home and would not return to work for more than 10 hours! The ground personnel discovered this new problem when they came to pick up the shipment—90 minutes before the Europeanwide telecast. To solve this additional crisis, the carrier called a number of people, first to find out if and how the shipment could be processed and then to persuade one of the customs agents to come in and help them out. Exactly 10 minutes before the show went live, the carrier delivered the promotional material to its destination and the ceremonies went off without a hitch.

The carrier's employees well understood the seriousness of the situation and demonstrated their personal leadership in doing whatever it took to satisfy this key customer. No standardized procedures would have worked, and nothing could have replaced this kind of individual commitment and understanding of the sense of urgency. To pull off something like this successfully, the employees must be customer obsessed, highly motivated, and committed to doing everything in their power to protect and preserve their organization through the fulfillment of customer needs—and they must be empowered to make it happen.

The Cost of Service Recovery

Earlier, the high cost of service failure was discussed. No matter what form of service recovery is chosen, a company will incur costs that are an inherent part of any service recovery effort. In the restaurant example, the cost of recovery is low—the wasted French fries. In the second example, Acme's simplest choice, the refund, would have cost the amount of the lost revenue as well as all the peripheral costs of delivering the training the first time—and the intangible and tangible costs resulting from a totally dissatisfied customer. With the more customized solution, the immediate costs are greater: specialized training delivery, perhaps costing overtime pay for training personnel, along with other peripheral costs. Clearly, the extreme measures taken by the European cargo carrier resulted in significant costs. In all three cases, the value of maintaining a solid reputation and the avoidance of all the negative word-of-mouth publicity and related lost revenue for current and potential customers makes the extra effort well worth all the costs in the long run.

The Impact of Service Recovery on the Organization

To most successful businesses, keeping current customers and building a strong and committed relationship with them is a key business strategy and a primary concern. Without a doubt, service recovery affects satisfaction and can therefore have a tremendous impact on the revenue and profitability of service organizations. This is particularly true in situations where the organization is highly dependent on individual employees' relationships with customers. For example, in many professional services, a customer's loyalty can be with a particular service provider—the individual, not the organization. Think about going to a hair salon or a medical office. You probably are loyal to your preferred hair stylist and physician rather than to their companies. If your hair stylist moves to another salon in the area, you would probably follow him or her, thus taking your business to that new organization. Whether a customer is loyal to an individual service provider or to the organization itself, loyalty is a product of satisfaction with services or, in some cases, satisfaction with service recovery.

The Impact of Service Recovery on Customers' Switching Behaviors

Although the majority of customers report they will remain loyal to a brand or service provider if a problem is properly handled, the seriousness of the problem can affect that decision. The more serious the failure, the more likely the customer is to switch to another company, no matter what recovery effort the company makes. According to a study done for the U.S. Office of Consumer Affairs,[133] when the purchase exceeded $100, 54% of customers would remain loyal to that company or product brand if a service failure were properly resolved. However, only 19% of the customers in the study said they would repeat the purchase if the problem were not resolved to their satisfaction. For less expensive problems (under $5), 3 out of every 4 customers would remain loyal if the problem were corrected; if not, almost half of them would not return to that organization or purchase that brand again.

Banks have long been institutions that have loyal customers—often because of the complicated process of switching accounts and banking activities to another bank, not because of customer satisfaction. However, this trend may be changing with increased options in the banking industry. For example, although most customers choose a bank based on convenience as well as its range of financial products, the fact that automated teller machines are widely available has made the convenience of the bank building itself much less important. In a survey of U.K. banks, 60% of the customers felt their banks could do more to improve customer service standards.[300] At the top of the most important issues list, in addition to prompt service, was the need for the banks to have better management of service failure resolutions. They stressed that employees at branches and other first-point-of-contact positions should have greater ability to resolve problems so they would not have to continuously go to colleagues in other departments or at the bank headquarters. Alf Saggese, the service processor for Europe, the Middle East, and Africa (EMEA) for the company Kana, said,

> This survey points to the future of customer service for banks. By concentrating resources—and accountability—on the front line, institutions can not only secure even greater customer loyalty, they can also transform the performance of branch networks and contact centres. . . . We know that the majority of the time and expense of delivering customer service actually goes on handling requests for information—as opposed to actually talking to customers themselves. This picture is totally upside-down.

In the same U.K. study, 80% of the respondents said they discuss their experiences at the bank with their friends and family.[300] This again emphasizes the ripple effect of each customer's satisfaction level.

Sometimes, service failures lead to a more serious problem than occurs when a customer simply switches, or takes his or her business elsewhere. If an attempt at recovery fails, "service terrorists" can emerge. They are customers who have become so dissatisfied that they actively engage in behaviors designed to criticize and get back at the company. Alarming statistics suggest that the most negative reactions to failed recovery attempts come from once-loyal customers.[302] For example, at a local eyewear store, one customer was so unhappy with the initial service and then with the lack of recovery on the part of the store that he made big placards with negative comments about the store on them. For 5 straight days, he marched in front of the eyewear store for all to see. Everyone who drove down this very busy street had the image of the placard-waving man solidly connected with the eyewear store itself. This is the worst kind of negative publicity, and it probably cost the store many times over in lost revenues what it should have spent just to fix this one man's problem. Another example is the person who bought a new car and was very unhappy with the fact that the car had some defects that the dealership just would not (or could not) fix. This car owner painted a big lemon on the side of the car with the phrase, "This lemon bought at Jack's Dealership!" (The name has been changed to protect the guilty.) He drove it around town for months—so everyone in the city got the message. From the eyewear company owner and car dealer's point of view, these were true "service terrorists."

As previously mentioned, a strong employee-customer relationship can greatly influence the customer's decision to stay or to take his or her business to a competing company. Newcomers and customers who do not have a "true relationship" with their service providers are naturally more likely to defect than others. In addition, some individuals are more likely than others to switch from one service provider to another, regardless of their level of satisfaction with how their service or complaint was handled. Low income, young age, desire for variety, and higher tolerance for risk are factors that can increase switching behaviors.[326]

Michael[208] highlights the main characteristics of service failures this way:

- Customer satisfaction generally decreases as a result of service failure and decreases in proportion to the acceptability of the failure.
- Customers' tolerance depends on the situation; for example, time, place, and price.
- Customer reaction is dependent on a customer's perception of how critical the service is to his or her well-being or financial loss.
- A negative service experience can be turned into a positive one if the problem is corrected in a timely, friendly, empathetic, and generous manner.
- A service recovery that exceeded expectations results in a higher level of customer satisfaction than that of customers who do not report a failure at all (recovery paradox).

The Impact of Service Recovery on Internal Customers

Manufacturing, purchasing, and quality control may never talk to the end user of our products yet they are vital in meeting the customer's needs. If we deliver an expensive product that doesn't work and we deliver it late, that affects customer service just as much as a rude salesperson.[155]

This is a good reminder that any organization must take care of its internal customers—the members of its own organization. Failure at this level can percolate throughout the company and affect the way service is delivered on the front line. Therefore, each organization must constantly analyze how well each part of the organization is servicing each other part and fix any part of the system that is not going well.

Harrison[132] gives the following suggestions for strengthening internal customer service orientation:

- Employees should never complain within earshot of customers. It gives them the impression your company is not well run, shaking their confidence in you.
- Employees should never complain to customers about other departments' employees. Who wants to patronize a company whose people do not get along with each other?
- Employees at every level should strive to build bridges between departments. This can be done through cross training and joint picnics, as well as day-to-day niceties.

- Use postmortems after joint projects so everyone can learn from the experience. Fences can be mended and new understandings gleaned when everyone reviews what went right or wrong. Not doing so can result in lingering animosities that will exacerbate future collaborations.
- Consider letting your employees become "Customer for a Day" to experience firsthand what your customers experience when doing business with you.
- Remember that service recovery applies to all customers—both internal and external.

The Impact of Service Recovery on Employees

Successful service recovery reduces employee turnover in service organizations. According to a recent study by Boshoff and Allen,[45] three key managerial actions that can enhance service recovery performance of employees are (a) setting and communicating clear goals that employees identify with, to foster organizational commitment; (b) empowering the front line to solve immediate problems; and (c) rewarding employees for service excellence. The tools to implement these steps are the managers' interpersonal and communication skills, along with the organization's internal marketing efforts. This internal communication must emphasize the importance of service excellence for the well-being of the organization and all of its members.

The Ritz-Carlton Hotels are the quintessential example of an organization that embodies service excellence. As a matter of fact, other organizations use the Ritz-Carlton as a benchmark to strive for. One way the hotelier achieves this customer service excellence is by hiring the right people and training them very well. It also treats its own employees the way they should treat their customers. Not only is the Ritz-Carlton motto "We are ladies and gentlemen serving ladies and gentlemen," but one of their service basics is "When a guest has a problem . . . break away from your regular duties to address and resolve the issue." Ritz-Carlton understands very well the notion that when guests have a problem and it is resolved quickly and satisfactorily, it can become a positive and memorable experience for that person. Therefore, they empower each employee to spend as much as $2000 without management approval to resolve a guest's problem. This empowerment makes the employee feel valuable and thus leads to higher job satisfaction. In luxury hotels, the median job turnover rate is 44%. At Ritz-Carlton, it is only 25%.[204]

The *internal* benefit of service recovery is its effect on employees. Just as occurs at the Ritz-Carlton, employees report higher levels of job satisfaction and are less likely to leave an organization if service recovery performance is good. This serves the purpose of building a strong service-oriented organizational culture. The organizational culture usually determines how employees react in situations where services fail, especially when the employees have some discretion in how to handle the service recovery.

> *Bless not only the road but also the bumps on the road. They are all part of the higher journey.*
>
> —Julia Cameron

Summary

In spite of best efforts of service organizations to *get the service right* the first time, services inevitably fail some time and to some extent. The cost of failure can be staggering, with lost customers, untapped future customers, and a damaged reputation, all of which negatively affect a company's bottom line.

Therefore, companies must prepare their systems, processes, and people to handle service failures and breakdowns. In fact, the preparation should be included in the organization's risk management or crisis management plans, as well as in overall organization strategies. The critical factor in a customer's reaction to a negative situation is how a problem is handled at the front line. The vast majority of complaints are reported to the frontline staff and it is their reaction to it that matters the most when it comes to maintaining customer satisfaction at the time of a service failure. Thus these strategies and tactics must be a key part of an effective training program for service providers throughout the organization—with special attention to frontline employees.

A number of variables must be taken into account to help an organization decide on appropriate recovery strategies. For example, it is essential to analyze the degree of standardization or customization of the service recovery efforts. This decision should be based on the severity of the service failure.

Various methods have been suggested to enhance the effectiveness of recovery attempts, such as measuring the cost of failures to get management attention, encouraging customers to voice their complaints, anticipating needs for recovery, taking preventive measures where problems are prone to happen, training employees to handle complaints and dissatisfied customers, empowering them to take corrective measures for the customer, and informing the customer about what has been done to correct the problem and to prevent it from happening again.

Because training is a crucial element in service recovery success, effective human resources strategies, from hiring the right employees to managing them skillfully, are essential. Other measures include establishing guidelines and standards for appropriate actions, providing easy access for customers to complain, and recording failures systematically to enhance organizational learning from past mistakes. Tactical maneuvers at times of trouble in the presence of customers include apologies, speedy response to the complaint, empathy, reimbursement or other symbolic acts, and a follow-up on the customer's level of satisfaction with the resolution of the complaint.

Research findings reported in this chapter emphasize that the benefits of a comprehensive recovery system to a service organization are great. These systems need to be reactive in the sense of responding to complaints and problems as they happen, as well as proactive in finding and preventing problems. It is essential for organizations to plan for and create a solid service recovery strategy and then to make wise decisions about tactics to use in implementing the strategy. Successful service recovery positively affects employee and customer satisfaction and loyalty, thus enhancing the organization's profitability.

PRACTICAL INSIGHTS

Pizza in the Sky:
Lessons Learned From Service Failures

Wolf J. Rinke

Wolf Rinke Associates, Inc.

I couldn't believe it! I was being put on my flight back home early! But wait; I'm getting ahead of myself. I had had a demanding but gratifying day. I delivered a motivational opening session in Rochester, NY, followed by an intensive sales seminar after lunch. And the day went GRRREAT! For both programs I received a standing ovation. So I was absolutely stunned when I arrived at the Rochester airport at about 4:30 pm and was told by the agent: "Dr. Rinke, we can put you on a flight right now. It will get you to Washington/Dulles 30 minutes early."

So I grabbed my McDonald's bag, and jumped aboard. Just before takeoff, the door was re-opened and we were told: "We have bad news for you. We've just been locked out from Dulles. Please go back into the terminal until at least 6:00 pm." I took this in stride. It gave me an opportunity to eat my cold McDonald's "unhappy" meal. However, several of the passengers were distraught. The reason: flight UA7578 had a scheduled departure time of 3:30 pm.

At about 6:50 pm everyone was asked to get back aboard for an "immediate departure." You guessed it. Immediate was not so immediate, because at 7:00 pm the pilot advised us that we had to wait a "bit longer." Continued thunderstorms were delaying all flights into Washington/Dulles. Finally at 7:25 pm we started our short 65 minute flight.

After we had been in the air for about 90 minutes, John, the pilot, advised us that we had been placed in a holding pattern. What was unusual was that John was very empathetic and "told us more than we wanted to know." He truly seemed sorry that this was such a fiasco. Also unusual was Amy, the young flight attendant, who was extremely cheerful and helpful throughout. Being responsive to every passenger who had a question, she was able to defuse a lot of apprehension and somehow made the flight not nearly as bad as it really was. She even began to serve free beer and wine. After circling the "friendly sky" for about two and a half hours, John told us that he was getting low on fuel and that we needed to land in Charlottesville, VA, to refuel. Once again, at 10:30 pm, we were asked to get off the plane. Sounded great, except the little Charlottesville, VA, airport had been virtually closed for the night, except a small boarding area. After about 50 minutes we were asked to get back aboard. No sooner had everyone fastened their seatbelt then the pilot told us that we had lost our "slot." And would we please get off the plane again. By then it was just about midnight and several passengers had been traveling for 18 hours.

So we went back to the waiting area hoping for a miracle. And it came when Amy cheerfully announced that she had ordered pizza and soft drinks for everyone. That seemed to cheer everyone up. Just as the pizza arrived some 35 minutes later, Amy told us that we had been given the go ahead. So Amy grabbed all the pizza boxes and soft drinks and told us: "No problem, I'll get this served en route." After we finally took off for the 15 minute flight, Amy served us our preference of pizza. In spite of the late hour she was very pleasant and cheerful.

Actually it felt more like we were at a ball game than in the air. When we finally landed at Washington/Dulles shortly after 1:00 am everyone thanked Amy and John for a job well done. Mind you, for most passengers the approximate 1 hour flight had taken 9½ hours!

Here is what we can learn from this: Don't fret about service failures! It's not the failure that will cause you to lose customers. It's how front-line service providers respond that will make or break your business. Research tells us that unsatisfied customers tell an average of 12 others about their unsatisfactory service experience. Unfortunately that's a very costly proposition since it literally destroys positive word-of-mouth, the only advertising that really works. It is also extremely costly since it costs roughly five times as much to attract a new customer compared to retaining a current customer. And you can increase profits by 25-95% by merely retaining 5% more of your current customers.

Here is what the crew did that is worth replicating:

- *Express Empathy*—Both Amy and John came across as really sorry.
- *Apologize*—The crew apologized repeatedly.
- *Take Ownership*—They took ownership by not blaming anyone else for the problems.
- *Fix it. When you can't, make it as pleasant as possible*—They served free wine, beer and even pizza.

- *Over-communicate*—At every opportunity the captain gave us detailed updates.
- *Tell the Truth*—They answered every question patiently and candidly.
- *Minimize Stress*—Withholding important information causes dysfunctional stress and contributes to customers going "ballistic."

Want to Do Even Better? "Plus Up."

All of us were inconvenienced in a big way. Serving pizza may have gotten us "minimally satisfied" but certainly will not generate positive word of mouth for United Airlines. However, if you "plus up" wronged customers, by, for example, giving customers a cash coupon, service providers can actually generate a greater level of positive word of mouth than if it had been done right in the first place. (Research tells us that a satisfied customer will tell about 3 others, but a recovered customer will tell about 5 others). The reason is that services that exceed customers' expectations are much more memorable than those that meet expectations. This causes more customers to come back and bring you more business.

SOURCE: From Rinke, W. J., *Don't Oil the Squeaky Wheel and 19 Other Countrarian Ways to Improve Your Leadership Effectiveness* (2004), McGraw-Hill, New York. See also: www.WolfRinke.com.

Key Concepts

Directions: The following are key concepts presented in this chapter. Write a complete definition for each one.

Service recovery

The recovery paradox

Switching behaviors

Risk management

Questions

1. Why is it more difficult to control the quality of service than the quality of products?

2. What is the recovery paradox? Give an example (from personal experience, if possible) of a situation in which the service paradox occurred.

3. Tax and Brown's model provides four steps for a successful service recovery. Briefly describe those four steps.

4. What role do customer expectations play in service recovery?

5. What steps do Haskett and Sasser recommend that an organization take to build a solid, proactive recovery system?

6. What impact does the customer–service provider relationship have on service recovery? Give an example to illustrate your answer.

7. What affects a customer's decision to switch to another service provider?

8. Service failures can occur with internal customers as well as external ones. Give an example of an internal service failure. How can that failure be resolved?

9. Why is it critical for organizations to break the silence of customers who are dissatisfied but who do not complain?

10. Think about a situation in which you have experienced a service failure that was successfully resolved. Use the list of key ingredients of a service recovery to recount the event. In case you have never had such an experience, use a hypothetical example to illustrate the ingredients.

Advanced Activity

Strategizing for Service Recovery

On their last trip to the Bahamas, three cruise lines (A, B, C) have had the unfortunate experience that some of the passengers aboard one of their ships got food poisoning. Approximately half of the passengers showed some type of symptoms of the food poisoning, ranging from mild to very severe discomfort. There were 950 passengers aboard each ship. The average price of medical treatment for each passenger was $800.

Company A gave those who got sick a full refund.

Company B gave those who complained a full refund.

Company C gave everyone aboard the ship a full refund.

Search the Web to find information on the average price of a cruise to the Bahamas and any other relevant information you can use. Assume that 35% of people return to take another cruise at least once in their lifetime. Use the information in this chapter to calculate which company made the best decision about how to handle this service failure.

Search the Web

Find examples of two service failures, either cases found in academic databases or cases published on corporate Web sites. Look at each company's Web site to try to find the company's service recovery policy. Write a brief report describing each failure and comparing how the companies dealt with the failure and attempted recovery.

Suggested Readings

Hart, C. W. L., Heskett, J. L., & Sasser, W. E., Jr. (1990, July-August). The profitable art of service recovery. *Harvard Business Review, 68,* 148–156.

Michael, S. (2001). Analyzing service failures and recoveries: A process approach. *International Journal of Service Industry Management, 12*(1), 20–28.

Parasuraman, A., Zeithaml, V. A., & Berry, L. L. (1985). A conceptual model of service quality and implications for future research. *Journal of Marketing, 49,* 41–50.

Designing Service Metrics

A hundred objective measurements didn't sum the worth of a garden; only the delight of its users did that. Only the use made it mean something.

—Lois McMaster Bujold[55]

Objectives

After completing this chapter, you should be able to recognize

1. What metrics are and how they apply to service organizations

2. Measures used in strategy formulation

3. Measures used to develop and monitor the service process

4. Measures used to develop and monitor service providers

Service Metrics

"To manage it, you need to measure it." This phrase has long been known in management literature. No service design process is complete without the development of appropriate metrics to measure the success of the design.

Wherever you are is the entry point.
—Kabir

Measurements can be one of the most powerful and motivational—but also challenging—tools at our disposal in the service industry today. The power of measurements results from the fact that they make performance visible and tangible and reveal the results of everyday action or inaction in quantitative terms. Measurements are elusive because it is difficult for organizational members to agree collectively on the right metrics for a given set of circumstances. At best, it is seldom easy.

The purpose of this chapter is to provide insight into the world of metrics, particularly as it applies to service organizations, and to draw attention to issues related to the use of data and methodology in developing and monitoring important elements in the overall operation of a company. Metrics can be a particularly useful tool in many situations relating to strategy formulation, service process design, and determination of the performance and attitudes of the service providers.

What are metrics? Metrics are in fact a collection of tools used for benchmarking organizational, divisional, or personal performance over a period of time. Metrics can also be used to provide a comparison with competitors, identify performance gaps, develop skills, and reward good performance. Most of all, metrics can help an organization and its members identify and focus on which issues need attention at a particular time and place. They also help organizations align their efforts to accomplish tasks needed to fulfill their objectives. That is precisely why organizations need to design their metrics carefully before they are put in place, both to make sure the right behaviors, attitudes, or tasks are being monitored and the metrics are actually measuring that for which they are intended.

All metrics have certain risks associated with them. Obviously, they can be manipulated and distorted if not carefully planned and correlated with what the organization wants to reinforce and emphasize. However, if applied correctly, they can create great value for the organization through increased focus, better decision making, and enhanced visibility of direction and performance.

Designing Metrics

In their book *Transforming Strategy into Success*, Shinkle, Gooding, and Smith[279] provide an excellent overview of various do's and don'ts for designing a system of metrics for any organization. They suggest criteria for the selection of the metrics, as well as practical information on commonly used metrics. Although they point out the fact that an organization should use as few metrics as possible to enhance the organization's focus, they stress the importance of metrics in monitoring progress toward the vision and objectives of the division or organization. They ask key questions, such as Will the metric or metrics drive the desired behavior and actions? Does the process of getting and having the information add value? and finally, In what way might organizational members behave improperly as a result of the metrics being introduced?

It is crucial that the organization make sure the metrics fit the company's culture, values, and its way of doing things. For example, an organization known for teamwork and a collective sales approach might decide to apply measures of individual performance and even go so far as to link payments to those metrics only if it wants to change its ways. Such measures could destroy rather than reinforce its traditional way of operating. Furthermore, the metrics need to address results and direct behaviors so they can be used to develop or enhance individual and group performance.

Overall, the set of metrics needs to be balanced. An organization cannot introduce a set of individual metrics that contradict each other or automatically create conflict between the items being monitored. Therefore the system of metrics needs to be looked at as a whole—whether it be in service performance, finance, individual behavior, quality, cost, or other factors. When examined in relation to organizational objectives, it is easy to determine whether the metrics system is helping to promote desirable employee behaviors or if it is causing confusion and conflict.

The value and usefulness of a system of metrics can be seen in the following example. Consider a service organization that wants to differentiate itself on the basis of low prices. To do that, it needs to emphasize rigorous cost control, and its metrics should reflect that. Simultaneously, the organization wants to maintain a certain level of service quality. The measures of service quality need to be aligned with the resources available for providing the designated level of service quality. Often, service organizations demand 100% quality in service delivery and measure it against that demand; however, their systems can never sustain such unrealistically high levels, due to the lack of resources available for or applied to the task. Therefore it is important never to put a metric system in place unless the organization is sure of its current status, has a vision of where it wants to be in the future, and, ideally, has identified milestones or objectives to help employees set their pace and measure their progress. Typical metrics can measure the following:

- How customers experience their encounter with the company or consumption of the company's products or services
- The development or growth of the organization
- The internal health of the organization; this is measured through the monitoring of organizational members' behaviors, attitudes, and values
- Traditional financial performance (in fact, in most organizations, metrics have been used *only* to measure financial performance)
- Both quality and quantity of products[279]

Table 8.1 shows examples of categories and typical metrics applied to each one. This is by no means a complete listing of possibilities, but it gives practical insight into the kinds of things being measured.

Strategy Maps and the Balanced Scorecard

To keep track of their strategies and to see them through, many organizations now apply strategy maps, an idea originally developed by Kaplan and Norton in the 1990s.[174, 295] A strategy map, shown in Figure 8.1, is a visual way of describing

Table 8.1   Use of Metrics in Organizations

Category	Metric
Customers	On-time response
	Percentage of on-time delivery
	Overall customer satisfaction
	Customer retention
	Number of complaints
People	Overall employee satisfaction
	Annual turnover
	Annual training hours
	Absenteeism
Productivity	Projects per year
	Cost per project
	Employees per project
	Value added per employee
Financials	Revenue
	Growth or market share
	Return on assets (RONA)
	Economic value added (EVA)
	Return on equity
Quality	Defects per product
	Person-hours of rework
Safety and environment	Number of accidents
	Lost time due to accidents
	Percentage of environmental inspections passed
	Hours of safety training per year

how an organization connects its goals and strategies in explicit cause-and-effect relationships with each other. The strategies are organized according to four perspectives: financial, customer, internal, and learning and growth.

The main principles behind strategy maps are the following:

1. Strategy balances contradictory forces.

2. Strategy is based on the proposition of differentiated customer value.

3. Value is created through internal business processes.

4. Strategy consists of simultaneous, complementary themes.

5. Strategic alignment determines the value of intangible assets.

The original purpose was to better understand how organizations in the information age create value. Traditionally, companies dealt with tangible materials and goods, making it perfectly logical to report progress and performance in financial terms. However, organizations are increasingly creating their competitive

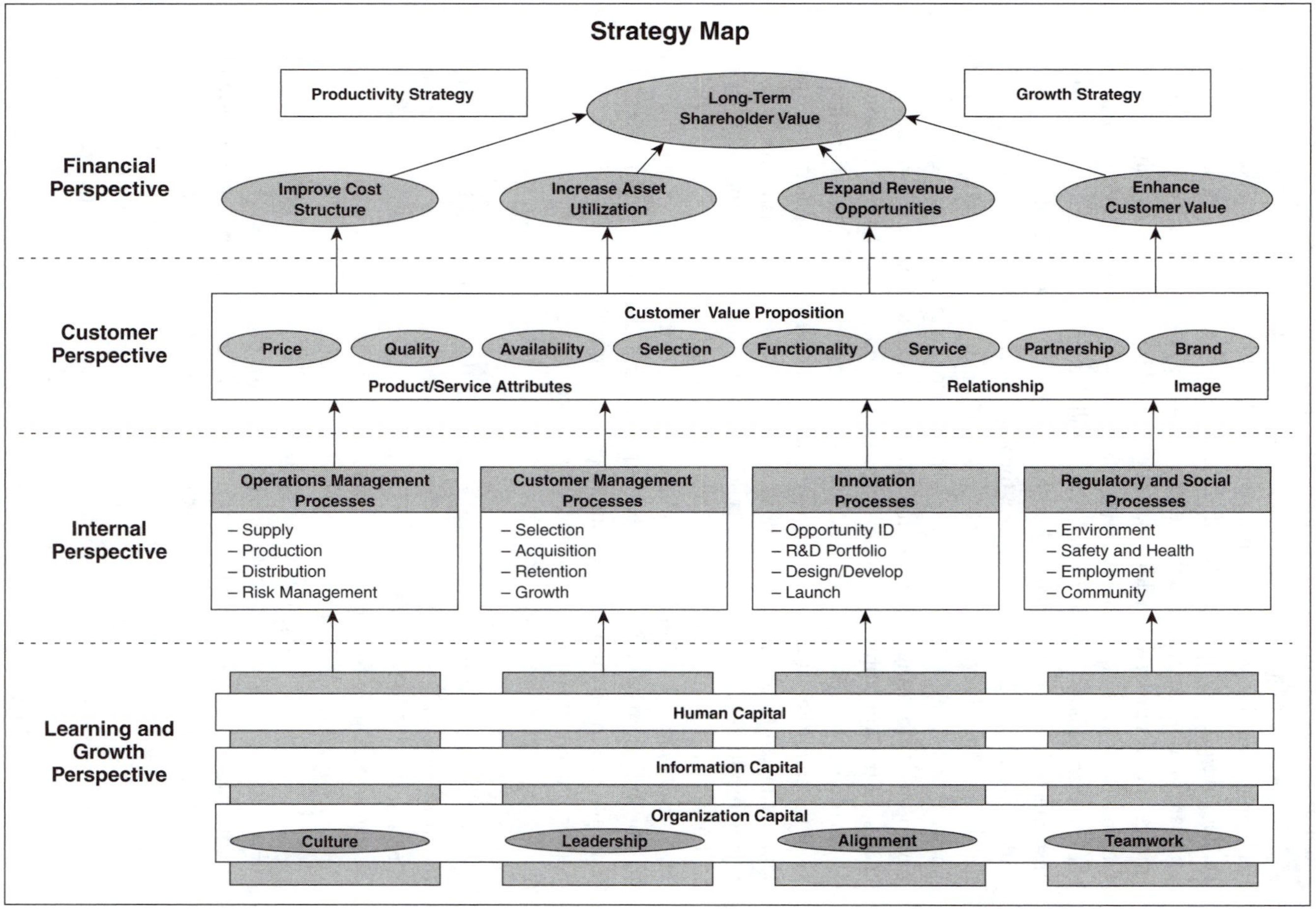

Figure 8.1   Strategy Map

SOURCE: From Kaplan, R. S., & Norton, D. P. (2004). *The BSC: Translating Strategy into Action*. Reprinted with permission of Harvard Business School Publishing Corporation. All rights reserved. See also:.www.valuebasedmanagement.net

advantages through other more intangible assets, such as customer relationships, employee knowledge and skill, technology, and even corporate culture, as discussed throughout this book. Therefore, organizations have had to adjust the way they monitor, track, and communicate their progress.

It is essential for all members of an organization to understand a strategy if they are going to be able to implement it successfully. This includes understanding the challenging process by which all of the intangible assets of an organization are translated into solid, measurable outcomes. Strategy maps can help all employees understand this process. In addition, strategy maps help organizations differentiate themselves from competitors by creating a venue within which they can focus on the issues that allow them to attract, retain, and deepen relationships with targeted customers. They can do this by achieving a clear picture of their customer-related and financial perspectives. They can then use those perspectives to help them decide how to achieve the competitive advantage in customer service and in its financial objectives. Finally, such maps emphasize the importance of growth and development, focusing organizational efforts on issues important for the future success of the company through capability, skill building, and continuous learning.

According to Kaplan and Norton,[174] strategy maps can help organizations implement (or craft) their strategies by giving employees a clear line of sight into how their jobs are linked to the overall objectives of the organization. As mentioned earlier, typical measures for such a map are generally divided into the four main categories of financials, customers, internal processes, and learning and growth. There are a number of ways these four items can be monitored. The necessary information can be obtained from sources that are both internal and external to an organization. Typically, new information can provide a variety of metrics for all of the categories. In addition, many organizations use marketing research, service audits, and employee audits to acquire important information on customer perceptions, image, and employee behaviors and attitudes.

The "balanced scorecard" is another method that Kaplan and Norton introduced to help an organization transform its goals and vision into strategies and then implement those strategies in the best way.[20, 174] A balanced scorecard, shown in Figure 8.2, uses the same four perspectives as the strategy map—financial, customer, business or internal processes, and learning and growth.

Each of the four categories requires its own kind of metrics. Frequently used measures for financial performance include return on investment (ROI) or economic value added, profitability of the operation, revenue and revenue growth, and costs. Frequent measures for customer perceptions and behaviors are market-share tracking, customer acquisition and retention, profitability, and customer satisfaction levels. When it comes to internal processes, most companies monitor quality, response time cost, and the frequency and success of new product introduction. Finally, learning and growth measures include employee satisfaction, retention, and productivity. Many companies also track employee training outputs, the number of hours spent on training, the value added through training, and even information system availability and use.

Some authors, such as Jack,[163] are proposing second-generation mapping solutions to help all members of an organization understand the value creation process.

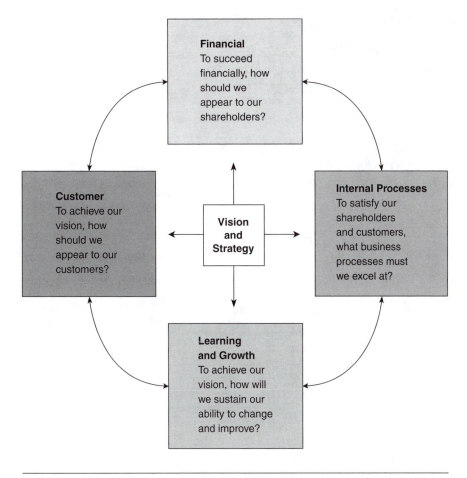

Figure 8.2   Balanced Scorecard

SOURCE: Adapted from Kaplan, R. S., & Norton, D. P. (2004). *The BSC: Translating Strategy into Action*. Harvard Business School Publishing Corporation.

Jack's model is the value map,[273] shown in Figure 8.3, which identifies and structures performance measures. As stressed throughout this book, the human contribution to the corporate bottom line is often undervalued, and Jack's value map purports to deal with that issue more effectively.

> It is the interface between measurement, management, and leadership that is crucial in ensuring that performance measures drive value creation. Communication is a central vehicle in integrating performance measurement with performance management and is placed at the core of the performance management solution.[163]

He also suggests that the value map can help both managers and employees change their negative opinions of performance measures and management decisions based on those measures.

> *It is good to have an end to journey towards: but it is the journey that matters in the end.*
>
> —Ursula K. Le Guin

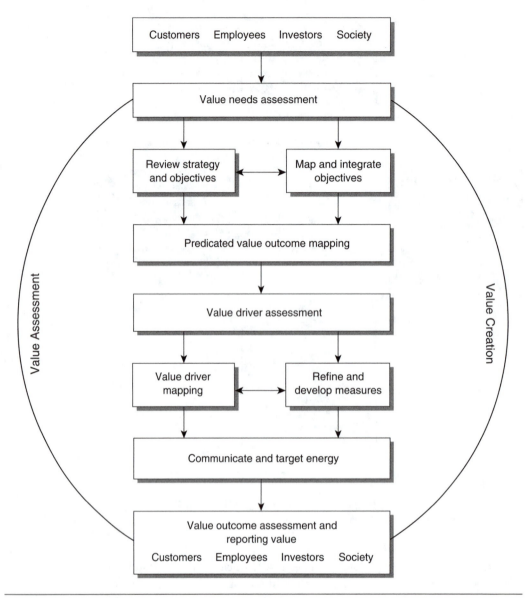

Figure 8.3   Value Map

SOURCE: Andrew, J. (2001). *Value Mapping – A Second Generation Performance Measurement and Performance Management Solution.* Business Excellence International Ltd.

Data and Methodology in Strategic Formulation

Service strategy is imperative for managing any corporation. An organization can enhance its decision making in the service process when it is based on service strategy. However, the strategy will need raw materials—namely, data that can be turned into useful information. Strategies, tactics, and decisions are worthless if they are not based on data and information. Where is the data? How can one obtain useful data? We can obtain them from either *internal* or *external* sources. Data can be either *primary* or *secondary* and can be collected using *qualitative* or *quantitative* measures. All of these are used in combination. For example, an organization can conduct internal primary research using a qualitative instrument. Let's see what these terms mean.

Internal Versus External Data

It is logical to classify sources of information according to their place of origin. Internal data can be obtained within the organization. External data are obtained from sources that are outside the firm.

Primary Versus Secondary Data

Sometimes useful data are "lying around" an organization; they have already been collected and exist as part of a corporate customer database. They may have come from a variety of sources and often have been summarized in reports. These kinds of data are categorized as secondary data, because our use of them is secondary to their original or primary purpose.

It is always a good idea to look for existing secondary data before deciding to collect new (primary) data. Although secondary data may not be as current as one would like or as specific or as well targeted as primary data, they have an obvious economic advantage in that they can often provide valuable information at nearly zero additional cost to the corporation. Finding these data can be a challenging project in its own right; knowing where to look is the key to success.

The first place to start might be to find reports that have been written earlier and check on whether they contain the information you need. Most corporations store huge databases about their customers that are too seldom used except for marketing purposes or for monitoring sales volume or tracking orders on each client. Numerous variables could be analyzed using fast data-mining software tools, which could yield unexpected and valuable information on topics of interest to service providers. Often the biggest problem associated with data mining in large databases is the cost of "cleaning" or formatting the data and making it accessible for analysis.

When the corporation has a customer relationship management (CRM) system in place, it will usually contain a wealth of information on how the corporation is servicing its customers. For example, customers' complaints should either be saved as a part of a quality system or stored in the CRM system. In addition to the previously mentioned data, it is highly likely that reports about customer complaints already exist. To find this information may take some digging or research into the relevant database, as existing data may be archived and essentially lost to corporate memory. Employees (including IT personnel and managers) are quick to forget what has been done or what information already exists. Sometimes a lack of communication between departments will complicate matters, especially in large companies.

There is a wealth of secondary data available for organizations to use to enhance decision making in the delivery of customer service. This is especially true in mature markets. A number of companies gather market information and store it in databases. One can then buy access to these databases or purchase ready-made reports based on this data. This approach can be very productive and is widely used in marketing. An example of this is customer profiling. Let's say a company in England is looking for older customers with large disposable incomes. It might use such a database and determine that Sussex would be an ideal market location.

Organizations that are thinking of expanding their markets into new countries should find out what trends exist in those countries. One example of this type of database service is Eurobarometer, for the European markets. Last, but not least, most countries have large amounts of information on their macroeconomic environment, information that is often free for corporations and other organizations to use.

When data are not available on a particular topic or when the data are not current enough, the company needs to conduct new research and turn it into valuable information, called primary data. There are many kinds of internal information that might be needed to formulate the service strategies. Part of that information is based on primary data; that is, management needs information on something specific within the organization but the data are not available. For example, management may need to find out how employees are servicing the company's customers. In this case, the company would need to obtain the required information through primary research.

Often the information the organization needs to improve customer service must be obtained externally, or outside the organization—that is, directly from the customers themselves. There are all kinds of external information available, both about customers and about the market in general. In addition, the company might want to know about future developments in the macroeconomic environment.

Often an organization needs to collect primary data for these areas. The most common kind of data collection is through the use of surveys, but other modes are also used, such as experiments, correlational studies, and expert reviews. Surveys would, for example, be employed to answer questions such as *How, where, and when are customers using a particular service? How does the company's performance compare to that of the competition? Why and under what circumstances are our customers willing to turn to the competition? What would happen to the demand for service if the company goes international?*

In the service sector, the factors of greatest importance involve the opinions and behavior of customers. Among the most important is customer satisfaction. Customer satisfaction affects the loyalty customers feel toward a company. In addition, the way customers feel about the corporate image and their expectations about service quality also affect their level of satisfaction. Each of these factors has to be measured and monitored. *What are the components of each factor? How is the corporation succeeding with them? Which of the components contributes the most to customer satisfaction?* These are questions a corporation has to ask, both for its own customers and for the competition's, so it knows what it has to do to stay competitive.

Despite the nearly endless possibilities for corporations to obtain secondary marketing data, primary data will always be the main way of strengthening service strategies and enhancing decision making about the delivery of service. In the service sector, the importance of primary data is due to the fact that corporations usually need up-to-date information that is collected specifically for their needs.

Qualitative Versus Quantitative

Whatever the source of information, research could provide qualitative (descriptive and not numerical) information or quantitative (numerical) data.

One example of a qualitative method is "mystery shopping." Here, the "mystery shopper," usually a person from a research agency, visits a company or business location and gathers data on various aspects of the service and the premises. The main objective of mystery shopping in a typical case might be to check on employees' behavior and to evaluate how well employees behave with regard to their customers. A secondary objective could be to determine the cleanliness and overall appearance of the facilities—two critically important factors in customer satisfaction, especially in organizations such as health-care facilities and restaurants.

Additionally, an outside consultant could conduct in-depth interviews with selected employees to determine how they go about servicing customers and even observe employees interacting with customers. An outside firm could also develop well-designed surveys for both customers and employees.

Undoubtedly, surveys are the quickest, easiest, and least expensive way of obtaining internal information on the delivery of customer service. Such surveys can be administered frequently—almost routinely—and as often as needed. How employees deliver service, their customers' responses, and their opinions on how well certain procedures are working are just a few of the questions that might be included in an employee survey. Although surveys of this type generally provide qualitative rather than quantitative data, the information derived from them can be quite useful in refining the customer service process if properly analyzed and acted on.

> *The real voyage of discovery consists not in seeking new landscapes, but in having new eyes.*
> —Marcel Proust

As mentioned earlier, quantitative methods produce statistical data. Although this kind of data is more difficult to collect and attribute directly to service, it has solid uses, such as measuring indicators of customer satisfaction and loyalty, discussed later in this chapter.

Measuring Customer Satisfaction

Whether they collect primary or secondary, qualitative or quantitative data, all organizations in the service industry must measure customer satisfaction. The kind of metric chosen depends on the objective of the measurement and on the research agency and its measurement conventions. Is the main purpose to track general changes in customer satisfaction, maybe in relation to marketing efforts? Is the purpose to go deeper; for example, to find predictors of customer satisfaction and reveal which of them has the greatest effect on customer satisfaction? Is the purpose to benchmark the service of the company or organization—to compare it with the competition? The answers to these questions will help to select or design the appropriate measurement tool. Let's examine these ways in more depth.

Customer satisfaction data usually come from both qualitative and quantitative methods of data collection. For the purpose of customer satisfaction, qualitative methods are mainly useful for generating ideas about what needs to be measured—often, focus groups or in-depth interviews are employed. Because of the nature of customer service and the difficulty of measuring such concepts as customer satisfaction, pure measurement is challenging. Think about measuring customer complaints. They are totally subjective; in other words, they depend completely on the individual who is reporting the complaint. Therefore, they are subject to a lot of variability. In light of this, analyzing customer complaints is a qualitative measure of customer satisfaction and could form the basis of more complex quantitative research on how to please customers.

Because the research on customer satisfaction has a history that spans several decades, one seldom needs to design new measurement tools. Focus groups, pretesting, reliability and validity tests, and other, similar instruments can be used. However, before designing a survey that will focus on customers of a specific company, one might want to conduct a few focus groups with customers to gain insight into what matters most from their point of view in the service provided by a given company or organization.

Tracking Changes in Customer Satisfaction

Every company and organization needs to know what the customers think of its service. It has been shown that customer satisfaction predicts how well corporations are doing, measured as market value added.[97] Thus it is extremely important to track changes in customer satisfaction to be able to respond when changes are seen, before they start hurting the business, as customer satisfaction directly affects an organization's profits. In addition, whenever a company engages in any kind of marketing effort, a measure should be taken before, during, and after the campaign. Strictly speaking, one measurement before and another after are generally not enough, due to possible threats to internal validity; that is, something other than marketing efforts could be operating at the same time.[58, 156, 219, 322] To avoid such a threat, the organization should take frequent measures, for example, once a month.

There are a few ways of measuring customer satisfaction for the simple purpose of tracking changes. The organization could use a 1 to 5 Likert-type scale (e.g., *Are you generally satisfied or dissatisfied with the service of Company X?* 5 = very satisfied, 4 = somewhat satisfied, 3 = neither satisfied nor dissatisfied, 2 = somewhat dissatisfied, 1 = very dissatisfied) or the 0 to 10 scale (e.g., *on a scale of 0 to 10, are you generally satisfied or dissatisfied with the service of Company X?*). The survey should include more than one satisfaction question each time so the measure will become more reliable. Additional questions could compare the company being evaluated with the "perfect" company in the same sector and ask how well expectations are fulfilled. The same scale should be used for all questions; then the questions can be put into one variable as a measure of customer satisfaction.

> *If you don't measure it, it will not improve; if you don't monitor it, it will get worse.*
>
> —Traditional

Going Deeper: Predictors of Customer Satisfaction

In general, it is not enough to measure customer satisfaction only. It is important to find out what affects it and determine how it can be improved. To make these determinations, several issues related to customer satisfaction need to be measured—things that can be used to improve customer satisfaction that are often related to the behaviors of employees.

A typical customer survey might include the following areas (several questions can come from each area):

- Assurance (employee knowledge and ability to inspire trust and confidence in the service)
- Empathy (employee concern for and individualized attention to customers)
- Reliability (employee ability to perform the promised service dependably and accurately over and over again)
- Responsiveness or speed of service (employee willingness to help customers and the customer's perception of the speed of service received)
- Tangible items (such as physical facilities, equipment, and the general appearance of the employees)
- Additional questions on the service that relate specifically to the corporation and its marketing and service sector

Two major things can be accomplished with a survey of this kind. First, the corporation gets a quantitative measure of several important factors that relate to its delivery of service. Second, through multivariate analyses, such as factor analysis, regression analysis, and even structural equation modeling, one can determine which factors affect customer satisfaction the most, what comes next, and how great the effects are.

Comparison of Customer Satisfaction to That Held by the Competition

Often it is important for corporations to obtain measures of customer satisfaction that are standardized; that is, measures that can be compared with those of other corporations. Such methods include the European Performance Satisfaction Index (EPSI) rating and the American Customer Satisfaction Index (ACSI). The ACSI measure dates back to 1994 and the EPSI measure to 1999. In both cases, the measures are carried out each time with the same questions and the same methodology, and they are analyzed in the same way. In both cases, the same three questions on customer satisfaction, with the same scale, are used. These questions are put together in the same variable on a scale of 0 to 100 to reflect a customer satisfaction index.

Standardized measures of this type have been done for large corporations in several European countries and in the United States and can be compared across corporations, sectors, and markets. At this time, many corporations have obtained several years of standardized measures that they can use to compare their own performance from one year to the next. Additionally, they can compare their customer satisfaction ratings with those of another company or competitor.

Standardized measures of customer satisfaction provide additional value by asking questions on several other issues dealing with corporate image, customer expectations, product and service quality, and value for money. A unique model of coefficients, found with structural equation modeling, is produced for each company or organization. Using such models, the organization can find the major predictors of customer satisfaction within the scope of the EPSI rating or the ACSI. When an organization can explain and predict customer satisfaction, it can use this information to help develop customer loyalty.

No matter how we measure customer satisfaction, we must try our utmost to keep the measure valid (is it measuring what we need to measure?) and reliable (is it consistent through multiple measurements?). To achieve this usually requires that a research professional or research agency conduct the measurement. Constructing a good questionnaire or survey is seldom easy, and there are several pitfalls on the way. For example, it is challenging to construct each individual survey question so it measures the right element and contributes to a reliable and valid survey. For this reason, and to maintain distance and objectivity, which is often difficult when measuring one's own company, it is a good idea to hire a professional to construct and carry out such measures.

> *The measure of success is not whether you have a tough problem to deal with, but whether it's the same problem you had last year.*
> —John Foster Dulles

Data and Methodology in Service Management

Customer-oriented behavior (COBEH) of employees includes positive attitudes translated into behaviors that benefit customers and, therefore, the organization. They include the tendency of the individual to learn and continuously improve on the job. These behaviors are discussed fully in Chapter 9, and additional information about measuring employee performance is found in Chapter 11.

There are several ways of measuring employees' customer-oriented behaviors. Three of these methods are discussed in this section: (a) employees' self-reported behaviors, (b) customers' perceptions of employees' performance, and (c) supervisors' evaluations of employees.

There are limitations to every approach, and no measurement exists in a vacuum. The potential limitations of survey research, some of which have already been mentioned, are well-known. Various intervening factors can influence the subjects' responses. Factors such as the respondent's need for social desirability can affect the accuracy, reliability, and validity of data collected. Social desirability is the tendency many people have to give an answer that makes them seem socially desirable. For example, when a survey asks a woman how much time she spends helping others outside the workplace, she may report a quantity of time and kinds of activities that would make her seem more the ideal person rather than reporting what she actually engages in. An additional limitation occurs when respondents are unable to recall accurately information about their activities, their behaviors in different circumstances, or even details about themselves. This can be caused by poor memory, confusion about the questions asked, or nervousness related to being involved in a research study.[110] Also, using self-reported data may lead to possible errors in assessment. For example, when assessing someone else's performance, people tend to discount situational factors. On the other hand, people tend to magnify such factors when assessing their own performance.[175]

Despite these limitations of surveys, research has shown that there is a high correlation between what people say and what they do.[200] In general, surveys are a powerful tool for obtaining reliable information for managers—a tool that has to be constructed with care, with the noted limitations in mind.

Employee Self-Reports

One way of assessing the extent of employees' customer orientation is to measure their actual service improvement efforts and helping behaviors toward customers, based on their own reports. An instrument was developed in the United Kingdom by Peccei and Rosenthal[231] to measure employees' self-reported customer-oriented behaviors. It contains 6 items and is measured on a 5-point Likert-type scale (1 = highly disagree, 2 = disagree, 3 = neither agree nor disagree, 4 = agree, 5 = highly agree). Employees are asked to evaluate their own performance using the scale, and the mean is calculated for their group, workstation, or department. The group mean can then be benchmarked against the overall organizational mean or against the last time the group's performance was evaluated using the same scale. The scale has been tested across various cultures and service industries. Longitudinal studies have shown it to be consistent and reliable.

A comparison with customers' perceptions of employees' service has also shown advantages in employees' self-reported service-oriented behaviors over supervisors' evaluations of those same behaviors. A high correlation has been found to exist between self-reports by employees of their customer-oriented behavior and customer perceptions of the provided services.[117, 120]

In addition to the known weaknesses of self-report measures, threats to any behavioral measure exist, including different kinds of variability and variance. However, Howard and colleagues[101, 154] have argued that although self-report measures are not perfect, the construct-validity coefficients of self-reports are superior to the validity coefficients of other measurements. Spector[288] has argued that the most frequently found sources of method variance in self-reports are acquiescence and social desirability. Research has shown that some measures are highly correlated with social desirability. This tendency toward social desirability makes it difficult to determine whether the intended construct is being measured. Various techniques have been developed to control for such threats to the instrument, such as including forced-choice items and screening out items that correlate highly with social desirability. The other suggested bias (acquiescence) is the tendency of participants to agree with certain items regardless of content.

Customer Perceptions

Another way of assessing employees' customer-oriented behaviors is to ask their customers. Both quantitative and qualitative methods can be applied. Quantitative measures include customer surveys, in which customers are asked to evaluate employees' performance on key factors of the service provided, such as those presented in the section on measuring customer satisfaction.

Such information on customers' perceptions helps managers better understand the impact of the employee-customer encounter on the overall service experience and therefore on customer satisfaction. Furthermore, results of customer surveys can then be examined in relation to either employee self-reports or supervisors' evaluations. In that case, an average of the customer survey of a particular department or other unit of the corporation constitutes a data point and is associated with the average of the self-reports of the same department or unit. They make a pair of related data points. An important note must be made that a considerable number of data points or pairs (employee-customer pairs or groups) are needed to obtain a meaningful statistical analysis of the relationship.

A similar framework can be adopted by qualitative methods such as focus groups or in-depth interviews with customers or with the mystery shoppers described earlier. Those results cannot be correlated directly with employee self-reports. On the other hand, customer surveys can be used to examine the validity of employees' evaluations. Qualitative information can, of course, provide valuable information and insight into important aspects of both employee behaviors and the overall service operation of the organization.

Supervisors' Evaluations

The third approach is to ask managers or supervisors to evaluate the customer-oriented behaviors of their employees. The same six-item scale applies here as in employee self-reports. Managers or supervisors evaluate their employees' helping behaviors and continuous improvement efforts. Known problems exist with supervisors' evaluations, such as the halo effect, central tendency, strict rating, lenient rating, last behavior rating, initial impression, and the spillover effect.

The *halo effect* is the tendency of a person to answer all questions consistent with to the way he or she feels about the person or subject being analyzed. For example, if a customer likes a certain employee, he or she may always rate that employee more highly than he or she would if the rating were strictly objective. The error of *central tendency* is the tendency to answer in the middle of a rating rather than give extreme answers. A *strict rating* means that the rater always gives ratings that are too low, whereas a *lenient rating* is just the opposite—always too high. The *last behavior rating* means that the rater is strongly affected by the last experience he or she had with a person or experience, and that last experience has a strong effect on the way he or she rates the current situation.

A similar situation exists with the *initial impression* weaknesses. Here, for example, the customer who had a very good first impression of a service provider would transfer that feeling to the way he or she evaluates that service provider. With a negative first impression, he or she would rate everything lower because of the lingering effect of that first impression. The *spillover effect* means that other, often extraneous, issues affect the way someone answers questions. Examples of spillover effects are a person's economic level, job, health, or family situation. These problems can never be completely eliminated, but they can be minimized if the evaluation is done with an objective questionnaire or checklist.

Evidence suggests that supervisors evaluate employees' customer-oriented behaviors differently than their employees and customers do. Employees and customers focus on helping behaviors directed toward fulfilling the current customers' needs. However, supervisors appear to overlook these behaviors and rate employees' performance by the number of suggestions or ideas they offer on how to improve the service, but not on their efforts directly related to serving the customers.[117] Known problems with supervisors' evaluations and the limited amount of research in this field make generalizations problematic. Further research is needed to establish and then enhance the application of the supervisor's evaluation as a valid predictor of employees' customer-oriented behaviors.

> The great thing in this world is not so much where we stand, as in what direction we are moving.
>
> —Oliver Wendell Holmes

In general, employees' self-reports are the most popular and advanced way of measuring employees' customer-oriented behaviors. In that area, there exists a wealth of tools to choose from, and most research agencies deliver or assist organizations in obtaining valid and reliable measurements of customer service.

Summary

The development of any service strategy and the plans for its implementation must include a plan for how the results of the implementation are to be measured. That requires the development of metrics that are appropriate for measuring each part of the service process.

The organization must choose metrics that fit the company's culture and values as well as its processes. The metrics an organization chooses must be designed with a global view. Rather than a disconnected set of measurements used in various parts of the organization, metrics should be viewed as a complete set of measures that fit together well and complement each other.

The most common metrics used by a service organization deal with the financial performance and overall growth of the company; the experiences and satisfaction level of the customers; the quality and quantity of the company's products and services; and the attitudes, behaviors, and values of the organizational members.

Strategy maps and balanced scorecards are two visual methods that can help the members of the organization see how the company connects its goals and strategies in a clear cause-and-effect relationship. Both of these tools also help all employees see how their individual jobs are tied to corporate objectives.

All organizations need solid data on which to base other strategies. Often, the company needs to collect primary data from original research. Other times, it can use secondary data, or research results and reports that already exist. Most organizations have huge quantities of data that are often unused or at least underused.

Both internal and external data are valuable to the company. Internal data, which are collected inside the company, include information about the processes themselves, as well as about employee behaviors and attitudes. External data, from outside the company, include critical information about the level of customer satisfaction as well as information about competitors' practices and performances.

Both qualitative and quantitative metrics are useful in service organizations. Qualitative data are descriptive, not statistical, in nature, and include such methods as interviews, surveys, and focus groups. Because of the intangible nature of service itself and the need to measure abstract concepts such as employees' attitudes and customers' satisfaction levels, qualitative measures are more widely used. This is due to the fact that quantitative, or numerical, measures, although extremely valuable, are much more difficult to obtain directly in most areas of the service industry. On the other hand, some quantitative data, such as increases in revenue, can be connected to customer satisfaction. This is a good example of applying readily available, but indirectly related, quantitative data from one area to evaluate performance in another area.

One of the most critical sets of metrics in this industry measures customer satisfaction, as it directly and significantly affects the company's profitability. An organization must conduct frequent measures of how satisfied its customers are, and it must track changes in customer satisfaction levels over time. In addition, the corporation should use data, such as the EPSI rating and ACSI, to benchmark itself against other similar organizations, both in the same country and in the global marketplace.

Another crucial set of metrics deals with the customer-oriented behaviors of service providers. Three measurement methods for this data are (a) employees' self-reported behaviors, (b) customers' perceptions of employees' performance, and (c) supervisors' evaluations of employees' behaviors.

When correctly designed and applied, metrics create great value for the organization because they help it analyze its strengths and weaknesses. This information then allows the organization to better plan its strategies and processes, because it helps the organization identify and focus on those areas that need the greatest attention. This, in turn, helps the organization better serve its customers, which can lead to higher levels of customer satisfaction. The ultimate result is what every organization seeks and needs—higher levels of profitability.

We would like to sincerely thank Dr. Thor Karlsson, the program director of the Business School at Reykjavik University and a former managing director of the research organization IMG Gallup, for his valuable input in the development of this chapter.

SAS Institute on Data Mining

One of the latest techniques to be adopted by the most ambitious service companies today is the science of "data mining." They use this statistical method and highly advanced software packages to reduce fraud, predict resource demand, increase sales, and efficiently align services with customers' needs and expectations.

The SAS Institute, one of the leading service providers in this field, defines data mining as "the process of data selection, exploration, and building models using vast data stores to uncover previously unknown patterns." By applying such techniques, companies can fully exploit data about customers' buying patterns and behavior to gain a greater understanding of consumer motivations. In practical terms, this means that information can be collected, merged, analyzed, and used by companies to make better informed decisions before taking actions to manufacture, sell, or reengineer goods and services.

Generally a model is built based on information about transactions, customer history with the company, and a variety of customer demographic information—some from within the company and other information from external sources, such as credit bureaus. Then these models are used to identify patterns in the data that can support decision making or predict new business opportunities. In addition to data, the SAS Institute now provides capabilities that enable companies to apply such analyses to text-based documents as well as numeric data. Data mining is most frequently used to

- Seek and retain the most profitable customers
- Segment markets for a targeted approach
- Predict the future and identify factors to secure a desired effect

Data Mining Reaches Across Industries and Business Functions

A wide range of companies now use data mining to enhance their bottom-line results and streamline their approach to their customers. According to the SAS Institute, telecommunications, stock exchanges, and credit card and insurance companies use this technique to detect fraud, optimize marketing campaigns, and identify the most profitable strategies. The medical industry uses data mining to predict the effectiveness of surgical procedures, medical tests, and medications. Retailers use this technology to assess the effectiveness of discount coupons, rebate offers, and special events, as well as to predict which promotions are most appropriate for different consumers.

Key Points

- Data mining allows companies to fully use their large databases to enhance decision making.

- It is a powerful statistical method of analysis.

- It can reveal previously unknown buying patterns and customer behaviors.

- It can be used to reduce fraud, predict demand, increase sales, and predict customers' motivations.

SOURCE: SAS Institute.[81, 264]

Key Concepts

Directions: The following are key concepts presented in this chapter. Write a complete definition for each one.

Service metrics

Strategy map

Value map

Predictors of customer service

Questions

1. How does the wise use of metrics contribute to the achievement of organizational objectives?

2. What are strategy maps? For what purposes are they used in organizations?

3. What is the difference between qualitative and quantitative measurements? Give an example of each.

4. What are primary data? What are two ways primary data about an organization's level of customer satisfaction can be collected?

5. What are secondary data? What are the main advantages and disadvantages of using secondary data?

6. Why should every organization obtain data from both internal and external sources? Give an example of each kind of source and explain why it is important.

7. Why should organizations track changes in customer satisfaction levels? How should that data be used?

8. What are EPSI ratings and ACSI? How should organizations use these indexes?

9. Briefly describe the three measures discussed in this chapter to measure customer-oriented behaviors.

10. What are five limitations in using any kind of self-report instrument for data collection?

Advanced Activity

Draw a strategy map in which customer relationships are intended to create added value for both customers and the company. Bring the map to class for discussion. Use Figure 8.1 or similar maps to guide your work. You can use an existing company that you know, or you can draw a map for a new company or service you might be planning to start in the future. (a) First, set the financial objectives for the company. (b) Identify customer requirements the company needs to fulfill to achieve its financial targets. (c) Identify critical internal processes needed to fulfill customer requirements. (d) Identify factors critical to the company's development and continuous improvement and learning.

Search the Web

Find the Web site of an online company that uses its site to advertise and sell its products and services. Find another Web site for a company that mainly focuses on selling its products and services through direct contact with customers in *traditional* facilities but uses its site to support its business. Examine the Web sites and find the major differences and similarities in the way the services and products are presented to customers. Pay particular attention to the tangible aspects of each Web site, such as how user-friendly it is, how detailed the information is, how appealing the company and its services and products are made to appear, and how customer focused they are. Write a short report on your findings.

Suggested Readings

Kaplan, R. S., & Norton, D. P. (2004). *Strategy maps—strategic communication.* Retrieved July 8, 2005, from the Value Based Management.net Web site: http://www.valuebased management.net/methods_strategy_maps_strategic_communication.html

Peccei, R., & Rosenthal, P. (1997). The antecedents of employee commitment to customer service: Evidence from a UK service context. *International Journal of Human Resource Management, 8,* 66–86.

Shinkle, G., Gooding, R., & Smith, M. (2004). *Transforming strategy into success: How to implement a lean management system.* New York: Productivity Press.

PART

three

Engaging the Providers

P art III focuses on the role of the service provider in the quest for service quality and competitive advantage. First, methods of enhancing employees' customer-oriented behaviors are explored; second, important issues in managing a service organization are discussed. Third, the crucial role of human resources in successful service organizations is dealth with. Finally, a step-by-step approach on how to build an effective service leadership culture is summarized.

The Power of the Providers

*General Electric Company
on Preventing Service Failures
in Business-to-Business Customer Service*

David Kirchner

*Program Manager,
GE Transportation
Rail Solutions, Train and
Yard Products*

G eneral Electric Company (GE) is a huge multinational corporation with a wide variety of businesses well beyond the light bulb or electricity connection on which the company was founded in 1878. Today, GE has operations in more than 100 countries, manufacturing facilities in 32 countries, and more than 305,000 employees worldwide. About 45% of GE's revenues come from its international business operations. GE has 11 primary business areas: health care, transportation, energy, advanced materials, NBC Universal, consumer and industrial services, equipment services, commercial finance, consumer finance, insurance, and infrastructure.

Customer service is a major concern of GE, and this multinational corporation realizes that this means more than just catering to the end user. GE believes there are three key elements in achieving quality for the customer: the customer, the process, and the employee. "Everything we do to remain a world-class quality company focuses on these three essential elements," states the GE Web site (http://www.ge.com/en/).

The Customer

GE's goal is to delight its customers. Customers are the center of the GE universe: They define quality. They expect performance, reliability, competitive prices, on-time delivery, service, clear and correct transaction processing, and more. In every attribute that influences customer perception, we know that just being good is not enough. Delighting our customers is a necessity—because if we don't do it, someone else will!

The Process

Quality requires us to look at our business from the customer's perspective, not ours. By understanding the transaction life-cycle from the perspective of the customer's needs and processes, we can discover what they are seeing and feeling and can identify areas where we can add significant value or improvement, from their point of view.

The Employees

People create results. Involving all employees is essential to the GE quality approach. (Discussed in Chapter 9, GE is an avid user of the Six Sigma techniques for quality.) Quality is the responsibility of every employee. Every employee must be involved, motivated, and knowledgeable if we are to succeed.

GE's Philosophy

Imagine, solve, build, and lead—four bold verbs that express what it is to be part of GE. For more than 125 years, GE has been admired for its performance and imaginative spirit. From the very beginnings of our company, when Thomas Edison was changing the world with the power of ideas, GE has always stood for one capability above all others—the ability to imagine. At GE, imagining is fused with empowerment—the confidence that what we imagine we can make happen. GE exists to solve problems for our customers, our communities, and ourselves. The products we invent and the businesses we build fuel the global economy and improve people's lives.

Our actions and our values are what unify us. What we do and how we work is distinctly GE. It's a way of thinking and working that has guided our performance for decades. It's about who we are, what we believe, where we're headed, and how we'll get there. It's how we imagine, solve, build, and lead.

GE is already synonymous with leadership. But with this mantle comes responsibility. And it's not just a responsibility to maintain the status quo or manage what worked yesterday. It's the bigger responsibility to change. Change is the essence of what it means to lead. It's a call to action that engages our curiosity, passion, and drive to be first in everything we do.

In the end, our success is measured not only by our ability to think big but by our attention to the small details that bring ideas to life. It's a way of thinking and doing that has been at the heart of GE for years. The worth of this framework is how we translate it into our own personal work ethic and then extend it to our teams, businesses, and cultures. It's permission to cast aside any approach that seems dated—to imagine, solve, build, and lead a better way of doing things.

While GE has always performed with integrity and values, each business generation expresses those values according to the circumstances of the times. Now more than ever, the expression and adherence to values is vital. More than just a set of words, these values embody the spirit of GE at its best. They reflect the energy and spirit of a company that has the solid foundation to lead change as business evolves. And they articulate a code of behavior that guides us through that change with integrity. They are our words and our values . . . in our own voice.

The International Perspective

GE Transportation is just one of GE's 11 core businesses. It includes aircraft engines, rail, and rail solutions in Melbourne, Florida. David Kirchner is the program manager of GE's Train and Yard Products.

As in many corporations, customer service at GE involves a business-to-business relationship that crosses many borders. As Kirchner points out, "The greatest challenge [in working with international clients] is to understand the culture and customs of the international customer . . . to have an understanding and appreciation of the social, political, economic, personal, financial, and business environment that your customer lives in every day and possess the ability to walk in their shoes, so to speak. This insight into your customer's mind-set will help you to understand his needs and permit you to meet those needs with your products and services. You must know what is most important to your customer and fulfill these critical needs to attain success. At GE, we defined these customer needs as 'critical to quality' needs."

Carefully fostering these relationships is the best way to prevent service failures, according to Kirchner. It is essential for customers to get to know you and to trust you before you can successfully conduct business with them. Internationally, it is essential to begin discussions through telephone calls, e-mails, or face-to-face meetings, with some personal discussions. Showing concern for the individual with whom you are communicating prior to discussing business is a good method to use for building a relationship. This can be accomplished by discussing some particular topic of interest such as a sport or hobby, asking the person how his family is, or achieving similar personal discourse. Also, it is important to maintain continuity with international customers to ensure that relationships grow and expand. One way to accomplish this task is to send the same "core" team for each meeting. This helps to give the client a sense of security and comfort, making it easier to cement the relationship.

In addition to building relationships that allow your business client to trust you, it is important to make sure there is a clear mutual understanding of the details of an agreement during the negotiating phases, something that is especially difficult across language and cultural boundaries. Kirchner uses a simple technique—the three-question technique—when a critical point, contract issue, or technical issue arises to assure himself that he and his client have the same understanding. In other words, during the discussions, he asks the same question three different ways. If the answers are consistent, he's sure he knows what his client needs and can therefore serve that client better. As Kirchner says, "to minimize problems with customers, first and foremost it is essential to clearly understand the problem. Due to language barriers or cultural differences it is critical to make sure that a problem exists and to define the problem clearly. This may require additional time and patience, but in the end it will save valuable time. The three-question technique can definitely be applied in this case to ensure you clearly understand the customer's problem [needs]. Ask many questions."

Part of the understanding process is dealing effectively with non-English-speaking clients. Kirchner pointed out, "Since GE is an international company, customer account executives are located around the world who speak the local language. I will provide the product expertise to them and they will manage the customer contacts. We possess company contacts that will translate documents for us if required. It is critical to observe nonverbal communications, such as facial expressions, body language, and other personal gestures, that help you understand the customer and the conversation. For presentations, proposals, and technical documents, a picture is truly worth a thousand words. Whenever possible, convey your message in a picture, graph, or concept diagram versus text explanations. There are universal symbols that everyone understands."

Using these techniques, along with all the other intercultural strategies, helps GE service providers such as Kirchner ensure the customer satisfaction of their many multinational clients within a true service leadership culture.

Activating
Customer Orientation

*In today's marketplace, customer service orientation and the
capacity of front-line workers are believed to be the keys to a
service organization's success or failure in responding to increased
competition and various external conditions.*

—Svafa Grönfeldt

Objectives

After completing this chapter, you should be able to

1. Define employee customer orientation and understand the differences in how the construct has been conceptualized over time

2. Identify core ingredients of employee customer-oriented behaviors

3. Understand the antecedents of customer-oriented behavior and managerial implications associated with them

4. Recognize challenges associated with implementation of customer orientation in an organizational setting

5. Realize the impact of customer orientation on organizational success

6. Understand the basic ways to measure customer-oriented behavior

Customer Orientation

Strong customer orientation is central to discussions of quality management,[190] human resources management,[233-235] the "excellence" approach,[47, 210] and service management.[324] However, in spite of the increased focus on the importance of employee-customer interactions and service orientation, the literature has given little attention to the conceptualization of customer orientation, its link to related constructs, and how it relates to an individual's performance and organizational service quality. The purpose of this chapter is to discuss the debate regarding the conceptualization of customer orientation and to examine related constructs and their development in the literature. A major part of the debate is disagreement about exactly what the concept of customer orientation entails. As a result of this debate, definitions of customer orientation vary across management, quality, and service literature; they can, however, be categorized into systemic, attitudinal, and behavioral terms. In this chapter, an overview of the various definitions is presented, followed by a discussion of the impact that employees' customer-oriented behaviors have on customers' perceptions of the service received. The primary aim of the chapter is to look for answers to the following questions: How can organizations increase employees' helping behaviors toward customers? How can organizations affect the extent to which their service providers work to improve their performance, service efficiency, and quality?

> *When enthusiasm is inspired by reason; controlled by caution; sound in theory; practical in application; reflects confidence; spreads good cheer; raises morale; inspires associates; arouses loyalty; and laughs at adversity, it is beyond price.*
>
> —Coleman Cox

Systemic Approach to Customer Orientation

To some, total quality management (TQM) provides a historically unique approach to improving organizational effectiveness.[124] A more skeptical view is that TQM is but one program in a long line of programs soon to be replaced with new management trends.[84, 315] Numerous service organizations have adopted a TQM philosophy and implemented TQM strategies in an attempt to enhance service effectiveness. The concept of customer orientation and employee attitudes is an important element in these programs.

Total Quality Management

TQM theory is a total process involving all operations. In TQM, every strategy relates to satisfying customers' needs and more actively involving all employees. Thus customer orientation is important at all levels of an organization. The universal approach of the classic quality writers, such as Deming,[85] Ishikawa,[159] and

Juran,[171] emphasized such an orientation as an aspect of human nature, to be uniformly "released" by appropriate systems and structures. These writers argued that the primary goal of organizations is to stay in business so that they can promote the stability of the community, generate products and services that are useful to customers, and provide a setting for the satisfaction and growth of organizational members.[124]

Hackman and Wageman[124] have pointed out that the TQM strategy is rooted in four interlocking assumptions related to *people, quality, organizations,* and *the role of senior management.* Although the assumption about people suggests that employees naturally care about the quality of work they do and will take initiatives to continuously improve their work, TQM recognizes that an organization must alter its employees' behavior to accomplish this desirable goal.

Moreover, the unpredictability of the customer service process makes it extremely difficult to *legislate;* that is, to provide the service according to a systematic set of rules operating under close supervision. Inherently, that kind of rule-governed behavior would hinder the required flexibility, initiative, and individualized care necessary to quality customer service. In fact, Hackman and Wagemen[124] suggest that organizations have problems motivating frontline staff toward continuous improvement and learning and simultaneously adhering closely to standardized best practices and procedures.

A central focus of TQM is that people at all levels of an organization are expected to *improve work processes continuously.* The method emphasizes an improvement in employees' behavior at work through three behavioral processes: *motivation, learning,* and *change.* Employees willing to work harder can be the result of increased *motivation; learning* implies that employees will become more capable by increasing their knowledge and skills; *change* implies that employees will act more responsively in meeting their customer's needs.

TQM is process oriented, and thus most TQM literature focuses on systems rather than individuals. Although service is a process and can be systematically analyzed through service blueprinting and service mapping, the service operation is less controllable than typical manufacturing processes because of the human element in service provision.

Two of the main principles of change embedded in TQM are (a) a focus on work processes and (b) the notion that uncontrolled variances are the primary cause of quality problems. Mullins[216] has argued that there has been too much reliance on systems in the service quality literature and that systems are only as effective as the people who design them. As a result of this, Peccei and Rosenthal[231] suggested that there is little evidence for the TQM assumption that appropriate systems and structures will cultivate a "natural" flow of employees' customer orientation, as suggested in the TQM literature.

In spite of the complex issue of employee-customer interaction, mainstream TQM literature underestimates the importance and complexity of the dynamics of the individual employee's customer orientation. Thus attention has been shifting to alternative definitions of customer orientation and solutions to ensure appropriate behavior in frontline service providers.

Lean Six Sigma for Service

Service organizations have increasingly been turning toward another systematic approach to service quality—the "Lean Six Sigma." Originally, two methodologies (Lean Speed and the Six Sigma) were developed for manufacturing in the 1980s at Motorola. In recent years, a fusion of these two has developed into a business improvement methodology for service that strives to maximize shareholder value. Its goals are aggressive, such as reducing costs by 30% to 50% in an attempt to dramatically improve a company's bottom line.

For many organizations, Six Sigma is a measure of quality that strives to achieve near perfection. Six Sigma's approach is data driven and highly disciplined. Its methods are used to eliminate defects in any process, including manufacturing, nonmanufacturing, and service processes. Interpreted literally, Six Sigma is reached when only 3.1 parts per million are defective—a daunting goal for manufacturing processes.

The use of Six Sigma for nonmanufacturing processes has been more challenging because of the nonstandardized nature of these processes, and some have questioned its applicability.

Jack Welch, former CEO of General Electric (GE), has been widely identified as the standard-bearer for the implementation of Six Sigma. His "Burning Platform" was to make GE "The Most Competitive Company on Earth." The philosophy of this dynamic and charismatic manager is detailed in his new book, *Winning*.[318] When he became CEO, Welch realized that GE's quality was not high and productivity was not up to par. To solve these and other problems, he launched the Six Sigma initiative in 1996. Much of it was applied to manufacturing processes, but it also helped GE expand its service offerings. In fact, Welch's business philosophy, which includes Six Sigma principles,[285] was put on a laminated statement-of-values card carried by all GE employees. Significantly, four of the nine points deal with customer service and related employee values:

1. Be passionately focused on driving customer success.

2. Live Six Sigma quality . . . ensure that the customer is always its first beneficiary . . . and use it to accelerate growth.

3. Prize global intellectual capital and the people that provide it . . . build diverse teams to maximize it.

4. Create a clear, simple, customer-centered vision . . . and continually renew and refresh its execution.

Certainly, using Six Sigma or Lean Six Sigma can quickly yield improvements in the speed and quality of service delivery, especially where service processes and delivery are fairly standardized. These improvements result in lower costs and greater customer satisfaction.

However, what works well for standardized processes does not necessarily work for most actual customer service encounters, where flexibility is a must. The same basic shortcomings apply to Six Sigma as to TQM when it comes to regulating or standardizing the actual employee-customer encounter. The fundamental objective of the Six Sigma methodology is the implementation of a measurement-based strategy that focuses on improving the process and reducing the variation through the application of Six Sigma improvement projects.[285] This creates a fundamental contradiction with the basics of good customer service. No amount of data input and analysis or processes control can regulate every customer contact and eliminate all variation. Furthermore, such an approach is likely to reduce both the flexibility and the leadership mind-set necessary at the front line, because employees are forced to follow procedures and prescribed service behaviors instead of relying on their own judgment for any given situation. Thus, the stated benefit—a much-needed decrease in variation in the process—often occurs at the high cost of insensitivity to customers' individual differences and needs and a lack of the flexibility needed to meet those individual needs.

> *The most infectiously joyous men and women are those who forget themselves in thinking about others and serving others.*
> —Robert J. McCraken

Attitudinal Approach to Customer Orientation

In the current service management literature, an alternative perspective to the systemic approach is an emphasis on employee attitudes toward service. The attitudinal approach holds that a strong customer orientation is embedded in the organization's culture. In a service context, customer orientation is viewed as "positive service attitudes," which involve the traits having to do with attitudes and personalities—psychographic characteristics, which can vary between individuals and between organizations. Positive service attitudes are viewed by some as a core element in an organization's goal of achieving competitive advantage because they lead to the development of long-term relationships between the organization and its customers.[178, 267]

Attitudes and their effect on behaviors are very complex and are by no means clearly related to the behaviors of individuals. Social psychologists point out that attitudes represent the interplay of a person's feelings, cognitions, and behavioral tendencies. Ajzen and Fishbein[2] have argued that behavior is more predictable when a person's intentions to behave are examined instead of his or her attitudes toward the particular subject. In short, attitudes and actions are two separate things.

However, such generalized concepts about the attitudes of service providers are often ambiguous and difficult to adopt in organizational settings, far more so than new technologies and systems. Furthermore, it is increasingly difficult to recruit, select, and retain service employees whose personal values match those of the organization, a topic that is expanded on in Chapter 10. This is especially true during times of favorable economic conditions, which

> *If what you are working for really matters, you'll give it all you've got.*
> —Nido Qubein

result in greater employee job mobility. Hence, it may be more fruitful, from both the theoretical and the practical points of view, to reconceptualize the customer orientations of frontline staff.

Behavioral Focus on Customer Orientation

No matter which approach to customer service is used, anything that is considered to be a core element must be a concern for meeting customer needs. Much of the quality and management literature assumes a direct relationship between employee attitudes and customer satisfaction. However, this assumption only relates to performance *if* and *when* it translates into desirable behavior, so just analyzing the attitudes of employees does not complete the picture. Therefore, the focus here is on the extent to which employees actually exert effort on behalf of their customers, not just on employee attitudes. This explicit behavioral approach to customer orientation has a direct connection to the behavior that is intended to enhance service performance and therefore fulfill customer needs.

This behavioral approach to customer service is congruent with the core of marketing thoughts that have developed over the past 30 years. Underlying it is the notion of an integrated, companywide approach where all activities are directed toward customer satisfaction and the cultivation of long-term, mutually beneficial relationships with customers. This perspective includes a problem-solving approach to service in which all parts of an organization are oriented toward solving customer problems and meeting the needs of the marketplace.[50]

Customer-Oriented Behavior

Peccei and Rosenthal[231] introduced the term *customer-oriented behavior* (COBEH) and defined customer orientation as the relative tendency of an individual to engage in continuous improvement and to exert effort on the job for the benefit of customers.

The COBEH approach contrasts with attitudinal and other behaviorally focused approaches to customer orientation, which emphasize the importance of the appropriate service orientations of employees. The behavioral approaches do not specifically identify a key element that is important for organizational success— employee participation in continuous improvement. The COBEH definition of customer orientation, on the other hand, includes *both* key elements of effective customer orientation; namely, (a) helping behaviors and (b) continuous improvement efforts.

The emphasis of the COBEH perspective on continuous improvement captures the notion that has been the central goal of quality management efforts. Simultaneously, the perspective embeds an emphasis on the key goals of human resources management. These goals are employee flexibility, innovation, and motivation manifested in a high effort on behalf of customers.[310] In summary, the advantage of the explicit behavioral perspective (COBEH) is a link to performance through the emphasis on two sets of behaviors, both identified as core elements in the management literature for organizational success and for achieving competitive advantage.

COBEH Challenges in Service Settings

Some elements of the COBEH definition need further clarification. COBEH could be hypothesized as a form of customer-oriented behavior reflecting employee motivation to exert an effort, which involves an active expenditure of energy on the part of the employee. Behaviors that are also important to service performance, such as employee flexibility and innovative approaches (both of which are emphasized in the quality and management literature), however, are not necessarily directly related to enhancing employee helping behaviors on behalf of the customers. Those behaviors that cultivate continuous improvement could be viewed as secondary factors or a subdimension of customer-oriented behavior. In other words, an employee can engage in customer-oriented behavior without engaging in continuous improvement efforts (or vice versa). For example, think about the employee who continuously puts forth ideas and suggestions for service improvements. For some employees, this might not be a conscious effort to satisfy customer needs but rather a strong effort to promote the employee's own career or well-being.

> *What do we live for if not to make life less difficult for each other?*
>
> —George Eliot

Two Core Elements of the Behavioral Approach to Customer Orientation

As discussed earlier, the explicit behavioral approach to customer orientation (COBEH) includes two core constructs: helping behaviors directed at customers and an emphasis on the quality perspective of continuous improvement. The following section provides a theoretical framework for these two constructs.

Helping Behavior: A Theoretical Framework

One of the first things a customer notices is the behaviors and attitudes of the employees he or she encounters. How helpful are they? How sensitive are they to the customer's needs at that particular moment? How much effort are they willing to put into satisfying those needs? These are extremely important questions for any service organization. Every day, managers strive to ensure the appropriate helping behaviors of their staff and to get them to improve their performance continuously. How can such behaviors be identified and enhanced? Many terms have been used to describe such behaviors, including *prosocial organizational behavior*,[50] *extrarole behavior*,[50, 107] *organizational citizenship behavior*, and *organizational spontaneity*.[107] As a result, there are many definitions for helping behavior.

Prosocial Organizational Behavior

Beginning in the late 1980s, there has been increased recognition of the importance of prosocial behaviors in organizational settings. In writing on this subject, Brief and Motowidlo[50] defined prosocial organizational behavior as a behavior which is (a) performed by a member of an organization, (b) directed towards an individual, group or organization with whom he or she interacts while carrying out his or her organizational role, and (c) performed with the intention of promoting the welfare of the individual, group, or organization toward which it is directed.

Thus, prosocial behaviors are a form of willingness or helping behavior performed to benefit or help other individuals. Such behaviors may be employee performance as a part of formal job requirements or as extra roles not formally required by management or rewarded by the organization. However, these extra roles are important to organizational success.

Organizational Citizenship Behavior

Various authors have tried to identify work behaviors that are sometimes overlooked by traditional definitions and measurements of job performance but still contribute (at least in the long run) to organizational effectiveness. Organizational citizenship behavior (OCB) is one such form of helping behavior. Bateman and Organ[31] have pointed out that early attempts to define organizational citizenship behavior emphasized that OCB is separate from job performance and should be viewed as an extra role that is organizationally functional. Organ[225, 226] defined organizational citizenship behavior as "individual behavior that is discretionary, not directly or explicitly recognized by the formal reward system, and that in the aggregate promotes the effective functioning of the organization." Note that both of these definitions emphasize that the organization does not directly or formally recognize or reward organizational citizenship behavior. For example, if an organization rewarded an employee for providing quality service to customers, then the employee's behavior would not be classified as organizational citizenship behavior. Hence, OCB includes some forms of helping behavior but excludes others.

Organ[225, 226] identifies the following forms of organizational citizenship behavior:

- *Altruism*—helping coworkers with specific tasks
- *Conscientiousness*—being willing or having the tendency to go above and beyond minimum required tasks
- *Sportsmanship*—avoiding "complaining, petty grievances, railing against real or imagined slights, and making federal cases out of small potatoes"
- *Courtesy*—being polite in a myriad of ways, including keeping people informed of decisions or commitments that might affect them
- *Civic virtue*—participating in the political life of an organization[115, 268]

According to Graham,[115] separation of in-role and extrarole behaviors in the context of organizational citizenship behavior is problematic in nature and varies across individuals, jobs, and organizations. Therefore, Graham presented another approach, based on citizenship research in philosophy, political science, and social history. In her view, organizational citizenship has a broader use as a global concept, which includes all positive employee behaviors that are relevant to the organization. These include traditional in-role job performance behaviors and organizationally functional extrarole behaviors, as well as political behaviors, such as participation, which were previously excluded in traditional organizational citizenship behavior definitions. In addition, Graham extended the conceptualization of OCB to include additional categories of behaviors having to do with employee obedience and loyalty in organizational settings.

Organizational Spontaneity

Organizational spontaneity describes a set of behaviors that is not included in role prescriptions. These behaviors are *impulsive* extrarole acts, performed voluntarily to contribute to organizational success. These actions are central to an organization's survival and effectiveness because no organization can proactively foresee every change in its external and internal environment. Katz and Kahn[177] argued: "The resources of people in innovation, in spontaneous co-operation (or helping coworkers), in protective and creative behavior are thus vital to organizational survival and effectiveness." George and Brief[108] identified the following five forms of organizational spontaneity: (a) helping coworkers, (b) protecting the organization, (c) making constructive suggestions, (d) self-development, and (e) spreading goodwill.

Notice that there is an overlap between organizational citizenship behavior and organizational spontaneity. However labeled, these behaviors are a great benefit to the organization and its culture. When a veteran employee helps a new employee through the learning stages, stays late to complete tasks, steps up to help a coworker meet a deadline, or contributes other such acts of kindness, everyone in the company benefits either directly or indirectly.

In almost all cases, these types of behavior we are looking for do not explicitly appear in the employee's job description. Nevertheless, because they are widely recognized as desirable behaviors for employees to exhibit, many employers (perhaps naively) may expect their workers to see their worth and exercise them. This may be implied or verbalized during new hire orientation; however, although these behaviors are expected and encouraged, they are seldom formalized in writing. There is no doubt, however, that when employees adopt a positive customer orientation, they aid their organization in accomplishing its service leadership goals and strengthen its competitive advantage in the marketplace.

Continuous Improvement

It is easy to see how helping behaviors benefit service organizations. However, there is also another element equally important to organizational success. That is the extent to which employees engage in continuous improvement efforts on behalf of the organization and its customers. Such behaviors could include improving their product knowledge; helping to promote and maintain a cleaner, safer work environment; working to better understand customer needs; and enhancing their own job skills.

Quality and management literature stress the importance of continuous improvement in attempting to improve, protect, and preserve the organization. One of four principles of the total quality management philosophy identified by Hackman and Wageman[124] is the concept of learning and continuous improvement. The pioneer quality writers Juran,[171] Ishikawa,[159] and Deming[86] emphasized the idea that the long-term health of an enterprise depends on treating quality improvements as a never-ending quest. The importance of continuous improvement has been emphasized by any number of other writers. For example, Hill and Wilkinson[146] state that employees will always have ways and opportunities to improve their performance. In addition, when they are dedicated to improvement, they will never stop learning about the work they do. They also stress that products and processes must be continuously improved to meet the requirements of both internal and external customers.

A key factor to establishing and maintaining continuous learning is an organization's use of effective human resources management, in which appropriate and necessary training initiatives should be an inherent policy. This aspect of continuous improvement is discussed more fully in Chapter 11.

A Proactive Way to Service

In today's constantly changing marketplace, satisfaction of customer needs calls for continuous improvement efforts (innovation and flexibility) to actively meet and proactively foresee changes in customers' needs and preferences to further enhance organizational successes. This means that some improvements must be made in areas that may not even be visible to the customer at the time of the employee-customer interaction.

The goal of total quality management is for the members of the organization to continuously improve work processes for the benefit of customers. Ideally, this calls for a proactive approach to service provision, in which each part of the organization keeps track of what is going on in the marketplace, as well as the changing needs and wants of the organization's customers. This enables the organization to have the ability to adapt its strategies in a timely manner and, in some cases, even stay a step or two ahead of customers' wishes.[75, 202, 215]

One challenging issue in employee proactivity is the fact that proactive behaviors are often contradictory to employees' natural inclinations to cling to routine. Because of the routines that are essential to the efficiency of any organization, a high level of proactive behavior is not common, even in organizations where continuous improvement is a core value. In fact, employees often do not inspect, reflect on, or consider their behavior, as would be expected where continuous improvement is emphasized. In addition, as Staw, Sandelands, and Dutton[291] have pointed out, employees are likely to maintain their routine behaviors more vigorously under stressful or demanding conditions—paradoxically, conditions that in fact demand

> *If I am not for myself, who will be for me? If I am not for others, who am I for? And if not now, when?*
>
> —Talmud

innovation and flexibility. Thus, although proactive behavior is a worthwhile goal, employees' reactive behavior to it can often make it difficult to implement.

Increasing Customer Orientation

As described earlier, helping behaviors and continuous improvement efforts can take many forms within an organization. What drives them? How can an organization increase these behaviors? Are employees helpful and continuously coming up with better ways to do their jobs because they are paid to do so, or do these behaviors depend on a more complex interaction of internal and external stimuli? These are important questions, to which we must seek answers.

In fact, individuals engage in customer-oriented behaviors for a variety of reasons. The theoretical and empirical literature on the possible reasons for such behaviors suggests that there are various *motivational* and *capacity* factors that affect how much employees are willing to engage in helping behaviors and how much effort they will expend on their own continuous improvement or that of the organization. However, the impact of these factors on such behaviors may very well be different for the two subdimensions of COBEH—namely, helping behaviors and continuous improvement efforts. In addition, the impacts usually vary within different organizational settings and type of service provided.

Peccei and Rosenthal[231] conceptualized a core model of customer-oriented behaviors. Their model draws on previous work in social theory,[188, 196, 265] standard models of rational action,[5, 173] expectancy theory,[32] and organizational commitment theory[209] and has been tested in various industries and across different cultures. The model includes four motivational variables designed to capture employees' willingness to engage in customer-oriented behavior. They are *affective, normative*, and *calculative orientations*, plus *organizational commitment*. However, the willingness or desire to provide service is not sufficient to ensure customer-oriented behavior— the capacity to provide the service is also needed. Thus capacity variables are also included in the model. They include employee knowledge and competence, supervisors' support, job pressure, and the way jobs are designed at the front line, as shown in Figure 9.1.

Willingness to Serve

The four motivational variables—affective, normative, and calculative orientations, plus organizational commitment—included in the top of the COBEH model direct attention to the different reasons why employees might engage in customer-oriented behavior. Let's take a look at these motivational elements.

Affective Orientations. Employees who are motivated to engage in customer-oriented behavior for affective reasons do so first and foremost because they derive personal satisfaction from the activity. They do not strive to please customers just

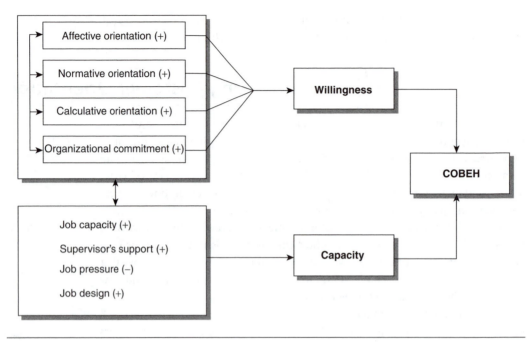

Figure 9.1   COBEH Core Model

SOURCE: Grönfeldt,[117] adapted from Peccei and Rosenthal.[231]

because they think engaging in such behavior is the right thing to do or because they expect rewards. In fact, they like their jobs and enjoy delivering quality service.

Normative Orientations. Employees' normative actions, on the other hand, are guided and conditioned by how effectively employees learn and internalize the service values and norms, often depending on the intensity and duration of their training and on how receptive they are to training about service values and norms.[231] These values and norms are also reinforced through continuing training and influence from the culture itself. In other words, employees are helpful and come up with better ways to do their jobs because they know it is expected and "it's the way things are done around here."

Calculative Orientations. The third motivational variable in the model covers employees' calculative orientation. In this case, employees calculate either unconsciously or rationally the possible benefits and costs associated with a particular task. In a service context, such behavior could be defined as an employee's pursuit of valued rewards or attempts to avoid punishment, in which he or she evaluates the costs and benefits associated with helping customers and continuously improving service efforts. This means that the employee behaves in a certain way because he or she gets paid for it or to avoid being fired or reprimanded in some way for not performing.

Organizational Commitment. This is the fourth and last motivational variable included in Peccei and Rosenthal's[231] model. Organizational commitment has been conceptualized in a number of different ways, but central to it is the notion of employee obligation, involvement, and loyalty to the organization. In a service context, customer-oriented behavior based on organizational commitment could be defined as individuals' feelings of obligation or loyalty, which get translated into service behaviors designed to benefit the organization as a whole. The behavior is conditioned by the relative strength of an individual's identification with the organization and perceptions of cost and benefits associated with the preservation and protection of the organization. In other words, employees go out of their way to behave in ways that are certain to benefit the organization because they are loyal to the organization and want only the best for it.

Capacity to Provide Service

In addition to the four motivational variables, the model includes four capacity variables important to promoting employee customer-oriented behavior. The capacity variables emphasize the notion that customer-oriented behavior should be a function not only of employees' *willingness* to engage in customer-oriented behavior but also of their *capacity* to provide the desired services. The capacity variables in the model are job competence and understanding of customer service requirements, supervisor's support, job design (job autonomy, job repetitiveness, etc.), and job pressure.

Job competence refers to employees' perceptions of their own knowledge and skills in relation to their performance on the job and to their problem-solving abilities. In addition, it addresses their understanding of customer needs and organizational service procedures and processes. Consequently, this attribute should be a fundamental condition for successful helping behaviors and continuous improvement efforts. An employee can engage in efforts on behalf of customers; however, without proper knowledge, understanding, and skill to perform, he or she will not succeed in providing the level or quality of service that the customer needs, wants, and expects.

Parallel to this concept is the notion of *continuous improvement*. An employee's suggestions and ideas on how to improve service can benefit neither the organization nor individual organizational members unless the ideas are based on relevant knowledge and sufficient understanding. However, the extent of employees' job competence and understanding largely depends on the effectiveness of various human resources procedures within the organization. These include selection, training and development, reinforcement of goals and expectations, and constructive performance feedback. The essential role of human resources in framing employee orientations, commitment, and job competence cannot be overstated.

Supervisors' support and *job design* are important in regard to customer-oriented behavior because employee-customer interaction in a service context is a "three-cornered fight" among the needs of the customer, the needs of the employee, and the needs of the organization.[117] This places difficult demands on supervisors and on job design in service organizations. When designing jobs, supervisors must take into consideration how much freedom or autonomy an employee is comfortable with, the extent of employee commitment to the service rendered, and possible obstacles to productivity or performance associated with the job design.[143] We already know that employees have little opportunity to show their initiative and be innovative when they are working under close supervision in narrowly defined and routine jobs. They simply have to do the set of tasks they have been told to do. They usually are not encouraged to break out of the routine or get creative about ways the job could be improved.

The final capacity variable in the model is *job pressure*. Kanter[173] argues that limited resources hamper employees' ability to perform their tasks, thus constraining their ability to exert effort and engage in innovative forms of behavior. Think about a service provider working in a small insurance company. Often, this employee has to multitask every day, as the small company cannot hire a variety of specialized employees. In this case, the employee is too often just trying to "put out fires" instead of having time to perform services creatively. In addition, employees working in high-pressure jobs will have difficulty providing high levels of individualized care to customers, and they will not have the time to deal effectively with customer demands that are not routine. This is true for anyone under pressure to accomplish a task or to meet a deadline. Under such conditions, the deadline almost always takes precedence over being innovative. This is no less true in the high-pressure, time-critical world of customer service delivery.

In summary, if an organization wants to develop a strong employee commitment to the organization, it must be accomplished through giving employees a solid purpose, trusting them, and instilling pride in their work. In addition, the organization must effectively communicate the organizational values and norms, clearly stating that helping behavior and continuous improvement are expected. It should take steps to make sure the employees enjoy their service-related tasks and should appropriately reward positive behaviors. In addition, the organization needs to use effective human resources processes to make sure the employees know their jobs and have the flexibility, time, and managerial support to continuously improve their own performance. The result will be motivated and capable employees who will exhibit customer-oriented behaviors, a fact that has been tested and has proven to be relatively consistent across both cultures and industries.

> *Knowledge is power, but enthusiasm pulls the switch.*
> —Ivern Ball

Willingness and Capacity Interaction

A recent study of seven European service companies conducted by Grönfeldt[119] examining the interaction between employee willingness and capacity to engage in customer-oriented behaviors has suggested that as job capacity increases, the *impact* of willingness decreases. In other words, if the employee is not very skilled at the job, an increase in willingness can make up for it. This employee will engage in customer-oriented behaviors in spite of his or her lack of skill or knowledge. Hence, willingness to engage in customer-oriented behavior has a greater impact among less skilled or less knowledgeable employees (for example, new hires) than among the more skilled ones.

Motivational factors are clearly very important. However, these results underline the importance of the cultivation and maintenance of job capacity in service organizations as well. Human resources procedures must include selecting appropriate frontline workers and then training them in practices that ensure employee participation and reduce job stress. These organizational practices will increase the capacity of employees to engage in desirable customer-oriented behaviors.

Different Perceptions

Do employees, supervisors, and customers agree on what behaviors result in quality service? Furthermore, does self-reported customer orientation of employees translate into positive customer perceptions? Several studies have attempted to answer these questions. In a study of 23 branch banks, customers were asked to describe the general quality of the service received at their branch; concurrently, branch employees were asked to predict how their customers viewed the quality of the service they had received.[117] The results show that a positive correlation exists between employee perceptions and customer perceptions of the service provided. In those branch banks where employees reported that their managers emphasized good customer service, the customers perceived the service to be superior and reported positive employee attitudes, low staff turnover, and overall satisfaction with the administration of the branch. Also, in a more recent study, supervisors and customers were asked about their perception of the quality of service provided in 18 full-service gas stations.[117] The results showed a high correlation between the employees' self-reported helping behaviors and the customers' own perception of the services provided.

It is important to realize that supervisors and employees do not seem to share a common understanding of what customer orientation involves and how it translates in the employee-customer contact. Basically, what employees perceive to be customer-oriented behavior is the extra effort they put into their jobs to try to satisfy customer needs. Supervisors, however, seem to underestimate or overlook the extra effort directed to customers and base their evaluations on more tangible items in the service provision process and on the visibility of the suggestions and ideas put forth by employees. It is not hard to imagine the potential problems that result during performance evaluations.

The Satisfaction Mirror

Although customers and employees view the service from different angles, their perceptions are, nevertheless, positively related. The "satisfaction mirror," developed by Heskett, Sasser, and Schlesinger[143] and shown in Figure 9.2, presents some important cause-and-effect relationships between customers and employees. The mirror also applies to supervisors or managers, showing them the impact of their behaviors on frontline service performance. The underlying assumption of the satisfaction mirror is that the more familiar an employee is with customer needs and the ways those needs can be met, the more likely the customer is to give repeat business to the company. This repeat business in turn increases the opportunity for the employee to become even more familiar with that customer's needs.

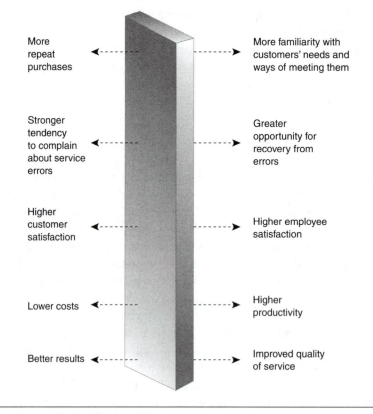

Figure 9.2   The Satisfaction Mirror

SOURCE: Adapted from Heskett, Sasser & Schlesinger. *The satisfaction mirror.* Free press / Simon and Schuster Inc.

An interesting side benefit is that customers who use a service more frequently are more likely to complain about service errors. Obviously, they feel comfortable enough to talk to the employee about something that is bothering them, probably because they feel a growing loyalty to the organization and they would rather have the problem fixed than have to switch to another company. In this situation, it is more likely that the employee involved will have an opportunity to correct these errors and thus "recover" a customer who might otherwise simply take his or her business to the competitor without even bothering to complain in the first place. This results in higher customer satisfaction and higher employee satisfaction in addition to lower costs, higher productivity, better results, and improved overall service quality.

The Cycle of Capability

Heskett and his colleagues[143] identified another important factor for service performance based on employee capacity, namely, the "cycle of capability," shown in Figure 9.3. The cycle points out the importance of high-quality employee training for both "job and life" and of well-designed support systems. These can include

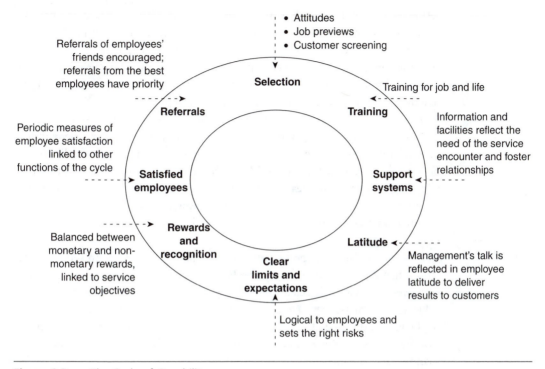

Figure 9.3   The Cycle of Capability

SOURCE: Adapted from Heskett, Sasser & Schlesinger. *Cycle of Capability.* Free press / Simon and Schuster Inc.

information and facilities that are expected to reflect the needs of the service encounter and are designed to foster relationships. The cycle allows for great latitude to meet customer needs but suggests clear limits on what is expected by and of employees. These behaviors are then supported by appropriate rewards and frequent recognition. The results are periodically measured and should result in more satisfied employees who are likely to refer friends to the organization.

> *This, indeed, is one of the eternal paradoxes of both life and literature—that without passion little gets done; yet, without control of that passion, its effects are largely ill or null.*
>
> —F. L. Lucas

Summary

Definitions of customer orientation vary, but they can be categorized into *systemic, attitudinal,* and *behavioral* terms. A main goal of this chapter is to answer the question "How can organizations increase desirable employee helping behaviors toward customers?"

Total quality management acknowledges the importance of maintaining a strong customer orientation at all levels of an organization. In fact, TQM has been defined as a total process involving all operations and in which every strategy relates to satisfying customers' needs. In TQM, people are expected to improve work processes continuously, work harder, and keep their customer needs in mind at all times. The challenges associated with this approach, as well as with other systemic approaches, such as Lean Six Sigma, are motivating frontline staff to continuously improve their performance and to keep learning as you encourage them to adhere closely to standardized best practices and procedures.

The alternative perspective to the systemic approach is an emphasis on employee attitudes toward service. In this approach, employees' customer orientation is viewed as positive service attitudes and is defined in terms of internalization of organizational norms and values. Many believe that positive service attitudes are important because they lead to the development of a long-term relationship between the organization and its customers. However, such general service attitudes are often ambiguous and usually prove to be difficult to implement in organizational settings.

Behaviorally based perspectives offer a more tangible approach to service orientation than do attitudinal perspectives because they tend to focus more on actual employee behaviors directed toward customers. Employee customer-oriented behavior encompasses two key elements for organizational service success: (a) helping behaviors directed at current customers to enhance customer satisfaction and (b) continuous improvement efforts designed to benefit future customers and gain a competitive advantage for the organization.

To enhance employees' customer-oriented behaviors, organizations must make sure that employees enjoy service-related tasks. To make this possible, the organization must carefully select, socialize, train, motivate, recognize, and empower its service providers. Through those same processes, the organization can build organizational commitment, which has also proven to be important for enhancing employees' customer-oriented behaviors. Managers must clearly communicate the organizational values and convey that all employees are expected to engage in helping behaviors and to improve continuously. In addition, human resources management needs to help employees know their jobs and give them the time, flexibility, and managerial support they need to continuously improve their performance. As a result, the organization will have a cadre of motivated, capable employees that will freely engage in desirable, customer-oriented behaviors.

Employees and customers share a similar view of the service provided. Employee self-reported customer-oriented behaviors can be used to predict customers' perceptions of the quality of service they receive. However, supervisors and managers seem more likely to use the employees' participation in continuous improvement efforts as a predictor of employee customer orientations.

Selection, training, support systems, and clearly defined limits and expectations are important for organizational service success. Human resources management procedures must be an integral part of any service system. These issues are discussed in more detail in the following chapter.

The Human Faces of Customer Orientation

Jon Didrik Jonsson

The Coca-Cola Company

From Singapore to Scandinavia and Malaysia to Eastern Europe, Jon Didrik Jonsson has worked in business development, marketing, and commercial management, as well as in rebuilding bottling operations for the Coca-Cola Company as an expatriate manager.

All over the world, people engage in service-related behaviors. They do it as a part of their job and as a part of their obligation to themselves and others. However, the extent of the effort and the reasons why, in my opinion, can vary greatly from continent to continent and country to country, even from city to city in some of the developing markets I have seen. The difference can perhaps best be identified in the way people view the end result of their efforts and the particular circumstances they find themselves in.

What I mean by that is, for example, in Southeast Asia, employees are very helpful and eager to please when the task is within their scope of authority or frame of reference. When a particular task is unknown or foreign to them, they become insecure. They may still be very friendly, but the outcome may not necessarily be the one you seek. Helping behaviors in many Southeast Asian cultures, such as in Singapore, are frequent; however, going against the grain, as required in continuous improvement efforts, is not an innate part of their being. The reason may be embedded in their *kiazu*. Kiazu is a governing norm—a drive for success and near perfection. What is interesting, however, is that people are motivated by fear of *not* succeeding, not by the ecstasy of winning. People are afraid of the unknown and prefer to master what they do know in their jobs. Everything works greater when you want people to add 2 and 2 and get 4. The trouble starts when you expect them to add 2 and 2 and get 5. If you go too far from the norm, you are entering hazardous waters. Their aim is to do what is expected faster and better than others. Making suggestions or daring to imagine the service differently is a risky business. They may be afraid of being wrong or making their manager look bad with constant suggestions of improvement. Losing face or causing others to lose face can be devastating to an employee in such cultures. Therefore, you must systematically communicate and reinforce what is expected and put in place a system that can cultivate and support not only helping behavior, but constant improvements as well. The famous Swedish film director Ingmar Bergman once said: "You need a detailed script to improvise." That most certainly is true about customer-oriented behaviors in some of the cultures in which I have worked.

Key Points

- Learn about the culture in which you will work.
- Give yourself time to adapt.
- Employ consistency and endurance.
- Use systemic approaches to build trust and a sense of security.
- Use selection, rewards, and training to breed creativity.

Going North

Going far north to the Scandinavian countries, Norway and Sweden, you find an interesting contrast between these two neighbors. In my experience, the Norwegians are not driven by the quest for success for success's sake, as I felt was so apparent in Singapore. They are helpful and diligent in their services, but moderately so. It was very difficult to get the sales force up and roaring like Vikings. Norwegians prefer stability, spending time with their families, and enjoying life. They make quick decisions and rely on their networks and good relations with their customers rather than plans and processes, resulting in flexible but inconsistent services. The Swedes, however, plan their service processes down to the slightest details—consider every angle. The decisions were sound and good, but implemented sometimes 2 years too late! They are much more systemic in thinking than the Norwegians. The systems worked much better. The problems came when the systems could no longer keep up with the changes imposed by the environment and competition. Under those conditions, the Norwegian ad-hoc way proved to be more successful.

Going East of the Wall

In the eastern parts of Europe, you find yet another example of standardization and improvisation in service. In the new capitalistic Poland, you can smell the drive created by passionate quest for a better life—a better life than past generations under communism had experienced. Since the early 1990s, international corporations have been entering the country city by city and mall by mall. Brand names are everywhere in the cities, and the rural areas are slowly giving way to a new, modern way of life. A hard-working new generation of Poles seeks monetary rewards, preferably reflected in status symbols and tangible proof of success. Still, decades of hierarchical organizational structures remain a part of their lives. Employees expect systems and structures to be in place, expectations to be clear, the authority of the leader to be beyond question. Once they believe you mean what you say and you give them the needed structure, nothing can stop them.

Think Globally, but Never Lose Sight of the Importance of Acting Locally

Differences in cultures of course put demands on the international manager to be able to put him- or herself in each employee's shoes. To understand why and how those particular employees see their own roles as well as the role of the manager is key to unlocking the paradox of applying international standard processes onto local ways of doing business. In a sense, you must think globally, but never lose sight of the importance of acting locally.

In many cultures, such as in Singapore and Poland, you really need to provide people with a structure. Your expectations must be clear, and you must develop a framework for people to work within. In a sense, you must plan the creativity just as carefully as the standard

implementation of processes. You create the conditions necessary for improvisation and creativity through careful recruitment, your management style, recognitions and rewards.

I always tell my staff, "It is better to apologize than to ask for permission." So act on your information or instinct and then take the consequences—good or bad. This takes a lot of determination on behalf of international managers, who really need to discipline themselves not to make difficult decisions for the employees. The mission of international managers must be to be able to move on to their next target knowing the local operation is fully functional without them. On the other hand, they cannot be too distant and hands-off, because that makes the locals, who are brought up in a hierarchical organizational manner and directive leadership styles, uneasy, and they begin to doubt the manager's leadership ability. This is a thin line you have to walk.

For different reasons, employees in these countries have a need for a systemic approach to service. The outcome is consistency in service and often high output or volume. In a way, you can say if you have a good plan, it will be beautifully orchestrated but hampered by the boundaries of the system. In some of the countries new to capitalism, the international corporations moved in so fast that the key account managers in my company had to service clients with needs they could never ever have imagined existed. In the fast-changing world, you need to foster employees' participation and confidence in going outside the norm and beyond what they know. In some cultures, that can be a challenging task.

Lessons From Service Management Across Cultures

The Main Lesson. Without a doubt, it is to take time to get to know what it is that really makes people tick. Have the patience and endurance to understand their motivations, fears, and ambitions. There is a whole breed of professional managers like myself who fly around the world putting standardized practices and procedures in place for their multinational corporations. Most of these "hired guns" get paid to go in with their technical knowledge and process know-how and get the job done—then "get the Hell out of Dodge"! The result is that the problem gets fixed, but the know-how is gone as soon as the international expert moves on to his next target. The local managers are left with processes and operations they may know but do not necessary understand. The result is a lack of implementation of the new processes and ownership by those who stay behind.

Key Concepts

Directions: The following are key concepts presented in this chapter. Write a complete definition for each one.

Customer orientation

Motivational variables

Capacity variables

Continuous improvement

Questions

1. Assume you are a service representative for a large multinational IT business that sells its services to large corporations. What behavioral processes would TQM use to improve your behavior toward these important customers?

2. Why are TQM and Six Sigma approaches often ineffective for improving the customer-oriented behaviors of their employees?

3. What are the challenges or difficulties associated with a systemic approach to employee-customer orientation?

4. What are limitations of the attitudinal approach toward engendering customer-oriented behaviors in service providers?

5. What is the COBEH approach? Why is it more suitable for customer service than systemic approaches such as TQM and Six Sigma?

6. What is the difference between general prosocial behavior and organizational citizenship behavior (OCB)? Give an example of how you might exhibit each of these on your job.

7. Why should the concept of continuous improvement be included in definitions of customer-oriented behaviors? What effect does it have on the organization?

8. Organizational spontaneity behaviors are proactive service behaviors. How are they exhibited by employees? From your experience, give two examples of employees exhibiting these behaviors. What was the effect on the organization?

9. Employees may have a number of motivations for delivering excellent service to their customers. What are three of these motivations? How does each one affect the organization?

10. How does the degree of an employee's knowledge of the job and ability to handle the requirements of providing good service affect the customer-employee interaction?

Advanced Activity

Be a customer for a day. Go to three different service companies and examine the level of customer orientation that the employees exhibit in their interaction with you and other customers. Use Figure 9.1 for the analysis. Write a report comparing and contrasting these companies' levels of customer orientation.

Search the Web

Find the annual reports of two major service companies. Determine whether and how they speak about (a) their customers and (b) their employees in their reports. Compare the two reports and try to evaluate the level of customer orientation in the companies. Underline sentences or comments made in the reports that you find particularly interesting and share them with your class. Use the sentences or comments as the basis for your analysis of the level of customer orientation. Write a short report with your findings.

Suggested Readings

Dean, J. W., Jr., & Bowen, D. E. (1994). Management theory and total quality: Improving research and practice through theory development. *Academy of Management Review, 19*(3), 392–401.

George, J. M. (1991). State or trait: Effects of positive mood on prosocial behavior, sales performance, and turnover: A group-level analysis in service context. *Journal of Applied Psychology, 76*(2), 299–307.

Managing Service Organizations

Human, not financial, capital must be the starting point and ongoing foundation of a successful strategy.

—Bartlett and Ghoshal[26]

Objectives

After completing this chapter, you should be able to

1. Understand why new management styles are needed in the new service organization

2. Understand the changes needed in managerial roles and objectives

3. Understand various models of strategy formulation

4. Understand why managerial communication is critical to organizational success

A Changing Managerial World

The past three decades have imposed dramatic challenges on organizations in general and on the managers within those organizations in particular. Virtually all managers are aware of the rate at which the world around them is changing, but many do not know how to react to these changes, much less how to be proactive in taking advantage of the opportunities and avoiding the disasters that change can bring. Intrusions from outside the organization call for different approaches to almost every aspect of the business and its internal resources. Implementing the necessary organizational changes is challenging, and research indicates that as organizations try to adapt to these changes, it is not the structure of the organization or its processes that have proven to be the most difficult to transform. The biggest barrier seems to be managers' outdated understanding of strategy, according to Bartlett and Ghoshal:[26] "Hierarchy has to be replaced by networks, bureaucratic systems transformed into flexible processes, and control-based management roles must evolve into relationships featuring empowerment and coaching."

> I believe that every right implies a responsibility; every opportunity, an obligation; every possession, a duty.
>
> —John D. Rockefeller

The need for identifying and learning how best to manage organizational and individual core competencies has become key to enabling organizations to respond to the rapidly changing business environment and to develop a unique and effective place for themselves in the current dynamic marketplace. In today's world, sustainable business success can only be achieved through innovation, along with the cultivation and application of knowledge, resources, and expertise.[109, 128] The unique blend of those elements allows an organization to differentiate itself from its competitors and forms the basis of the organization's competitive advantage, built on its core competencies.

Managers must move away from the security of well-known structures and familiar processes that for decades have been largely concerned with the acquisition and allocation of materials and financial resources. With human capital becoming ever more important, managers now must move into the unpredictable human side of business. This has placed challenging demands on the strategies, structure, and management principles under which organizations operate. It is difficult enough to change the orientation of an organization; it is even harder to change the mind-set of its senior managers, as Bartlett and Ghoshal stress in their article "Building Competitive Advantage Through People":[26] "today's managers are trying to implement third-generation strategies through second-generation organizations with first-generation management."

> Democracy . . . is a charming form of government, full of variety and disorder. It dispenses a sort of equality to equals and unequals alike.
>
> —Plato

No matter how one looks at it, service organizations are dependent on people, their most strategic resource. Employees' expertise and knowledge of customers' needs often drive new-product development. They use their interpersonal skills to create and maintain relationships with clients—an asset of critical importance for any organization. Hence service organizations must be built and managed on a foundation that values and rewards its intellectual capital. As organizations have come to realize this fact, we have witnessed a major drive to acquire talent. This has resulted in heavy competition for capable people who possess specialized knowledge, superior skills, or unique talents, and who are highly motivated.

In this chapter, we will examine why new management styles are needed in the new service organization and provide insight into the changes managers need to make in their roles and objectives. The chapter also presents some useful strategic management tools and concludes with the reasons effective communication is so important to any service organization.

The Changing View of Management's Role

Today's managers must redefine their relationships with their employees and design new battle plans. To many, it seems as if they are moving from a comfortable, stable organizational setting with definite rules, tangible resources, and clear lines of authority into a nebulous and often temperamental world of employee empowerment. To succeed in this new order, organizations have been forced to revise drastically the role of management to be better aligned with their new environment. Today's managers must compete for more than product markets or technical expertise. Now they must win the hearts and minds of talented and capable people. Then, after persuading them to join the enterprise, management also must ensure that those valuable individuals become committed to the company's aspirations.[26, 43]

Changes do not happen overnight, and in this case, change is closely associated with a transformation of organizational cultures and values. It requires active engagement in the act of leadership from top and middle management, as well as at every organizational level. Leadership is particularly important in times of crisis, but that does not mean leadership is not needed at times of relative certainty and normalcy.

Challenging the status quo can be vital for a successful service organization. Leadership behaviors in service organizations are in fact designed to push the envelope and carry the organization forward, although the resulting actions sometimes happen more rapidly than the systems, processes, and some people can handle. Organizations simply cannot stand still if they want to be innovative and achieve excellence. They require leaders who will always be alert for market changes, ready to adapt and change where necessary, and eager to improve their company's competitive position.

As emphasized throughout previous chapters, organizations must be infused with leadership principles at all levels. Organizational leadership cannot only be imposed from the top. A critical position is that of the middle manager who is responsible for day-to-day operations and lives the values and culture suggested by the organizational strategy. Without middle managers' acts of leadership, movements are sluggish and reinforcement and implementation of the strategy slows to a halt. Especially in service companies, where the personal touch is a key element, inspired leadership at the point of service is crucially important.[40]

Managers provide leadership by inspiring a clear vision for the organization as a whole and setting standards of excellence by their own behaviors. More important, they inspire and cultivate leadership behaviors in others. They put the right people in charge by careful recruitment and selection and then teach them how to reach their full potential as leaders through training and coaching. There are, in fact, few decisions in a service organization more important than determining which characteristics and skills the management team should embrace and foster.

Therefore, the greatest benefit management can bring to an organization is to inspire employee self-confidence and empower all organizational members to exercise constructive leadership behavior. To do this requires a fundamental change in the way organizations think about leadership and the roles of their managers.

It has been suggested that CEOs must make the following three major changes in their points of view to successfully run their businesses in the new service era. They must change their perspective on (a) their strategic resources, (b) their organizational values, and (c) the role of senior managers.[26]

The Changing View of Strategic Resources

Since the earliest of times, it has been said that money makes the world go around. This may still be true today, but the vehicle for making the money that boosts an organization's annual profits is the result of a unique combination of interpersonal skills, knowledge, and application of that knowledge by the people within the organization. However, most organizations still have a long way to go to fully appreciate this fact. All organizations state that their people are their most valuable asset, but many do not act as if they really believe or understand what they preach. For example, most annual reports only state the organization's financial performance, leaving out key elements such as customer satisfaction and retention or employee satisfaction and turnover.

The same is true for corporate acquisitions and takeovers. Financial information and monetary performance are of course important, but additional parameters that give important indications of the organization's health and future growth potential must now be considered. Financial statements do not paint a complete picture of today's service organizations. We cannot deny that the wise use of financial resources is essential; however, growth is usually limited for reasons other than just the lack of capital.[26]

The *sacredness* of the *bottom line* on financial balance sheets is deeply embedded in the mind-set of many managers and most investors and is, therefore, the hardest to alter. Managers' time and efforts have been strongly focused on achieving financial goals for so long that it is almost impossible for them to comprehend that their value to the organization can very likely be enhanced by focusing on the resources that ultimately create the monetary rewards in the first place: their employees and the *intellectual capital* they contribute to the organization.

As organizations move away from competition for products and markets through competition for resources and competencies, especially in the area of competing for "talent and knowledge," their strategic objectives must change. Their focus must shift from maintaining defensible product-market positions to acquiring sustainable competitive advantages through core competencies, resource-based strategies, and networking organizations. The final goals are continuous self-renewal through vision and values, flexibility, innovation, and frontline entrepreneurship and experimentation. These goals can only be accomplished through acquiring, developing, and retaining superior intellectual capital. The elements and value of effective human resources management are discussed in Chapter 11.

> *The first requisite in running a major corporation is the ability to pick good people.*
>
> —Lee Iacocca

The implication for top management is a transfer of human resources issues to the top of the management agenda, where they should become the core of the organization's strategic priorities. Financial resources, performance evaluations, and monetary reward systems have to be redesigned to support the growing strategic importance of human intellectual capital.

The Changing View of Organizational Values

The first step in changing the way management defines value is to recognize that the organization's most valuable resources exist in the minds, hearts, and skills of the employees. In the early 1980s, strategic thinkers such as Michael Porter saw the world in terms of a "zero-sum game." According to this view, when a fixed and finite amount of any resource or commodity is divided between two or more entities, some will receive more, and others, by necessity, will receive less, because less remains available to go around. The simplest example would be two people sharing a pizza. If one takes a large piece of the pizza (say 60%), then the other person will receive a smaller piece (in this case 40%), because both pieces must add up to 100%. Therefore, during the 1980s, management spent much of its time engaged in a zero-sum battle with suppliers, customers, and resources (including potential employees) to capture the greatest economic value possible.[26] However, the rules of the game changed as the focus on unique internal capabilities shifted the emphasis from *value appreciation* to *value creation* and as information and knowledge became the key to competitive advantage. "When individual, group, and organizational values are in sync, tremendous energy is generated. Commitment, enthusiasm, and drive are intensified: people have a reason for caring about their work."[187] This has called for a shift in the way employees are treated and rewarded. It is also true that, unlike financial capital, knowledge increases in value when shared, thus canceling out the zero-sum game.[114]

More and more organizations are realizing that those who create the value expect and deserve to take part in the organization's financial success. As an example, a number of companies turn employees into owners by offering employee stock option plans. This kind of employee participation helps the organization earn the trust of its workers[40a] and encourages them to be fully committed to the organization. As we shall soon see, aspiring to achieve employee loyalty is a highly desirable goal for any organization. If the company does not give employees the opportunity to share in the fruits of their labors—namely, increased profits—they will go where they have the opportunity to do so, typically to new, less tradition- bound companies.[114]

The Changing Role of Upper Management

A company cannot accumulate specialized knowledge in its managers the way it accumulates its financial resources. This kind of knowledge is spread through the organization within individuals and teams. In fact, much of it is within those service providers who are closest to the customers, the competitors, and the technology. To mobilize individual strengths, knowledge, and expertise in the organization, senior managers must rethink their role in shaping strategic direction. Now they must include their people as they structure the organization's purpose and processes. "The philosophical shift requires executives to expand beyond strategy, structure, and systems to a simultaneous focus on the company's purpose, process, and people."[26]

Top management's main contribution to an organization needs to shift from deciding the strategic content of the organization's operation to *framing the organizational context.* However, keeping everyone working at a high level continuously means that human resources must be carefully planned, which requires superior leadership abilities.

> Value-driven leaders infuse their values into the fabric of the organization. They lead not with commands, not with a thick rulebook, but with a set of core values—what the firm represents and aspires to be. The more these values tap into an employee's own values, the more they guide individual decision making and inspire personal achievement.[40b]

This means that managers must create a sense of purpose for all organizational members. The purpose *provides a framework* for employee initiatives and establishes a sense of meaning and belonging to a common cause or community.

Managers may not yet understand that they need to be more and more "the guy on the side or the man in the stands" rather than "the sage on the stage." This emphasizes the new reality that the role of management is becoming less authoritarian, less "top-down," and is moving toward a more supportive and participative role of recognizing, encouraging, empowering, and rewarding desirable employee behaviors. In short, managers in the new service era are becoming more like a combination of coach, cheerleader, and team member. Figure 10.1 contrasts the new role of managers with the older, more traditional view.

The Service Profit Chain as a Management Tool

To excel in the new service economy, organizational management must devote much more of its time and attention than ever before to customers and to the frontline workers who interact with them. The short version of the story is that satisfied frontline employees produce satisfied customers, who, in turn, become loyal, repeat customers of the organization. The longer version of the story identifies a chain of cause-and-effect events that arises from the interactive relationship that exists between the service provider and the customer. This concept, introduced by Heskett, Jones, Loveman, Sasser, and Schlesinger,[142] is called "the *service profit chain.*" It ties

The Manager as	Traditional Role	New Service Era Role
Coach	Top-down management Authoritative Clearly the *Boss*	Mentors and trains Empowers Encourages

Cheerleader	Occasionally gives formal
	  recognition of outstanding
	  performance
	Gives special awards
	Recognizes through raises and
	  bonuses
		Frequently recognizes good
		  performance
		Supports
		Encourages by attitude
		Helps all organizational
		  members feel good about
		  themselves and their
		  role in the company

Team member	Never!	Participates actively Does his or her part Leads by example

Figure 10.1   The Changing Role of the Manager

employee satisfaction, loyalty, and productivity to customer satisfaction and, ultimately, loyalty to the organization. This is the service part of the chain; the profit portion comes from the repeat business derived from satisfied and loyal customers.

In their book *The Service Profit Chain,* Heskett and his Harvard University colleagues[142] assert that managers at a number of outstanding companies stay on top by "managing the service profit chain." This claim is based on 5 years of research and includes Southwest Airlines, Fairfield Inns, Ritz-Carlton Hotels, Merry Maids (a subsidiary of ServiceMaster), American Express Travel Services, Banc One, Taco Bell, USAA (insurance), Intuit (software), Waste Management, and British Airways. In these companies, the authors were able to establish a set of quantifiable relationships directly linking profit and growth to customer loyalty and satisfaction, as well as to employee loyalty, satisfaction, and productivity. The strongest relationships discovered during this research were those linking (a) customer loyalty and profits, (b) employee loyalty and customer loyalty, and (c) employee satisfaction and customer satisfaction. It is interesting, if not surprising, that these relationships were found to be mutually reinforcing. For example, employee loyalty contributes to customer loyalty and vice versa. Similarly, companies with satisfied employees tend to have satisfied customers, but, conversely, customer satisfaction tends to reinforce the employee's level of job satisfaction. Obviously, trying to correlate and quantify such complex, interactive relationships of this type can be very complex.

Let's examine this very important concept and see how management's role becomes that of "making it all happen."

There are seven fundamental steps that form the links in the service profit chain, shown in Figure 10.2. It should be pointed out that each link consists of two parts—a cause-and-effect pair in which each causative factor produces or yields a particular effect.

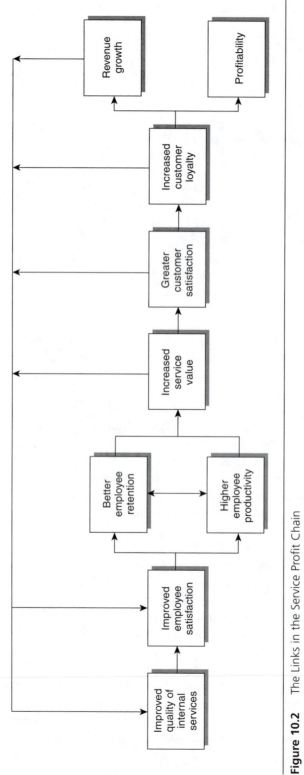

Figure 10.2 The Links in the Service Profit Chain

SOURCE: Adapted from Heskett, Jones, Loveman, Sasser, & Schlessinger (2004). Putting the service profit chain to work, in *Harvard Business Review*, March-April.

Let's discuss each of these links in the following order:

1. Internal quality yields employee satisfaction.

2. Employee satisfaction yields employee loyalty.

3. Employee loyalty improves productivity.

4. Improved employee productivity yields higher value for the customer.

5. Greater value to the customer yields greater customer satisfaction.

6. Improved customer satisfaction leads to customer loyalty.

7. Customer loyalty drives corporate profitability.

Understanding the relationships among the seven links will help managers define their own roles in the overall process; furthermore, it will guide them in developing appropriate strategies at each stage (link) of the chain. Taken together and sequentially, these cause-and-effect links lead to the final effect in this series—*profitability*. Of course profitability itself can lead to its own set of desirable consequences—namely, corporate growth, a more secure company, satisfied and well-rewarded investors (shareholders), and a greater competitive advantage for the corporation. Clearly, if the service profit chain is a valid concept, it behooves management at all levels to work hard to facilitate and encourage all employees (not just those on the front line) to make it work. Obviously, two key ingredients in making this happen are *enlightened managers* and *superior employees*.

It should be pointed out that the service profit chain in its broadest sense is a complex, theoretical concept. Sometimes its complexities are ignored, and it is reduced and simplified down to its basic components, leaving little or no opportunity for development of individual components. Sometimes the links between the steps that form the model are assumed to exist even in the absence of adequate proof. In such cases, it is possible that the available evidence, data, or observations will be made to fit the assumptions, and little or no thought will be given to see what other factors could be responsible for the observed results. Silvestro and Cross[284] feel that due to the complexity of the theory and the nature of its links, pieces can be broken apart and disproved, bringing into question the theory as a whole. There are reports that the service profit chain has been applied both successfully and unsuccessfully by a variety of organizations. Until more research has been done, perhaps the safest position to take is one of cautious enthusiasm, without relying on this theory entirely.

In fact, a lot of good things can and have been said about the service profit chain. Many feel that it provides a solid theoretical foundation for the development of an outstanding strategic service vision and can serve as a model for managers to use in building more focused operations and marketing capabilities. So important is the service profit chain concept that having managers understand it well is a critical step toward achieving true service leadership for the organization. With this in mind, let's now briefly examine each of the seven links or steps in the chain.

1. *Internal quality drives, yields, or produces employee satisfaction.* Here, internal quality refers to all things in the employee's working environment that contribute to his or her happiness and satisfaction. Anything that makes the employee feel wanted and appreciated; that makes the work easier or more interesting; or makes the working environment safer, cleaner, or more comfortable will contribute to internal quality. Inevitably, these improvements will generate greater employee satisfaction.

2. *Employee satisfaction will produce loyal employees.* It is obvious that a happy and satisfied employee will become a more loyal employee. It is simple human nature to respond positively to attentive managers who care about their people and who work to make things better in the working environment. This personal loyalty will and should transfer to the organization if the employee feels that the values of the corporate culture are worthwhile and beneficial to his or her interests.

3. *Employee loyalty improves employee productivity.* Again, this link in the chain seems intuitively obvious; namely, an employee loyal to the organization will work harder and therefore be more productive. We might say that a loyal worker will "go the extra mile" for the company. If a special effort is needed to finish a project, or if extra hours are required, it will be the loyal employee who will step in to "get the job done." This is especially true if he or she feels that the efforts will be appreciated and that it is for the good of the organization. An additional benefit is that organizations with loyal employees have a much lower employee turnover rate. Many organizations only measure losses caused by high employee turnover in terms of the direct costs associated with recruiting and training new hires. They often fail to understand the fact that the real losses are the indirect costs that come with loss of productivity and decreased customer service.

4. *Higher employee productivity yields greater value to the customer.* The bottom line is that higher productivity translates into lower costs; hence products and services can be delivered to the customer at lower prices.

5. *Value drives customer satisfaction.* It follows that most customers know when they receive greater value in the form of improved products or services delivered to them even without price considerations. Equally or more greatly appreciated will be lower prices. Although the customer may not immediately recognize value in the form of improved products, almost everyone can immediately evaluate what they experience personally. Therefore, when service is delivered quickly and efficiently by knowledgeable and helpful frontline employees, the customer will instantly recognize and value it. It is not hard for us to understand how customer satisfaction is a direct result of value added to products or services received.

6. *Customer satisfaction leads to customer loyalty.* Although all satisfied customers do not necessarily become loyal customers, it is highly unlikely that dissatisfied customers will become loyal to the company. Therefore, customer satisfaction is a necessary (if not sufficient) condition for customer loyalty.

Figure 10.3 (originally introduced in Chapter 2 as Figure 2.6) shows a typical relationship between customer loyalty and customer satisfaction. In this figure,

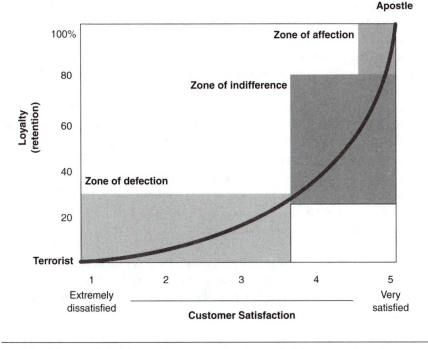

Figure 10.3   Typical Relationship Between Customer Satisfaction and Customer Retention

loyalty is inferred from customer retention expressed as a percentage. By examining this figure, one can see that the loyal customer occupies a very special place at the upper right of the curve and represents an invaluable asset to any organization.

A few comments are in order concerning Figure 10.3. Although it is no surprise that an extremely dissatisfied customer can be a very damaging entity to any organization, it is interesting to note how low the retention rate is (approximately 30%) for all customers who reported that they were "less than satisfied" with the service they received. These customers, whose dissatisfaction ranges from "slight" to "extreme," fall in the "zone of defection," where they are very likely trying to take their business somewhere else. From the chart we can see that only about one out of three customers in this category will be retained by the organization. Next comes the middle region—the "zone of indifference"—where the retention rate is still no better than three out of four customers (75%) who have reported that their level of satisfaction is just below "very satisfied." Customers who fall in the "zone of indifference" feel no special loyalty to the organization and will defect relatively easily. Customers who said they were "very satisfied" are now very likely to become long-term customers. Such customers have moved into the "zone of affection," where approximately four out of five, or about 80%, of these very satisfied customers will be retained. These are the truly "loyal" customers.

7. *Customer loyalty drives profitability.* Think customer retention, repeat business, and good recommendations and word-of-mouth referrals when you think of customer loyalty. The ultimate achievement in any business that depends on sales or services for its survival and profitability is to transform as many customers as possible into *loyal* customers. The word *loyalty* makes a big difference here—a customer, even a satisfied one, is not necessarily a loyal customer. Once a customer crosses the line and becomes a loyal customer, he or she will most likely become a customer for life. Heskett et al.[141] state that a 5% increase in customer loyalty can boost profits by 25% to 85%. According to Xerox Corporation, customers rated as *very* satisfied were six times more likely to repurchase company equipment than were customers who were merely satisfied. Heskett et al. also point out that although the lifetime revenue from a loyal pizza customer can be $8000, it can reach $332,000 for a loyal Cadillac customer, and hundreds of millions of dollars for a corporate purchaser of commercial aircraft.

It is important that managers fully appreciate the potential benefit to be gained by understanding the service profit chain concept. Managers of frontline employees should explain to their people its significance and encourage them to use it to help move the organization toward service leadership excellence.

The Service Profit Chain Audit

Data and information useful to managers can be obtained by an audit of the service profit chain. Managers who conduct a service profit chain audit are better able to (a) determine what drives their profits and (b) initiate those actions that can lead to long-term profits. Managers should use the audit to answer a number of fundamental questions and investigate what efforts are being or have been taken throughout the organization to obtain these answers. Some of the questions may at first appear to be trivial, simplistic, or obvious, but their answers can and will be quite revealing. Heskett et al.[142] suggest that managers use the results of the audit to answer the following questions:

- How does the company define a loyal customer?

  Loyal customers don't just happen. It takes time and effort on the part of (possibly) many frontline employees before a customer can be considered a "loyal" customer. These customers provide a disproportionately high percentage of the sales and profit growth of successful service providers.

- How much does the company spend on customer retention programs?

  Many companies concentrate too much of their effort on attracting new customers and too little on retaining existing customers. This is clear evidence that many companies simply do not appreciate the value of a loyal customer. Managers should take proactive steps to ensure that good customers become loyal customers.

- What are the main reasons that customers defect?

  It is critical for managers to know who the defecting customers are, where they go, and why they defect. Was it due to high prices, low value received, or poor service? Answers to these questions are important in determining how well existing strategies are working. Because top managers will not be the first to see the answers to these questions, it is imperative that they encourage frontline service providers and lower level managers to pass this information "up the line" without fear of retaliation if the answers do not support the prevailing mind-set and preconceived ideas of top management. The rule should be "don't shoot the messenger just because you don't like the message!"

- What are the sources for obtaining customer feedback?

  Although there may be many sources for obtaining this information, the main sources will include letters of customer complaints, reports from sales representatives and service personnel, and audits of the logs of telephone service representatives.

- How does the organization measure service value?

  Although value is usually subjective, it can be either tangible or intangible. For example, a better (tangible) product will have greater value to the customer than will a product of lower quality or poorer performance. Similarly, if two products are virtually identical in every way except price, then most customers would say that the less expensive one offered better value for the money. Service (an intangible) rendered quickly and courteously by a knowledgeable and helpful service provider will almost certainly be valued very highly by most customers. Service value is always relative, elusive, and difficult to quantify. It is relative because it is largely based on customers' expectations, interpretations, feelings, or perceptions of how the service was or should be delivered. Simply speaking, not all customers will rate identically delivered services or assistance received the same (indeed, this is a hypothetical situation in the first place, as services are like snowflakes—no two are identical!). When a company tries to determine service value, it will usually measure the level of satisfaction expressed by the customers themselves. From these results it will then try to infer the value customers place on the service they received. Although this method is a bit indirect, in many cases, it may be the best that can be done. See Chapter 8 for more details on service metrics. In any event, managers should know the many subtleties and pitfalls involved in this important area of customer service.

- Does the company do enough to recover from customer service failures?

  No matter how hard one might try to achieve excellence in service delivery, failures will inevitably occur. As any carpenter will tell you about cutting lumber, "Measure twice, cut once." Too many companies have it backwards, thereby doubling the amount of resources needed to achieve the same result. Service organizations, like carpenters, must strive to do things right the first time to minimize errors. At the same time, however, managers must organize and plan for recovery from those inevitable service failures. Organizations known for outstanding service delivery almost always have solid plans in place to meet service emergencies. Managers play an important part in this process when they are committed to anticipating problems before they happen, finding potential problems in the pipeline, and then resolving problems satisfactorily as they occur. Enlightened managers will give frontline employees the authority, resources, latitude, and encouragement to resolve service emergencies and problems as quickly as possible. Chapter 7 presents more information on recovery from service failures.

These questions are only examples of the many issues that managers will want to explore during the course of a service profit chain audit.

The Loyalty Effect

In his book entitled *The Loyalty Effect*, Frederick Reichheld[254] presented the thesis that successful companies have three things in common: loyal employees, loyal customers, and loyal owners. He stated that a 5% increase in the customer retention rate can increase lifetime value to a company by as much as 75% over a wide range of industries, such as banking, insurance, and transportation services. If one has loyal customers, many desirable things begin to happen:

- Customer loyalty and retention levels increase.
- Customer referrals go up.
- Customers become less price sensitive.
- Spending rates increase.
- Initial processing and servicing costs go down.
- Product returns and losses due to service failures are lower.
- Profits increase.

The loyalty effect itself, although simple to understand, correlates many complex events and circumstances in a complex and interactive web. It is illustrated in Figure 10.4 and, at first glance, appears to be a random and disorganized collection of things and events. Closer inspection reveals that it is much like the service profit chain. For one thing, both models consist of a set of cause-and-effect events—the main differences between the two are the items included and explicitly shown and the particular end result achieved (or emphasized). Reichheld[254] emphasizes building loyal employees, customers, and investors by starting with the *right* new employees, retaining the *right* new customers, and attracting the *right* new investors. All of these loyalties will lead, directly or indirectly, to the customer receiving superior value for the product or services purchased. This superior customer value leads to customer loyalty, which in turn makes employees feel good about the work they are doing, thereby raising their loyalty to a company they have pride in and motivating them to work harder or serve the customer better. Indeed, this sets up a *virtuous cycle* of self-sustaining and mutually beneficial actions and

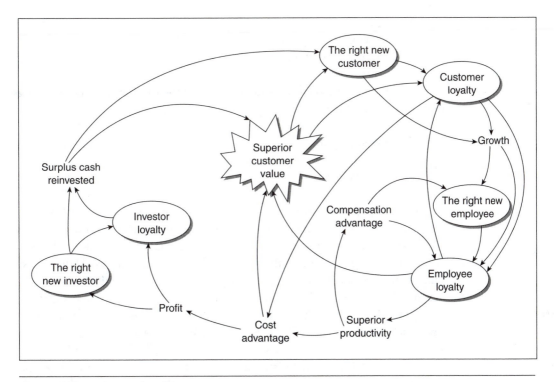

Figure 10.4   The Loyalty Effect

SOURCE: http://www.mori.com/pubinfo/pfh/how-to-focus-on-the-customer.pdf

behaviors between the employees and the customers. As this all takes place, complaints fall, satisfaction increases all around, cost advantages increase, competitive advantage is achieved, and profitability and company growth occurs. It is largely, but not exclusively, these last two positive economic benefits that will attract the *right*, loyal investors.

These same fundamental goals are found in the service profit chain—only with different descriptors, and the events are linked together in a more formal cause-and-effect, linear, chainlike fashion. In many respects, the complex and interactive nature of these events may be better represented in Reichheld's[254] modeling of the loyalty effect. The main benefit of the loyalty effect may be as a strategic tool to help managers and other members of the organization visualize the essential elements of the process and how they interconnect.

The Gallup Path

A company that developed its own version of the service profit chain is the Gallup Organization. The Gallup Path,[69] as it is called, consists of eight steps, as follows:

- Identify strengths.
- Find the right fit.

- Have great managers.
- Develop engaged employees.
- Acquire engaged customers.

These five steps are the causes (actions). They then will lead to the following three results (benefits); namely,

- Sustainable growth
- Real profit increase
- Stock value increase

The Gallup Path (which may be seen at http://www.gallup.com/content/default.aspx?ci=1528)[103] emphasizes the culture and human relationships within an organization. Although Coffman and Gonzalez-Molina[69] believe that the world's greatest organizations all know that their employees and customers are their most valuable resources, they also believe that the very best organizations understand that people are emotional first and rational second. From this it follows that for an organization to reach its full potential, its employees and customers must be emotionally engaged. The Gallup Organization feels its research supports this view and that the Gallup Path provides a model for creating and managing an "emotional economy." Gallup's experience has taught it how to build relationships one employee and one customer at a time. Furthermore, this company feels that almost any organization that values and develops its employee and customer human relationships will undergo a transformation that will lead to real financial advantages.

The Importance of Effective Managerial Communication

The concept of leadership has been central to this text. "Effective leadership can move organizations from current to future states, create visions of potential opportunities for organizations, instill within employees commitment to change, and instill new cultures and strategies in organizations that mobilize and focus energy and resources."[36] An essential notion is that communication is the vehicle in which to transmit these elements of leadership.

No matter which strategic model a company uses, managers must figure out effective communication strategies to make employees understand the vision, mission, service strategies, and implementation processes of the company. Managers must also communicate results effectively and remain open to feedback. Strong managerial communication practices within an open corporate communication culture strengthen the chances of an organization's success. The culture—and the managers who strongly influence its character—must encourage open, honest exchange of information among all members of the organization.

Managerial or organizational communication is a field that has been expanding and gaining influence. Eisenberg and Goodall's book *Organizational Communication*[92] summarizes much of the theory in this area. They propose the following view of communication within the theories of organizational culture:

- Communication is a core process by which culture is formed and transformed.
- Culture reflects patterns of behavior and their interpretation.
- Everyday communication is just as important as more notable symbolic expressions.
- Organizational communication encompasses not only words and actions, but also all types of nonverbal communication, including machinery, artifacts, and work processes.
- Each organization's culture is a cultural nexus of national, local, familial, and other forces outside the organization, and their communication reflects that.

All theories reflect the changing role of all members of an organization as a result of movements toward empowerment and all the associated implications. With greater participation at all levels, traditional lines of communication have drastically changed. This also means that access to information must be more open. As a matter of fact, managers who believe that empowered employees are more productive also recognize how crucial communication is in the process toward greater productivity. Within the service leadership culture, the relationship between communication and productivity is dialogic, emphasizing a mutual, two-way communication between managers and employees working together to accomplish complex tasks. This relationship, shown in Figure 10.5, demonstrates that a sense of urgency is usually a mediating factor. As Eisenberg and Goodall[92a] summarize, "Sharing business information, encouraging employee participation in decision making, and providing employees with feedback about the successes and failures of their efforts lead to increased levels of identification, commitment, and involvement, which in turn increase worker productivity."

In spite of what appears to be a free flow of information in both directions—to and from employees and managers—there is little doubt that managers and others in superior positions tend to have different views from their employees and those in inferior positions. This difference can be labeled the *semantic-information distance.*

Although managers spend from one to two thirds of their time communicating— usually verbally—with their employees, the communication process and its topics are often perceived differently by managers and employees. This is especially true for perceptions of organizational issues[162] and perceptions of participation in decision making.[132] Significantly, the perceptions of managers and employees about communication are quite different.

> Whereas supervisors tend to believe that they communicate with employees more frequently and effectively than they actually do, employees tend to believe that supervisors are more open to communication than they actually are. Employees also tend to believe that they have more persuasive ability than their supervisors believe that they possess.[68]

The crucial part of this semantic information distance is that neither of the parties tends to be aware of its existence. It is interesting that some studies have pointed

Feedback from managers about results

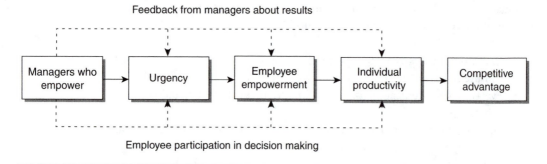

Employee participation in decision making

Figure 10.5   The Empowerment-Productivity Relationship

SOURCE: Adapted from Eisenberg and Riley.[93]

> *Take calculated risks. That is quite different from being rash.*
>
> —General George S. Patton

out that the perception of agreement may have almost as positive an effect as might occur if both parties really understood and agreed.

Communication is the lifeblood of an organization's culture. Through managers, as well as other organizational members, communication frames and directs all the activities of an organization and its culture. In addition, the organizational communication climate affects how employees communicate with customers, thereby having a significant effect on customer satisfaction and, ultimately, the organization's profitability.

Summary

The dramatic changes facing today's service organizations require that managers abandon many traditional concepts and rethink the way they organize, manage, and carry the organization forward through the allocation of people and their intangible resources, which we call *intellectual capital*. Most managers understand that a change is needed in the way companies are organized and managed, because there is an increased demand for speed, flexibility, and continuous self-renewal. The new service era requires motivated and highly skilled employees whose talents, skills, and knowledge can be integrated into the fabric of the organization and efficiently applied to create a competitive advantage. Only then can an organization have a chance to receive a positive return on its investment in people through its investment in the selection, training, and facilitation of its employees.

The biggest barrier to this change has not been organizational structure or processes but the mind-set of top managers and their formulation and application of old strategies in new times. Therefore, the major changes in the role of the manager are not only the need for leadership at the managerial level but also the manager's initiative to inspire a leadership mind-set and behaviors at every level of the organization. Thus managers must lead the organization in (a) determining its purpose; (b) designing the processes needed to realize that purpose; and (c) selecting, training, and inspiring people to become fully committed to that purpose.

The increased emphasis on each employee's unique contribution to the creation of a competitive advantage has generated significant pressure on workers. Increased investments in people call for a demonstration of results and the added value each employee brings to the organization. This in turn creates demands for innovation, creativity, empathy toward customers' needs, participation in continuous quality improvement efforts, and other behaviors that benefit the organization's delivery of quality service. How can this be done? Read on!

The service profit chain (developed by Harvard Business School service experts) is a theory of linked causes and effects whose basic tenet is that employee satisfaction leads to customer satisfaction, which is linked to profit. Complexities aside, possibly the strongest argument for the service profit chain is that, as a management tool, it makes sense and is easy to understand. In its simplest form, it can help managers achieve organizational profitability by aiming for employee satisfaction, loyalty, and productivity, which, in turn, lead to customer satisfaction, loyalty, and repeat business. Today, many companies—both large and small—are "managing the service profit chain." Many feel that it provides a solid theoretical foundation for the development of an outstanding strategic service vision and can serve as a model for managers to use in building more focused operations and marketing capabilities. The concept of the service profit chain is so important that having managers who understand and apply it can be a critical step toward achieving true service leadership for the organization.

Effective managerial communication is essential to successful management. Communication is used for everything from instilling the corporate vision in all organizational members to discussing specific tactics of service delivery. Communication influences the way strategies are developed, decisions are made, and information is shared. As discussed in other chapters, within any strategic organizational model, managerial communication must be open, supportive, motivating, and empowering. It is also important for managers to realize the impact of perceptual differences and to maintain open information exchange to maximize agreement among organizational members.

The ability to communicate well is critical for success. Great service leaders also realize that to achieve a competitive advantage they must constantly build and nurture a desirable organizational culture, empower and encourage their employees, and never forget their customers. The ultimate success of these important elements is determined by how well they are articulated and communicated.

PRACTICAL INSIGHTS

Gallup on Employee Engagement and Customer Loyalty

In the late 1990s, when one of the world's largest home improvement retailers set out to become number 1 in the world, the management team laid down a solid strategy focusing on customers and employees. The employee-customer-profit chain was used as their operating model in the belief that recruiting talented employees and keeping them engaged would lead to higher levels of customer loyalty, hence creating return business and increased number of referrals by customers to others.

To monitor whether the strategy was working, the company turned to the Gallup Organization in the United States to assess and improve employee engagement and to measure its influence on customer loyalty. The program consists of measurements, analysis, executive consulting, manager training, and manager intervention components. Employee engagement levels are measured every 6 months, and customer loyalty is measured monthly. Twice a year, managers receive a balanced scorecard with their employee engagement and customer loyalty scores. Bonuses are awarded based on the scorecard results. Through a business impact analysis, Gallup identified critical links between employee engagement, customer loyalty, and business growth and profitability. Employee engagement levels for each store were analyzed against four key productivity measures: inventory shrinkage, customer complaints, employee absences, and staff turnover.

When comparing the stores scoring in the top 25% on employee engagement and customer loyalty to the stores that performed in the bottom 25%, the top stores consistently outperformed the bottom ones across the four productivity measures. Also, 10,000 customer complaints per year were attributed to the underperforming stores. The financial impact of this underperformance is estimated to be more than $82 million yearly in shrinkage and turnover costs alone.

The Link to Business Growth Measures

To further examine the impact of employee engagement on important business parameters, an effort was made to link employee engagement to three measures particularly important to the growth potential of the business. The objective was to examine the linkages between engaged employees, loyal customers, and key business growth measures. The measures were per-store sales, per-store profitability, and sales per full-time equivalent employee. Again, stores in the top 25% significantly outperformed those in the bottom 25%. Stores in the top quartile outperformed the others on all the financial measures applied.

SOURCE: Gallup Organization.[149]

Key Points

- The employee-customer-profit chain affects the bottom line.
- Employee engagement and customer loyalty are directly proportional to productivity utcomes.
- Customer complaints increase as employee engagement decreases.
- Financial implications can run into millions of dollars annually.

Key Concepts

Directions: The following are key concepts presented in this chapter. Write a complete definition for each one.

Strategic resources

Intellectual capital

Framing the organizational context

Service profit chain

Questions

1. How are management roles changing with respect to managers' relationship with their employees?

2. Why does the theory of the zero-sum game not work in a service organization?

3. What philosophy challenges the "sacredness of the bottom line"?

4. Why is the service profit chain such an important tool for managers? Why is it also a useful tool for employees?

5. What role does loyalty play in the service profit chain?

6. What is the purpose of a service profit chain audit?

7. How are the service profit chain and loyalty effect models similar? How do they differ?

8. Describe how the loyalty of the employee to the company can affect the loyalty of the customer and vice versa.

9. Why is effective communication critical to success within a service organization?

10. Do employees and managers share the same opinions about communication topics and implications? Explain your answer.

Advanced Activity

Interview a recruitment agency or human resources (HR) manager about what he or she looks for when recruiting service managers. Ask if and how those requirements have changed over recent years. Drawing on the results of the interviews and lessons you have learned throughout this book, write a job description for a managerial position in a leading service organization. Briefly describe the position's major responsibilities and tasks. Identify the qualifications, skills, and abilities required for the position.

Search the Web

Find online ads for managerial positions in service organizations using job banks such as monster.com. Analyze the requirements for the job—the abilities, education, and experience needed. Is there any explicit request for leadership abilities or customer orientation in the candidates? Print out the ads, make a note of your findings, and discuss them in class.

Suggested Readings

Bartlett, C. A., & Ghoshal, S. (2002, Winter). Building competitive advantage through people. *MIT Sloan Management Review, 43*(2), 34–41.

Hamel, G., & Prahalad, C. K. (1990). The core competence of the corporation. *Harvard Business Review, 68*(9), 79–91.

11

Implementing Human Resources Policies for Service Organizations

Human, not financial, capital must be the starting point and ongoing foundation of a successful strategy.

—Bartlett and Ghoshal[26]

Objectives

After completing this chapter, you should be able to

1. Understand how the role of human resources is changing

2. Know why recruitment and selection are critical for service excellence

3. Realize the importance of continuous learning at all levels of service organizations

4. Understand how human resources managers assess the effectiveness of their hiring policies and training programs

The Changing World of Human Resources Management

As organizations move away from competition for products and markets toward competition for resources and competencies, especially in the area of competing for truly talented and driven people who share the corporation's values and visions, their strategic objectives must change. As discussed in Chapter 10, management has had to shift its focus from a purely financial analysis of corporate value to a realization that their employees are the resources who ultimately create profit for the company. Management focus must shift from maintaining only defensible product-market positions to acquiring sustainable competitive advantages through core competencies, resource-based strategies, and networking organizations. Table 11.1 provides an overview of the ever-evolving role of human resources in the service industry as the focus transitions to competition for talents and vision—for the very best employees for every position. These days, the race is not only for certain kinds of knowledge or ability to perform a task. Now the winning formula involves finding people who not only are technically competent but share the company's values, vision of the future, and understandings of how to get there, allowing the company's culture to strengthen to the point of creating a competitive edge. During the process, the organization must continuously

> You have to learn to treat people as a resource. . . . You have to ask not what do they cost . . . but what can they produce?
>
> —Peter F. Drucker

Table 11.1   The Evolving Role of Human Resources Management

	Competition for Products and Markets	Competition for Resources and Competencies	Competition for Talents and Vision
Perspective on employees	People viewed as factors of production	People viewed as valuable resources	People viewed as talent
HR's role in strategy	Implementation, support	Contributory	Central
Key HR activity	Administering of recruitment, training, and benefits	Aligning resources and capabilities to achieve strategic intent	Building human capital as a core source of competitive advantage

SOURCE: From Barlett, C. A., & Ghoshal, S., Building competitive advantage through people in *MIT Sloan Management Review*, Winter 2000, reprinted with permission of Tribune Media Services.

renew itself through its vision and values, flexibility, innovation, and frontline entrepreneurship and experimentation. These goals can only be accomplished through recruiting, training, and retaining superior intellectual capital.

Service managers must rely on the tools and processes of human resources to maximize the likelihood of bringing the right people on board to carry the organization forward. This ensures that those skills and abilities needed to successfully meet customers' needs faster and better than the competitors are integrated throughout the organization.

If managers at all levels are now faced with changing roles, then human resources (HR) managers are no exception. Human resources management must transform the way human resources will be operated now and in the future. However, like all other managers, HR professionals are not comfortable with having to transform their current personnel practices or with questioning the assumptions and principles on which they are based.

Human resources managers who want to create a competitive advantage are faced with the following issues:

- A building challenge: recruitment and selection
- A linking task: knowledge management through social networks
- A bonding process: culture-loyalty, commitment, and a sense of belonging[26]

The role of HR managers must shift to support the new service organization. Their perspective on employees must change from viewing people as a part of production or as just another resource. This puts HR right in the center of the organization rather than on the fringes with only a supporting role. Because of that, HR activities must now build human capital as a core source of competitive advantage. This requires them to align their resources and capabilities with the strategic intent of the organization. That may be a major shift for many of today's HR managers, because, by definition, the cornerstone of the human resources function has been centered on the *job* and the *individual* who will fill that job. Even in the recent past, organizations attempted to make jobs as fixed as possible and, by so doing, remove as much employee variability as possible.[109] Today's changes and new rules require quite the opposite from management and employees.

Today's conventional wisdom maintains that employee loyalty no longer exists. It has been replaced by a free-agent talent market that requires companies to hire employees using short-term contracts rather than building long-term, trust-based relationships with employees. Organizations in the service industry have long accepted high employee turnover that goes along with low-level jobs. Because these organizations have often had a low regard for their service employees, they have decided to use temporary help or have outsourced their service delivery. They have seldom realized the full consequences of such shortcuts.

According to Bartlett and Ghoshal,[26] "If a company can outsource services or hire temporary expertise, so can its competitors. Such actions, therefore, are unlikely to lead to any competitive advantage."

This is a key concept in evaluating how organizations actually create a competitive advantage. If the use of temporary help and outsourcing do not help, then what must organizations do? Do they have to accept the fact that employees are not loyal to the company they work for? Do they need to change their operating policies and human resources processes? This chapter deals with those questions and examines the changing role of management in service organizations as a result of the growth in the importance of human resources. First, the changes needed in the managers' roles and daily activities are examined, followed by a discussion of the increasing importance of the transformation of the human resources function within organizations. Then the chapter provides a practical overview of important practices and guidelines for recruiting and selecting new staff, indoctrinating them to the organizational ways of doing things, and fostering continuous learning at every level to enhance employee motivation, skills, and commitment.

> *You have to think of service workers as your colleagues in the business of life. Service jobs are never easy, and service workers can be some of the more tolerant, professional, and polite people working today. Learn from them.*
>
> —Donald Trump

The Redesign of Human Resources Procedures

Bartlett and Ghoshal[26] reject the notion that loyalty among today's employees is dead. They argue that organizations must accept the challenge of creating an environment that will attract, keep, and motivate those who join the organization. Yet another major strategic task imposed on HR managers is to help management do so.

To truly benefit from an investment in people, organizational processes and management practices need to be redesigned to support the development of that investment. To do this, organizations must recruit, train, and retain the best people. They must first do everything in their power to *get employees off to a strong start* (recruitment, selection, and socialization). Second, they must foster *continuous learning* through training and coaching, and finally, they must create conditions that cultivate *ownership attitudes* through rewards, performance feedback, and result-oriented cultures.[40a]

Let's take a look at one company that is succeeding magnificently in investing in its people. The Container Store, founded in 1978, is a chain of stores located across the United States. It is devoted to helping people streamline and simplify their lives by offering them a selection of more than 10,000 storage and organizational products (see their Web site at http://www.containerstore.com). This 27-year-old firm has had annual sales growth of at least 20% for each of the years it has been in business. Within the housewares industry, where average employee turnover is more than 70%, the Container Store has less than a 10% turnover for its full-time employees and about a 30% turnover for its part-time employees. How has it achieved this remarkable record? "This company is in total harmony, from the sales floor to the distribution center."[244] It believes that the only way to create a great place to shop is to create a great place to work. The Container Store has a total management commitment to making sure the right employees are selected and trained thoroughly and that the total work experience is one that makes employees want to stay—and makes them want to have their friends work there with them.

Recruitment and Selection

In the service industry, there is no buffer between the customer and the rude, uncaring, frontline service provider. Because of this, the recruitment, selection, and training of employees are extremely important for the service firm. Unfortunately, service organizations too often do not set high enough standards for the recruitment of frontline staff in the belief that the lower level jobs do not justify a rigorous and aggressive recruitment process. Too often, the first "warm body with a heartbeat" gets the job. The consequence is high employee turnover, service failures, and related costs that often go undetected by the organization. Under these circumstances, employees take little pride in their work, and their self-confidence and commitment to the organization are low. These negative attitudes often lead to a bare minimum job performance. Thus, one of the most important tasks of service managers is the *recruitment and careful selection* of their staff.

Selecting the right individual for the organization—not just for a particular task—from a sizable pool of applicants enhances the possibility of a more efficient operation and better quality. The saying "garbage in, garbage out" rings particularly true in this context. Setting high standards for employee selection at all levels of the organization, the front line included, enables managers to make better use of the organization's human resources development dollars. If an organization truly hopes to benefit from an investment in its people strategy, it must not recruit individuals who are merely average. Instead, the very best candidates must be recruited and hired. Those employees who come in with the qualities and values emphasized by the organization stay longer, produce better results, and benefit more from performance improvement programs, such as service training.[117] In addition, when a company has a cadre of employees who are indeed the very best for their jobs, it will be able to maintain this kind of employee, because "like attracts like." In other words, skilled and talented people want to work with people who have these same characteristics. That helps to explain why very successful firms can continue to hire outstanding candidates.

The Container Store has been at or near the top of *Fortune's* "Best Companies to Work For" list for several years. As mentioned earlier, one way to accomplish this is through the organizing principle for human resources: turning the company's best customers into loyal, top-performing employees. The Container Store's own employees are one of the best sources of its new hires. In fact, each employee, from those who stock shelves to managers, carries recruiting cards in his or her pockets. When employees talk with customers, they can encourage those who they know are enthusiastic about the company's products and who they feel would share the company philosophy to apply for a job. Also, employees are rewarded with nice bonuses for carrying out this in-store recruiting—$500 for each full-time hire recruited by an employee and $200 for every part-time hire. The company's director of training and recruiting notes that this practice is so successful, the company often goes 6 to 8 months without having to place a classified ad.

Knowing how critical the selection process is, why do many organizations make their frontline selection decisions routinely and sometimes carelessly, from a small pool of less-than-stellar applicants? As mentioned earlier, management often believes that low-level jobs do not justify a rigorous selection process. However, those decisions can be expensive if recruiting costs, training costs, and cash flow of the expected future salary stream and benefit payments are counted. Because poor hires usually have limited loyalty to the company, the turnover rate is high. Therefore, the company must incur recruiting and training costs over and over. As a result of a bad hire, other, more crucial costs are also incurred—those that are associated with service failure and the resulting damage to an organization's image.

With sloppy recruitment and careless selection, organizations lose the opportunity to obtain competitive advantage through their hiring decisions. On the other hand, if employee recruitment and selection are regarded as strategic tools, then standards are set and evaluation of the new recruit's performance is systematically conducted. Only if these steps are taken will human capital investments be made with the same rigor and respect as financial capital investments.[26] This is clearly demonstrated when one examines many of the leading service organizations in the world. They aggressively seek out the best pool of applicants for every position and give themselves time to find the right person to fit into their organizational culture; as a result, they are able to deliver the services expected by and promised to their customers.

Coffman and Gonzalez-Molina[69] recognize this in their new model for Gallup:

> Great organizations create an environment in which their best performers can do what they excel at, over and over again. These men and women are so tuned in to what they are doing, and so effective at responding to the needs of customers, that profits and growth flourish, as do the employees. These men and women are referred to, with gratitude, as being emotionally engaged employees. When engaged employees utilize their natural talents, they provide an instant, and constant, competitive edge. They build a new value: emotionally driven connections between employees and customers.

It's no wonder that, with this recognized value in human capital, organizations must tailor their recruiting and hiring policies. As an additional element, when strategizing for the selection process, organizations must move away from job descriptions toward accountability statements, competency profiles, and result-based employee performance measures such as quality service and initiative, not just task or work order completion.[109]

One great person equals three good people.

—The Container Store

The starting point is to conduct an analysis of values, tasks, attitudes, and characteristics critical for successful performance on the job and within the organization. The criteria for employee selection need to be clear. The focus must be on specifications of skills and abilities the candidates should have and on any of their past behaviors that would indicate a possible fit with the organization's profile and needs. Let's take a look at the process of recruitment and selection of applicants for service organizations.

Evaluation of Applicants

Evaluation of applicants in service organizations can be organized into steps, sometimes referred to as the multiple hurdle approach, whereby the applicants go through a series of procedures or steps designed to eliminate all but the most appropriate applicants for the job. The first step in this process, preselection, usually begins with examining an employee's past using information found on the application form and resumé. This includes education, experience, and recommendations from former employers. However, the future value of the applicant to the organization lies in his or her DATA, an acronym that stands for the *desire, ability, temperament,* and *assets* that he or she brings to the job.[125] Therefore, the evaluation process must be designed to uncover the applicant's skills, as well as his or her temperament and suitability for the company. In addition, the selection process should try to discern whether the applicant is motivated, not only to provide excellent service, but to go well beyond the basic job requirements.

Testing is the second step in the evaluation process. Testing should focus on the basic skills required for the job and on the applicant's service orientations. Further testing may analyze specialized skills, such as foreign language proficiency or specific knowledge that is required for the job. Following this preliminary screening, the third step is to interview the remaining applicants using standardized interview techniques. In Step 4, a second interview (a follow-up interview) is conducted with those applicants remaining after the first round of interviews. The Container Store handles this by having the follow-up interview conducted by a team of 10 employees. During this interview, the candidate has to perform one or more job-related tasks, such as pitching a product. In addition to seeing how the applicant fits into the group, managers can get an indication of the candidate's sales skills, potential customer service behavior, and enthusiasm for the job itself.

A fifth step in the hiring process may include formal tests, including on-the-job performance of the applicant in simulated circumstances. For some positions or kinds of jobs, psychological testing is also required. For example, if testing reveals that a candidate has attention deficit disorder (ADD), then that individual should not be placed in a job requiring close, tedious attention to detail.

The number of steps taken in the evaluation process depends on management's commitment to a selection strategy of excellence. One or more steps can be omitted, depending on the level of screening needed to identify the most appropriate applicants.

A useful and relatively easy way of measuring selection performance in the organization is to keep track of the so-called selection ratio. The term *selection ratio* refers to the number of qualified applicants as a percentage of the number of positions being filled. By calculating the selection ratio, the organization can keep track of the results of its recruitment efforts.

Socialization and Continuous Learning

Getting new employees off to a strong start lays a foundation for the future. Much rides on getting the selection right the first time to avoid costly employee turnover and service failures that may occur as a consequence of a bad selection decision. New recruits need to be properly integrated into the organization through carefully thought out socialization processes. In most jobs, the first few days or weeks of employment offer the new recruit critical and valuable opportunities to learn about the company's values, traditions, history, strategy, customers, competitors, policies, and procedures. "Like actors on a stage, service providers need to know the play; furthermore, to perform their role well, they need to know where and how their part fits into the overall performance."[40]

Therefore, after an employee has been successfully selected, the important first steps of his or her socialization process into the organization can commence, usually with a comprehensive orientation program. After the organization has acquired top talent, human resources functions must constantly help those talented individuals develop and progress through continuous learning.

The Container Store maintains that customer service is its core competency, so it actively recruits employees who are self-motivated and team oriented, and who have "a passion for customer service." Next, the company goes above and beyond the usual industry practices for training of its employees. Although the majority of its employees are college educated, each first-year, full-time salesperson receives more than 235 hours of training that is customized to each individual and job function—this in a retail industry where the industry average for such training is about 7 hours. In addition, all employees receive continuous training during their career at the Container Store.

Continuous employee learning is important for at least four reasons: (a) Continuous learning reinforces the organization's core values; (b) education motivates employees by building their self-confidence and know-how; (c) no one is ever fully trained or fully knowledgeable; and (d) continuous learning professionalizes the service delivery role. In fact, learning is "an alternative to staleness, boredom, burnout, and ineffectiveness."[40]

However, individual and organizational core competencies cannot be developed solely through training and organizational development initiatives. This devotion to the continuing development of all employees must be fostered by all members of the corporate culture. Any knowledge management program must clearly demonstrate that top management, line management, and employees have a common and consistent purpose. Without it, the organization will not be able to achieve either core or individual competencies in its human assets.[109] Top HR executives must take the lead in developing the social networks that are vital to the capture and transfer of knowledge, because that requires an understanding of organizational design, process management, interpersonal relationships, and trust-based culture.[26]

In addition, the organization must actively link the various pockets of individual knowledge and expertise so it will not risk losing the return on its investment in its talent pool. Therefore, leaders must be sure to take an active role in the process of being sure that knowledge is really being transferred and used. This is critical for yielding the expected return on the investment in people. Leading the knowledge transfer process is the responsibility of upper level management. In fact, senior executives must be willing and able to teach, coach, cultivate, and mentor others so that continuous learning is woven into the fabric of the organization and leaders are continuously created. This results in "an environment where leaders are teaching leaders."[305]

Weeding the Garden

All good gardeners know that pruning and weeding are essential to promote healthy growth. The same is true with managers. Because employee selection is not an accurate science, mistakes cannot be avoided. Various tools and processes of employee selection can help to increase the accuracy of the process, but in case a selection failure occurs, for whatever reason, managers must not be afraid to admit and correct those mistakes. Jack Welch, former CEO of General Electric, is one of the foremost advocates of this approach. He emphasizes the importance of the employees living the values of the organization and of management's paying close attention to their performance on the job. In his book *Jack: Straight From the Gut,*[317] he identifies the following four categories of employees.

First, the *stars* of the company are the ones who strongly share the values of the organization and perform beautifully. The second group is composed of employees who can be helped to improve their performance through training or coaching. They live the company's values but lag behind in performance. The third group, however, should be immediately dismissed. Employees in this group are those who do not share the values of the company and whose performance on the job is not up to standard. The fourth and final group is more of a puzzle for most managers. These are the high performers who constantly provide results but unfortunately do not share the organizational values and act accordingly. These talented but often difficult employees are usually kept of until they leave of their own accord. Welch points out the danger of their disruptive influence on the organization and on other employees. Although employees in the fourth group may themselves be performing well, their behavior or attitude might hinder the performance of the organization as a whole. Because of this, Welch maintains that they should be discharged regardless of individual performance levels.

The organization must continually check to be sure that the evaluation methods used do indeed predict the applicant's suitability and job performance. To monitor the quality or success of selection decisions, managers can keep track of employee performance to determine "true and false positives." *True positives* are the ratio of applicants that a manager predicted would perform well if hired, and the applicants' job performance has supported that prediction. *False positives,* on the other hand, are the ratio of applicants a manager predicted would have a good performance record, but on-the-job performance did not support that view. This analysis

> *When you hire people who are smarter than you are, you prove you are smarter than they are.*
>
> —Robert H. Grant

should be connected to the groups listed earlier so managers can make the most informed decisions about which employees should be kept and which ones must be discharged.

Evaluation of Training Initiatives

The increased emphasis on each employee's unique contribution to the creation of a competitive advantage has generated significant pressure on workers. Increased investments in people call for a demonstration of results and the added value each employee brings to the organization.

Since the 1990s, training and performance improvement programs have become mainstream practices in the service industry. However, comprehensive measurement and evaluation processes within those organizations have lagged behind. Fortunately, in recent years, there has been a growing interest in determining the business impact of human resources development programs so their importance can be demonstrated in language that all stakeholders understand.

Managers need to know whether learning is taking place and if not, why not. Although there can be many possible explanations for poor employee performance, the following are three very common reasons for this: (a) The employee may have learned the skills but does not have the support or resources needed to perform well; (b) the program may have been too difficult, or the person did not have the necessary background training or education needed to comprehend the material, much less to be able to apply it on the job; and (c) the program may have been poorly designed or disorganized, and the instructor may have been unable to communicate the material adequately.[147]

If learning *has* taken place, then managers need to find out whether it is benefiting the customers and creating added value for the organization. Questions such as these can be answered by comparing employee performance evaluations with customer feedback surveys.

Organizations need to be sure that their evaluation programs are fully integrated throughout the organization. This requires a solid partnership between HR managers and key operating managers. The measurement of training and performance-improvement programs helps to link the organization's strategic goals with the training initiative. "The organization funds training at the expense of other organizational needs, and the results influenced by training can be elusive without a focused evaluation effort to address the outcomes."[237] Measurements make the result of the initiative more tangible, thereby enhancing the commitment of managers to using human resources development tools and techniques.

As has already been emphasized, performance-improvement initiatives must be aligned with organizational strategies and values. To accomplish this alignment, a number of objectives have to be put in place before a new training program can be launched. Hodge[147] has identified the following three objectives as important for this task.

- *Business objectives* specify what the participant will accomplish as a consequence of the application of skill and knowledge in measurable business terms.
- *Performance objectives* provide precise, measurable statements of the behaviors that the participant will be able to demonstrate on the job.
- *Learning objectives* describe what participants will be able to do at the end of their training or intervention program. These should match the performance objectives as closely as possible.

Finally, Hodge[147] recommends a *needs assessment* as the first step in any carefully planned HR initiative. The most important contribution of such an analysis is to define objectives for the program or initiative. The assessment addresses questions such as the following:

- What is the problem that needs a solution?
- Why does the organization want the program or training to accomplish?
- What is the problem to be corrected or the opportunity to be captured?
- Which key business results does the organization want to change?
- How will you know you have been successful as a result of the program or initiative?

Comprehensive measurement and evaluation processes must capture the contributions of human resources development and establish accountability. For this to happen, objectives should be precisely stated in terms of participant behaviors. They should begin with active verbs—such as *adjust, assemble, build, calculate, list, recall, repair,* and *perform*—that indicate the desired activities. The objectives must be stated in terms of *measurable* participant behaviors. When the objectives have been clearly set, the *program design* is carried out.

A Framework for Evaluation

Phillips and Stone[237] have presented a framework for evaluating training and educational programs, human resources programs, organizational development or change initiatives, and technology initiatives. The framework draws on the work of Donald Kirkpatrick,[182] a pioneer in the field. Phillips and Stone use Kirkpatrick's four levels of evaluation and add a fifth (see Figure 11.1). The levels measure (a) the participants' immediate reactions to the training, (b) the amount of learning that has taken place as a result of the training, (c) the extent to which the new skills or knowledge are applied on the job after the training, (d) the business impact of the initiative, and, finally, (e) the potential return on investment (ROI) in monetary terms. Let's look at each of these levels in more detail.

Level 1: Reaction. The first level measures the reaction of participants to the training program. It is intended to capture their level of satisfaction and their plans for

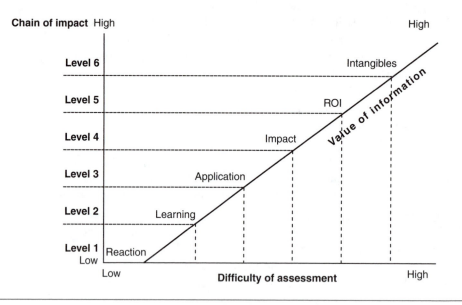

Figure 11.1   The Impact of the Assessment Method on Information Value

SOURCE: Based on Phillips and Stone[237] and the original work of Kirkpatrick.[182]

putting the training into action. Here the focus is on the training program itself, the facilitator, and the perceived application of the program in general. Reaction data reveal what the participants think of the program and should be used to adjust or refine the training content, design, and delivery. Most training programs today are usually evaluated at this first level by having the trainees answer generic questionnaires or surveys.

Level 2: Learning. The second level focuses on the participants and the support mechanisms for learning. The intent is to "measure the extent to which desired attitudes, principles, knowledge, facts, processes, procedures, technologies, or skills that are present in the training have been learned by the participants."[237] It is more difficult to measure learning than reaction. The data are used to explore the extent to which the participants have learned what was intended in the first place. A typical way of evaluating Level 2 would be to give the participants a test to discover how much of the subject matter they know after they complete the training program. However, a positive measure at this level does not guarantee that the training will be applied in the work setting. It only reveals the participants' knowledge of the content being presented or the skill being taught.

Level 3: Job Application or Implementation. The third level focuses on the participants' work setting and support mechanisms for applying learning on the job. The evaluation measures behavioral change on the job and is generally measured after the participants have been given some time to implement their new skills or knowledge on the job. The data are used to evaluate how effectively knowledge acquired on the job is applied. Managers also need to use the data to determine whether the application is working as intended. Work samples, customer surveys, or "walk-throughs" can usually be applied to measure Level 3 outcomes. Although successful application of course material is important, it still does not guarantee that it will have a positive impact on the organization.

Level 4: Business Impact. This level focuses on the impact of the training process itself on specific organizational outcomes. Usually, training programs or performance improvement initiatives are instigated because business results have fallen below expectations, because of competitors' advancements, or because certain factors threaten an organization's ability to meet its goals. This level of evaluation determines the training's influence or impact on improving organizational performance. It often yields objective data, such as cost savings, output increases, time savings, or quality improvements. It also yields subjective data, such as increases in customer satisfaction, customer retention, and improvements in response time to customers. This fourth evaluation step, together with the other three, provides a comprehensive view of the success of a particular training program or initiative in question. The ultimate goal of the training is usually to create a positive business impact for the organization. However, the training or program might have been too costly for the organization to justify when compared with the value it created. That is why Level 5 comes into play.

Level 5: Return on Investment. The fifth and final level focuses on the monetary benefits as a result of the training compared with the training costs. This level shows the true value of the training program in terms of its contribution to the organization's performance objectives (for a summary of studies on levels of assessment for selected training programs, see Strother[296]).

There is a *sixth type of data* that can be used to evaluate the benefits of training and other organizational performance initiatives: the intangible benefits. Intangible benefits focus on added value of the training in nonmonetary terms. According to Phillips and Stone,[237] "Intangible data is data that either cannot or should not be converted to monetary values. This definition has nothing to do with the importance of the data; it addresses the lack of objectivity of the data and the inability to convert that data to monetary value." Examples of such data are increases in customer satisfaction or employee satisfaction, customer retention, improvements in response time, organizational commitment, improved teamwork, improved customer service, reduced conflicts, and reduced employee stress. If an impact of performance improvement initiatives cannot be measured in monetary terms, it cannot be compared with the cost of the program. Therefore, an ROI analysis or cost-benefit ratio cannot be determined. As seen in Figure 11.1, each level has different characteristics and presents a different set of values to the organization.

The most common method of evaluation, the reaction level, produces the lowest level of value to the organization; its main benefit is that it is easy to measure and focuses on the participants who actually go through the program. It is the fifth level that provides the most value to the organization because it focuses on the ROI,

> *There is a way to do it better. Find it.*
>
> —Thomas Alva Edison

but unfortunately, this level is the most difficult to measure. As a result, it is infrequently used.

As discussed in Chapter 8, to manage anything, you need to be able to measure it. No matter how an organization hires and trains its employees, it must find appropriate ways to assess the effectiveness of its hiring policies and training programs.

Summary

To be successful, organizations must capitalize on their human resources—their intellectual capital. However, too many organizations have accepted high turnover in service jobs and continued to hire people who are poorly qualified, to use temporary employees, or to outsource their service components. A key concept is the consequences of these actions. If an organization can use these shortcuts, so can its competitors. This means the company gains no competitive advantage by just saving some money in the short term with these inadequate solutions.

The changing role of managers at all levels calls for a shift in the human resources manager's role toward a more strategic approach, in which human resources are regarded as strategic tools, not merely as tactical resources used to produce goods or services. This requires a real focus on the hiring, training, and retention policies and procedures of the company.

First, a higher standard for recruitment and employee selection procedures must be implemented throughout all levels of the organization. Higher quality applicants must be solicited for crucial frontline positions. From these applicants will come the service providers—those who are in contact with customers and who can strongly influence (for better or worse) each customer's satisfaction level. Then applicants must be put through the multiple hurdles required to filter out the best candidates.

Once the best candidates have been identified and hired, the company must take the responsibility to train them carefully for their jobs and to socialize them within the corporate culture. The process should start with a comprehensive orientation program, including preliminary training for job-specific skills. This process then should be transitioned into a continuous learning program to reinforce the organization's core values, motivate the employees, and make the service delivery as efficient and professional as possible.

All of these initiatives help an organization retain the best employees as well as helping with the decision to remove those who are not providing a solid benefit to the company.

All training programs, which should be integrated throughout the organization, must be aligned with the organization's business and performance objectives. In addition, as important as the training program itself is, measuring its results is even more critical and should be done carefully.

With these policies and processes in place, any organization should be able to recruit, train, and retain the best employees, which translates into customer satisfaction and corporate profitability.

The Gallup Organization on Talent Development

In the April 2002 edition of the *Journal of Applied Psychology*, the Gallup Organization published an article on a comprehensive research study indicating that a more engaged employee is more productive, more profitable, more customer focused, safer, and less likely to abandon the organization. How can these findings be applied to enhance organizational performance?

According to Gallup, 70% of U.S employees are not engaged at work, and the longer they stay within an organization, the less engaged they become (measured by the Gallup Q12 question survey of employee engagement). Furthermore, Gallup suggests that many of the HR solutions currently being used, such as competency-based selection, competency-based performance appraisal, competency-based manager development, and gap-driven training needs analysis, all feeding into an integrated performance management IT platform, are in fact making matters worse.

On its Web site (http://www.gallup.com/), Gallup answers the following two questions: (a) How much can we change a person after he or she has been hired? and (b) given a finite amount of time and money, where are we likely to see the most improvement? Furthermore, Gallup argues that everything we do to engage our people—how we select them, position them, measure their performance, develop them, channel their careers, pay them, and terminate them—is affected by how we answer these two questions.

Gallup bases its answers to the questions on recent advances in neuroscience, suggesting that "between the ages of roughly 3 and 15, a person's brain organizes itself by strengthening the synaptic connections that are used frequently, while those that are used infrequently wither away." In the words of Dr. Harry Chugani, professor of neurology at Wayne State University School of Medicine, "roads with the most traffic get widened." Therefore, after our midteens, the architecture of synaptic connections in our brain does not change significantly.

This means that a person's recurring patterns of thought, of feeling and of behavior do not change significantly. If he is empathic when he is hired, he will stay empathic. If he is impatient for action when he is hired, he will stay impatient. If he is strategic, always asking "What if?," he will stay strategic. If he is competitive, he will stay competitive.

These characteristics or traits of the individual are not likely to change after the person is hired. Of course, none of this implies that a person cannot change, but it sends a strong signal that we must be extremely careful whom we select.

Key Points

- The majority of U.S. employees are not strongly involved in their work.
- The longer those workers stay within the organization, the less engaged they become with their work.
- An employee's talents do not change much after he or she is hired.
- People will improve the most in their areas of greatest talent.
- An organization should base its performance strategies on selection and talent-based development.

Who Will Learn the Most, Change the Most, and Improve the Most

Neuroscience tells us that if we want to develop a person, the best thing to do is identify where his or her talents lie and then expose him or her to skills, knowledge, and experiences that build on those talents to create consistently excellent performances—what Gallup refers to as strengths. In neuroscience terms, one could say, "to create new buds on his existing branches [in the brain] rather than creating totally new branches."

The underlying premises are that a person is believed to improve the most in his areas of greatest talent. Therefore, Gallup researchers argue,

We must teach managers how to distinguish between talents—which cannot be transferred from one person to another—and skills and knowledge, which can. We must build performance management systems that label a person's talents his "areas for development" and that encourage him to "work on" strengthening his talents with the relevant skills and knowledge. And we must stop promoting people out of their areas of talent, and instead build alternative career paths that encourage them to grow within their areas of greatest talent.

SOURCE: Gallup Organization.[102-104]

Key Concepts

Directions: The following are key concepts presented in this chapter. Write a complete definition for each one.

Human resources' role in service

Recruitment and selection

Socialization

Training evaluation

Questions

1. The text calls for a shift in the human resources manager's role, toward a more strategic approach. List at least three things that HR managers should do to accomplish this.

2. Explain why outsourcing services and hiring temporary workers are strategies that are unlikely to help a company gain a competitive advantage in the new service era.

3. How would you define "frontline" staff? Give three examples of jobs they might perform. What are the consequences to a service organization if it sets low standards for the recruitment of frontline staff?

4. Someone once said, "It is far better to have one average worker with a good attitude than a dozen geniuses with bad work attitudes." How might you improve the performance of the average worker with a good attitude?

5. Welch advises dismissing employees who fall in two of the four categories of employees. What are the characteristics of employees in these two categories? As a manager, how would you determine that an employee falls in one of these groups? In other words, what formal and informal methods could you use to classify your employees?

6. Think about an organization for which you work or have worked. What makes its recruiting, training, and retaining policies effective, or what prevents them from being effective?

7. Why do successful firms have a better chance of hiring outstanding candidates?

8. How do customers of a service organization benefit from continuous employee training?

9. What are three kinds of objectives that should be put into place before a new training program is launched? What is the philosophy or purpose behind setting each kind of objective?

10. Assume you are a manager and you want to evaluate the results of a recent employee training program. Using Kirkpatrick's four levels and Phillips and Stone's fifth as the framework, briefly describe how you might measure employee learning at each level (for example, using tests, supervisor observations, surveys, or other methods).

Advanced Activity

Choose a local service company. Write a short description of a typical service training program for that company. Align the training program with the company's organizational strategies and values. Align the program by putting a number of objectives in place before the new training program can be designed and launched.

a. Set *business objectives* (the overall business effect of the training program—e.g., to the company's bottom line).
b. Set *performance objectives* (precise, measurable statements of the behaviors that participants will be able to demonstrate on the job).
c. Set *learning objectives* (what participants will be able to do at the end of their training or intervention program; match the learning objectives to the performance objectives as closely as possible).

Search the Web

Find the human resources mission statements of (a) a major service company and (b) a typical government agency. Examine the statements for differences and similarities. Based on your findings, what practical implications do you think the two *official* HR mission statements have on the day-to-day operations of the company and the government agency? Write a short report summarizing your opinions.

Suggested Readings

Berry, L. L. (1999). *Discovering the soul of service: The nine drivers of sustainable business success.* New York: Free Press.

Godbout, A. J. (2000). Managing core competencies: The impact of knowledge management on human resource practice in leading-edge organizations. *Knowledge and Process Management, 7*(2), 237–247.

Kirkpatrick, D. (1979). Techniques for evaluating training programs. *Training and Development Journal, 33*(6), 78–92.

12

Building and Maintaining an Effective Service Leadership Culture

The frightening uncertainty that traditionally accompanied major organizational change has been superseded by the frightening uncertainty now associated with staying the same.

—Cameron and Quinn[57]

Objectives

After completing this chapter, you should be able to

1. Understand what organizational cultures are based on

2. Realize why organizational culture can be, in itself, a powerful strategic tool

3. Know the main characteristics of effective organizational culture and how the culture can be built and maintained

4. Understand the need for alignment of culture, strategy, and leadership

5. Better understand the strategic application of leadership through service leadership culture

E very organization has its own culture, identity, and character—its own history and its own way of doing things. In this chapter, we examine the application of organizational culture as a strategic tool in an effort to shift the focus from strategy formulation to strategy execution. As crucial as organizational culture is, it was not until the 1980s that anyone began to pay serious attention to it. The reason may be that all cultures are a collection of values, assumptions, and collective memories that are simply taken for granted. Most people are not even aware of the culture that they are surrounded with until it changes—for example, a person may experience another culture or have his or her own culture made explicit in one way or another. There are many types of cultures and subcultures—national or regional, gender based, religious, professional—all of which are reflected through language or specialized jargon, symbols, and ethnocentric feelings.

> Soldiers generally win battles; generals generally get credit for them.
>
> —Napoleon Bonaparte

Cultures will form in any organization. The big question is whether the culture helps or hinders the organization's ability to execute its strategic objectives. An organization cannot ignore its culture and just hope it develops well. An organization must be proactive about using its culture to fully execute its strategy and inspire creativity and innovation. Although most managers are fully aware of the importance of cultural management, they may be unable to develop policies that have the clarity, consistency, and comprehensiveness needed to achieve the desired effect on employees. In fact, organizational cultures have turned out to be more than most managers bargained for, both as an enabler of competitive advantage and as a stumbling block for organizational efforts to improve processes and performance.

The three main organizational change initiatives that have been practiced in the last 20 years are total quality management (TQM), downsizing initiatives, and reengineering initiatives, many of which have failed. Research suggests that the most common reason reported for failure of organizational improvement efforts is neglect of the organizational cultures. In other words, when a company failed to change its culture, all of the other changes that the organization attempted were doomed. Cameron and Quinn[57] suggest that without a fundamental change in the organizational culture, there is little hope that lasting improvement in organizational performance will occur.

> And when you have reached the mountain top, then you shall begin to climb.
>
> —Kahlil Gibran

The purpose of this chapter is to explore the elusive phenomenon of organizational culture and its potential for achieving service leadership. We examine the concept of organizational culture and discuss how to build and maintain an effective culture, including issues that arise from an international perspective. The need for cultural change and a process of incorporating that change are then discussed. The chapter wraps up with a discussion of the strategic use of service leadership cultures in today's service organizations.

Organizational Cultures

Organizational or corporate culture is "the glue that holds an organization together, or the rock on which it stands."[24] The concept is difficult to describe and even harder to understand. Organizational culture has often been described as "the way people think about things around here" or "the way things are done around here."[57] A culture is a system of shared values and norms. Values are common beliefs that the organization and its members accept as important for individual and organizational success; norms define the attitudes and behaviors needed to achieve that success. Thus, organizational culture can be regarded as "a set of assumptions, values, and beliefs which determine the nature of truth" or "the way an organization exerts control over its members and how behavior is regulated."[242]

Strong cultures enhance organizational performance in two ways. They energize employees by appealing to their higher ideals and unified values, and they shape and coordinate employees' behaviors and decisions. A successful corporate culture is clear, consistent, and comprehensive. If the culture is aligned with organizational objectives, it has a powerful impact on performance.[67]

No organization has one pure culture throughout the entire organization, but all successful organizations are believed to have a core culture. That core culture is fundamental to the way an organization functions. Without it, the focus of resources and organizational operations is lost and energy is wasted as people, systems, and processes work out of sync with one another. For the organization to succeed, the core culture must be aligned with the organization's strategy and its core leadership practices.[271]

Different Types of Cultures

There is no single culture that is "the mother of all cultures." In fact, each one has unique characteristics imposed on it by the environment in which it originates. In addition to being largely determined by the environment in which the organization operates, it is affected by national values and characteristics, as well as business, economic, and customer considerations. To manage or change culture, organizations must be able to identify the determinants of culture and understand the way in which they interact with each other. Schneider[271] describes four core cultures:

- *Control cultures,* based on military systems, with power as the primary characteristic
- *Collaboration cultures,* in which the underlying premise is affiliation
- *Competence cultures,* governed by the will to achieve extraordinary things
- *Cultivation cultures,* motivated by growth or self-actualization

As seen in Table 12.1, strategy, culture, and leadership are interrelated and need to be aligned for the organization to succeed in strategically applying culture as a tool for competitive advantage.

Culture of Control

According to Schneider,[271] the culture of control "fundamentally exists to ensure certainty, predictability, safety, accuracy, and dependability." Organizations

Table 12.1   Strategy, Leadership, and Culture Interaction

Culture	Strategy	Leadership	Epistemology

Control	Market-share dominance
	Commodity
	Commmoditylike
	High distribution intensity
	Life and death
	Predictability
		Authoritative
		Directive
		Conservative
		Cautious
		Defensive
		Commanding
		Firm
			Certainty
			Organizational systematism:
			  fundamental issue is to
			  preserve, grow, and
			  ensure the well-being and
			  success of the
			  organization per se

Collaboration	Synergistic customer
	  relationships
	Close partnership with
	  customer
	High customization
	Total solution for one customer
	Incremental, step-by-step
	  relationship with customer
		Team builder
		First among equals
		Coach
		Participator
		Integrator
		Trust builder
			Synergy
			Experiential knowing:
			  fundamental issue is the
			  connection between
			  people's experiences and
			  reality

Competence	Superiority
	Excellence
	Extreme uniqueness
	Creation of market niche
	Constant innovation to stay
	  ahead
	Typically, carriage-trade
	  markets
		Standard setter
		Conceptual visionary
		Taskmaster
		Assertive, convincing
		  persuader
		Challenger of others
			Distinction
			Conceptual systematism:
			  fundamental issue is the
			  realization of conceptual
			  goals, especially superior,
			  distinctive conceptual
			  goals

Cultivation	Growth of customer
	Fuller realization of potential
	Enrichment of customer
	Raising of human spirit
	Further realization of ideals,
	  values, higher order purpose
		Catalyst
		Cultivator
		Harvester
		Commitment builder
		Steward
		Appeals to higher
		  level vision
			Enrichment
			Evaluational knowing:
			  fundamental issue is the
			  connection between the
			  values and ideals of the
			  organization and the
			  extent to which those
			  values and ideals are
			  being operationalized

SOURCE: W. E. Schneider (2000). *Strategy culture and leadership connection.* Reprinted with the permission of Emerald Group Publishing.

seeking control cultures apply the strategy of market share dominance and high distribution intensity. They regard their goods or services as commodities. The leadership style is likely to be authoritative, directive, and commanding. Managerial practices would include downsizing, customization, statistical process control, process reengineering, activity-based costing, decision trees, and simulation. The fundamental issue is to preserve growth and ensure the well-being and success of the organization itself.

Culture of Collaboration

In cultures of collaboration, the name of the game is synergy. Synergy can be thought of as a situation in which the whole is greater than the sum of the parts—in which people working together produce a far better result than would result from of each working alone. This kind of culture fosters unity and is extremely dedicated to the customer. Organizations seeking to maintain collaborative cultures generally have high customization, emphasize total solutions for customers, and form close partnerships. The leadership style is likely to be based on team building, participation, and trust. Managers or team leaders are regarded as "first among equals." The organization seeks customer loyalty through teams and open book management. Other management activities would typically be the application of high performance work teams, participative management, brainstorming, and group facilitation, all of which create synergy.

Culture of Competence

Organizations seeking distinction from their competitors seek to build a competence-based culture. This kind of culture is totally focused on ensuring that the organization's products or services are unique and unmatched in the marketplace. To accomplish this, the organization applies a strategy of superiority, excellence, creation of market niches, and constant innovation. The function of leadership is to challenge others, set standards, and persuade others to believe in leadership's vision. Critical management practices needed for this culture are knowledge-capital measures, benchmarking, continuous improvement, performance-based compensations, and reliance on core competencies. The fundamental issue is the realization of superior goals.

Culture of Cultivation

A culture of cultivation is all about enrichment. The corporate strategy is to contribute to the growth of the customers and to help them reach their full potential. Also, there is a belief in realizations of ideals, values, and higher order purpose. The leaders are catalysts, cultivators, and commitment builders who help the organization reap the benefits of human interactions and ideals. The management activities would best be characterized by empowerment to ensure employee commitment and by emphasis on the quality of work life. The fundamental issue is the connection between the

> *Plus ça change, plus c'est la même chose [the more things change, the more they remain the same].*
>
> —Alphonse Karr

values and ideals of the organization and the extent to which those values and ideals are being operationalized.

An International Perspective

The international dimension adds to the complexity and makes organizational cultures even more difficult to comprehend and manipulate. That in turn creates a number of implications for cross-cultural management and vendor relationships. How much can we generalize about the characteristics of a given culture without falling prey to stereotyping? Is there really a Japanese or a German "way" of doing things that makes them more successful just by virtue of their national character?

Baron[24] identified four types of cross-border management styles, based on a foreign office's relationship with its home headquarters and its organization's approach to people and systems. The four categories are (a) centralist, (b) local autonomous, (c) value driven, and (d) pioneer.

Centralists like to develop their policies and procedures for doing things in their home base, which usually is located in the organization's country of origin. Then the messages and policies are introduced to the branches or international sites, to be implemented in accordance with company procedures. These organizations tend to have strong identity and be fairly directive in their operations. The centralist approach can work well if it is flexible enough for its policies to be communicated effectively to the local employees. An example could be an international retail store selling fashion clothes and accessories. Every detail of the store and all tangible items are designed centrally and sent to the various locations. The approach ensures common appearance and establishes a sense of familiarity for customers across geographical and cultural boundaries.

Local autonomy entitles the home base and the company's international sites to maintain their own identity and operate policies and practices that are developed locally. Operational parameters are frequently used to ensure that the business strategy is consistent, but local management issues are generally left to managers on site, who, more often than not, are natives of the country in which they operate. For many organizations, this local approach to cross-cultural management has produced significant value. They feel that a strong local identity is beneficial to the company, and they treasure the resulting diversity in the organization. When companies apply this approach, the goods may be manufactured centrally and sent to the local sights where they are marketed, serviced, and even branded according to local preference and needs.

Value-driven organizations develop a set of values that they expect everyone in the organization to adopt completely. These values normally shape the global strategy of the organization. However, as long as local offices or divisions stay within the framework of overall organizational values and strategy, they are allowed to develop detailed policies of implementation that are acceptable to national values and practice. Many international companies see this as an effective way to create and maintain their company culture across borders. A set of company values is identified and reinforced throughout the organization. By managing through values, companies can avoid making rules and regulations about every little detail, instead relying on a set of values to guide employee behavior. In other words, everything is allowed unless it is specifically forbidden. This is in contrast with rigid organizations, in which everything is forbidden unless it is specifically allowed. For example, a company might foster the values of ambition, flexibility, proactiveness, teamwork, and efficiency to ensure that the level of customer care remains high enough to stay ahead of the competition. This method of management tells the company's employees that they should be unafraid to change the way they do things and come up with new ideas that improve the company's service. The emphasis on the efficiency and teamwork values ensures that employees do not engage in costly tasks or changes—or not, at least, without consulting with others.

Pioneer organizations are usually just starting up in their overseas operations. They employ expatriate managers who are usually responsible for developing local policies. Their local policies usually reflect the home organization's corporate culture because these managers already believe strongly in it.

There is no right or wrong way of dealing with cultural issues in cross-border operations. However, the trend seems to be for organizations to move away from the centralist or pioneer approaches to a more value-driven style of international management. The main reason is the growing emphasis on globalization and flexible policies and procedures that can be successfully implemented in different national cultures and accepted by local staff. Human resources personnel have at least two important roles in cross-cultural efforts. At the strategic level, personnel professionals are involved in developing policy frameworks that are relevant to the business strategy and can enable business objectives to be achieved. At the local level, this is translated into processes that are acceptable to local workers and their national cultures.

In conclusion, an important note must be made. Organizations that successfully manage the cross-cultural aspects of their business are not necessarily knowledgeable about every aspect of the culture or cultures in which they operate. They are, however, culturally aware and open to the notion of the difference itself. In addition, they are often willing to defer to a more diverse management group, which possesses the local cultural understanding and skills to manage in a global world.

> It takes an entire village to raise a child.
>
> —African proverb

The Power of Culture

Porter[243, 57] maintains the predominant view in management theory that successful organizations are subjected to certain conditions, some of which are considered to be critical. Successful organizations need to be operating in a market where there are *high barriers to entry,* such as high cost, technology innovations, and proprietary knowledge. They should have *nonsubstitutable products* or provide unique services or expertise. Also, a *large market share* enhances success. *Low levels of bargaining power* from buyers and suppliers give these organizations additional advantages and leverage. Finally, *rivalry among competitors* deflects attention away from head-to-head competition with the organization, making those competitors less focused on any potential weaknesses the organization may have.

It is an amazing fact that, over the past several decades, none of the most successful U.S. firms, in terms of profitability and financial return, have had any of these competitive advantages or so-called *prerequisites for success*. According to Cameron and Quinn,[57a] "The major distinguishing feature in these companies, their most important competitive advantage, the most powerful factor they all highlight as a key ingredient in their success, is their organizational culture." Because organizational culture is more powerful than anything else, it has been suggested that no management idea will work in practice if it does not fit the organizational culture, which is "so powerful in fact, that its impact supersedes all other factors when it comes to organizational performance."[186]

For the last decade, strong organizational cultures have been believed to be critical to bottom-line performance in large organizations. Commitment-based organizations packed with people who fit the organization's values perfectly have repeatedly outperformed other organizations. The traditional belief has been that the older and more successful an organization is, the stronger its culture, characteristics, and identity become.[224, 271] New evidence now suggests that even for relatively young organizations, developing a strong, strategically relevant culture is the strategy offering the greatest possibility of success.[67]

O'Reilly[224] has suggested that cultures have two main characteristics: (a) the amount of agreement among employees about what is important for individual and organizational success and (b) the level of passion the organizational members have for these values. If everyone agrees with the organizational values, believes in their importance, and is really passionate about upholding them, then the culture is unified and strong. However, if agreement is low and passion is lacking, then the values do not really govern employee behaviors or inspire employees to achieve extraordinary performance. As a result, the culture becomes very weak and ineffectual. If there is high passion and low agreement, then we may see a mismatch of cultures forming in the organization wherein not all people support the organizational objectives.

> *If you think education is expensive, try ignorance.*
>
> —Derek Bok

Building an Effective Culture Through Shared Values and Norms

We now know that culture can greatly improve organizational performance; however, the content of the culture must be strategically relevant to organizational objectives. Cultures are multidimensional, but only one dimension appears to be universally applicable across organizations regardless of their size, industry, or age—that is, innovation.[67] Kotter and Heskett[186] performed a longitudinal study of 207 organizations spanning a period of 11 years. They found that the organizations that had developed a strong culture that was supportive of their strategy performed better than others in the long run. What these organizations had in common was that their cultural norms and values encouraged innovation and change.

Shared norms are powerful because they affect how everyone in the organization works with each other. The concept of norms implies some level of social control, because norms reinforce confirming behaviors and punish behaviors that do not conform. The right kinds of norms are a positive factor within an organizational culture; *rules*, however, which are explicit formal directions regarding behavior or attitudes, are usually not. In the words of Chatman and Cha, "Relying on formal rules, policies and procedures will not result in anything outstanding, be it customer service, innovation, or quality."[67, 224]

Cultural values appeal to peoples' ideals and inspire them. They clarify expectations by demonstrating the way in which the organization expects its members to approach their work, customers, coworkers, and other stakeholders. For example, organizational values of integrity and ambition state that employees should be ambitious in their work but not at the expense of their own integrity or the organization's integrity. The closer the organizational values are to those important to individual employees, the more comprehensive their implementation will be at the organizational level. One of the key tasks roles of leaders is to make sure that all employees clearly understand the key cultural values of the organization. At the same time, employees must be allowed to interpret organizational values by adding their own layers of meaning to them.

A major pitfall in implementing or changing organizational culture occurs when management fails to "walk the walk" or just gives lip service to cultural values and norms. Values become little more than cheap talk if they are not lived every day. Employees watch management and get real evidence about what counts and what behaviors of their own will probably be rewarded or punished regardless of what printed vision statements and policies say. This is especially true for organizations whose mission and vision statements are more a declaration of political correctness than a real statement of values to be lived by.

The Role of Human Resources

Baron[24] has suggested that human resources personnel can be described as the "guardians of culture." Strategies for compensation and the measurement of performance are instrumental in shaping individual expectations about the workplace. Human resources tools are also instrumental in managing and maintaining effective cultures. As discussed previously, the three key tools for assisting in making the corporate culture clear, consistent, and comprehensive are (a) recruiting and selecting people who fit the culture, (b) managing the culture through socialization and training, and (c) managing the culture through the reward system.

Building and maintaining an effective culture is a challenging process. Many stand in the way of success by resisting attempts to alter behaviors, systems, or structures that have been in use for quite some time and have provided a sense of security for those involved. One of the most important elements of successful cultural management is the ability to tolerate and manage tensions brought about by change.

Human resources personnel can significantly contribute to any cultural management initiative for change. Baron's[24] research suggests that HR personnel have been active in the delivery of the change processes but have been concerned primarily with the "people implication" of change rather than with the change itself. In other words, they have spent more time formulating a response to change than coming up with ways of helping to shape the change and make it happen. Human resources professionals can assume a more active role in strategic development by identifying what is appropriate in cultural terms and predicting what impact the initiative might have. When communicating organizational reinforcement of values and norms, they can ensure that the information gets disseminated and understood by all members of the organization.

When strategizing for change, human resources personnel should be flexible in the use of their tools and procedures. They must also ensure that initiatives are correctly translated into national culture and value systems so that the management of the culture occurs at both the global and the local level.[67] All personnel policies and procedures need to be assessed and reviewed regularly, but it is especially important to do so at the very beginning of a culture change program. If not, the human resources personnel run the risk of becoming "the guardians of an outdated culture by reinforcing the behaviors the organization seeks to change."[24]

Managing the Culture Through Hiring Policies

As discussed in Chapter 11, an organization must choose the right people and then train them well if it is to maintain its competitive advantage in the marketplace. When an organization designs its selection strategies specifically to target people with the particular organizational culture in mind, it sometimes calls for a trade-off. For example, certain desired skills may be sacrificed for a better personal fit of the individual to the culture. Technical skills and know-how can be more easily developed than employee characteristics that are deeply embedded in the employee's own personal value system. Chatman and Cha[67] suggest an approach to selection that contrasts with typical approaches to selection by emphasizing a person-culture fit in addition to the person-job fit. Their approach requires anticipating whether the organization's culture will be rewarding for potential recruits.

Finally, Chatman and Cha[67] argue for the need to tailor the selection process to the organizational culture by (a) developing selection criteria that target candidates who best fit the organization's goals and values, (b) benchmarking to make sure the process is effective in attracting and selecting top talent, and (c) targeting "passive applicants." These are the people who are satisfied in their current jobs and are not job hunting but who might be recruited to the organization given the right incentives.

It is interesting that Chatman and Cha[67] warn about the "similarity-attraction effect," which is a fundamental theory in psychology that suggests that we are likely to pick people who are just like us. The message is simple but important: Be careful which people you send out to do your recruiting, because you will get more of them in the company.

Managing Culture Through Socialization and Training

The organization must get its new recruits off to a good start through the socialization process, during which the organization clearly communicates to new hires the fundamental mission and values of the organization, in addition to their own role within that structure. Values and norms are communicated and reinforced through socialization and training, but employees must be allowed to interpret the way the values and norms affect their jobs and responsibilities to ensure their acceptance of the message and indoctrination into the corporate culture. This process helps to align their behavior and expectations with organizational values and norms and allows each employee to become a true member of the organization.

Managing Culture Through Rewards

Culture is, in fact, the organization's informal reward system and needs to be connected to formal ways of rewarding and reinforcing employee behaviors. These rewards need to be clear, consistent, and comprehensive, as well as perfectly in tune with the organization's goals, purpose, and culture.

> *Know your limits, not so that you can honor them, but so that you can smash them to pieces and reach for magnificence.*
>
> —Chérie Charter-Scott

Strategic Application of Leadership Through Culture

For every strategy, there exists a set of core cultures and leadership practices. Chatman and Cha[67] pointed out that "the irony of leadership through culture is that the *less* formal direction you give employees about how to execute strategy, the *more* ownership they take over their actions and the better they perform." This ties in perfectly with the theoretical framework of this book, which links ideas about the strategic application of corporate culture and leadership to enhanced service performance.

A Service Leadership Culture

As introduced in Chapter 1, service leadership is the culture that empowers the organization to strategize its *promises*, design its *processes*, and engage its *people* in a proactive quest for competitive advantage. The concepts of a service leadership culture are based on three assumptions, all of which are grounded in service management theory and extensive research evidence collected in recent years. First, organizations can achieve competitive advantage in service through a collective leadership mind-set based on the strategic application of processes and people to design and deliver the service *promise*. Second, the *process* ensures competitive advantage through the speed and accuracy of the service delivery and enhances an organization's efficiency by maximizing its resources. Third, the *people* ensure competitive advantage through proactive adaptability to change created by innovation, flexibility, and determination to move the organization forward. Organizational cultures can be created and maintained for the strategic purpose of creating a commitment to a cause and aligning employee attitudes and behaviors to that purpose.

A *service leadership culture* is, therefore, a strategy designed to carefully select and design service processes with active participation of customers and employees in the design processes. This strategy is built on collective leadership efforts at every level to fully benefit from an organization's investment in people.

Collective Leadership Mind-set to Serve

Four critical processes have been associated with leadership: (a) setting the mission, (b) actualizing goals, (c) sustaining commitment and cohesion, and (d) adapting to change.[250] As discussed in Chapter 3, our understanding of leadership has been evolving from one of individual power, authority, and influence to a broader concept of leadership as a process, task, and purpose. These new ideas about leadership have pointed out the obvious—one person cannot do it alone in today's complex and fragmented world. These ideas suggest that more power is realized if the leadership phenomenon is regarded not as a title, a person, or a position but as an act or initiative designed to create a positive change. In fact, leadership means that actualizing goals, sustaining commitment, and adapting to change is a part of everyone's job.

The primary responsibility of today's organizational leaders, including all those who *engage in the act of leadership* at every level within an organization, is to help to create and maintain shared values to guide and fine-tune the organizational culture and, hence, its performance. A survey[271] examining the reasons that CEOs fail in their attempts to reach goals revealed that one of the major reasons for their failures is that they have not successfully implemented their strategies. This emphasizes the fact that an alignment of strategy, culture, and leadership is critical for organizational effectiveness. Because organizational culture is the channel through which strategies are implemented, it is crucial for organizational success.[271]

The power realized by simultaneously cultivating the conditions for the formation of a strong culture and actively encouraging organizational members to engage in the act of leadership to protect and preserve the organization can therefore be enormous. Service leadership means that an organization can achieve optimal efficiency without running the risk of undermining service quality or overinvesting in the service delivery by using employees and customers in service process design and in the selection of processes that are standardized, outsourced, offshored, automated, or self-serviced.

When an organization optimizes the speed, accuracy, and efficiency of the delivery system, its resources can be spent on investment in talented people. The company must recruit the best of the best at every level—those possessing core competencies critical to the organization. These treasured employees will be able to build profitable relationships with customers and customize service where needed, hence making the services unique and impossible for competitors to imitate. Only then has the organization truly benefited from its most valuable asset—the service providers.

Application of service leadership culture allows an organization to implement its strategy through its process and its people, resulting in actions designed to bring the organization closer to the customer and farther away from the competitors. We noted earlier in this text that almost 80% of people employed in industrial societies work in services. Fifty years ago, nearly 40% of American citizens earned their living in manufacturing; however, as a result of outsourcing, automation, and globalization, only about 10% of all U.S. workers today are in the manufacturing sector. According to Karmarkar,[176] there are signs that the service industry might be faced with a similar trend. Information from a report made for the World Bank suggests that about 1 of every 10 jobs in the G7 countries (the United States, Canada, Germany, Japan, the United Kingdom, France, and Italy) can now be automated, outsourced, or moved offshore. Because automation and outsourcing can also be used by competitors, those actions do not create a competitive edge per se. However, they can be used strategically to ensure that core functions are accomplished faster or cheaper than before. Each company needs to analyze carefully the degree of complexity of its service offerings, as well as the amount of standardization or customization to which it is able or willing to commit time and resources. As shown in Figure 12.1, the interaction of these elements will help a company decide on the most efficient and cost-effective process to adopt for its service delivery. This allows the organization to focus even further on improving its remaining human resources through selection, continuous learning, and leadership, thus enabling it to build better relationships with customers and be more innovative and more adaptable to change.

The increased role of leadership in an organization calls for a paradigm shift in the way we define and engage in leadership activities. Focusing on the collective leadership mind-set of the entire organization does not mean that the "great leader" concept is dead. Indeed, the paradigm shift from "great man" theories to collective leadership does not mean that one is necessarily better than the other. In fact, collective leadership is but one possibility. Leadership can manifest itself in many different forms at different times. It is also needed in different forms at different times and places.

The conditions under which today's service organizations usually operate call for changes in the way many service organizations have been managed for them to be able to differentiate themselves from their competitors and firmly place themselves in the hearts, minds, and pocketbooks of their customers. The strategy of a service leadership culture is an alternative that has the power to release more power from cumulative leadership acts than is possible with individual leadership.

However, there are obstacles on the road to adopting this approach. First, it requires changes in management roles. Managers have proven to be far more

	Simple Process	**Complex Process**
Customized Service	Automation Self-service End-to-end service Captive offshoring Selective outsourcing	Insourcing, onshoring Deintegration, decoupling Selective automation Selective outsourcing
Standardized Service	Offshoring, outsourcing Globalization One-stop shopping End-to-end service	Captive offshoring In-house automation Selective outsourcing Globalization

Figure 12.1   Dimensions of Service Complexity

SOURCE: From Karmarkar, U. Will you survive the service revolution? in *Harvard Business Review, 82*(6), 2004, reprinted with permission of Harvard Business School Publishing Corporation. All rights reserved.

difficult to change than systems or structures. Second, we still have to consider the financial aspects. There are difficulties in fully comprehending that today's primary currency is not money but highly skilled individuals at all levels of an organization. These people create the monetary value with their attitudes, behaviors, and innovative ideas. Collective leadership ideas are still so new that they are barely understood, and we may not be ready to let go of the comforting idea of the single leader. It is interesting that Raelin[250] has pointed out that we live in a democratic society—which none of us would want to give up. At the same time, most of us have no reservations about working in an authoritarian business world. Perhaps we just have to implement more of the democratic philosophy to achieve the notion of collective leadership in our organizations. This will help our organizations succeed in their quest for competitive advantage in the service arena.

On Rewarding Performance

Gunnar Haugen

Behavioral Psychologist, Deloitte Consulting

"Now why should I reward my employees?" a manager once asked me. "I know it will only bring discontent, and then the ones I'm rewarding will use it to ask for a raise."

"Yes, but . . ." I said, an employee who is rewarded will know what you value in his performance, he will feel appreciated, he is less likely to be looking for another place to work, and he will be more willing to go the extra mile. Any appreciated employee should know that he is valued by the company, and if that individual asks for a raise, it is an opportunity to discuss performance and what needs to be done in order to increase salaries. In addition, it is better to increase the salaries of those who perform rather than to increase everybody's pay regardless of performance. Rewarding employees is something that will allow you to increase productivity and service with relatively little input of effort. However, to reap the benefits of rewards, it is necessary to follow a few simple rules.

For rewards to be effective, they must be

- Timely
- Relevant
- Personal
- Linked to performance

What Are Rewards?

Rewards can be anything; the only requirement a reward has to fulfill is that it is wanted by the recipient. This requires the manager to know a little bit about the individuals he or she wants to reward. For some, tickets to a ballgame may be just the thing, whereas for others the tickets would be unappreciated or even insulting.

Another requirement for rewards is that they should not be something that an individual would necessarily need as a part of his or her daily routine. An effective reward sticks out and is remembered because it is special.

Informal rewards are very efficient in the sense that they allow spontaneity and can be delivered whenever you feel like it. The problem with informal rewards is that they tend to go to those people we like best, not necessarily the ones who deserve them.

Combine Feedback, Goal Setting, and Rewards

A very effective method for using rewards is to combine performance feedback and measures with rewards. That is, reward your people when they meet or exceed goals. By setting realistic goals (and no stretch goals), you will create a culture that considers goals a challenge to be met and conquered.

Key Points

- Rewarding employees is something that will allow you to increase productivity and service with relatively little input of effort.

- A reward can be almost anything, but it must be special to the recipient.

- Reward your people when they meet or exceed goals.

- In today's complex organizations, everybody's performance is linked to everybody else's performance.

Whenever stretch goals are used, the probability that a goal will be achieved is diminished, and prolonged use of stretch goals will most likely train employees to ignore them.

The Many Faces of Rewards

Not every reward needs to be tangible. Many of the best rewards can be comments regarding an employee's performance. When a supervisor, a manager, or a coworker comments positively on somebody's performance, it can be, and often is, taken as a compliment. Compliments work wonders and do not cost anything. For a compliment to be an effective performance enhancer, it needs to be made in relation to job performance. The most effective manner in which to give an enhancing compliment is for the manager to give a short description of the exemplary performance he or she may have seen or heard the employee doing.

Timing Is Everything

Whenever you observe or hear of exemplary performance, you need to use that information as soon as possible. Rewards are most effective when they are delivered close in time after the employee's performance. Whenever a manager decides to reward somebody later, he or she takes the chance of forgetting to do it. Then the employee will perhaps feel unappreciated for super performance, or the employee may botch things up in the meantime.

Do It Often, Do It Small

The act of rewarding someone's performance is a very powerful performance enhancer. The more often it is done, the more effective it is. A reward that fits the recipient does not need to be expensive or tied to a numeric achievement.

Group or Individual?

Use both! Whenever you have the opportunity to reward individual performance, do so. However, achievements are rarely realized by individual performance. In the broadest sense, everybody's performance is linked to everybody else's performance.

What Not to Do

You should never reward somebody to fulfill a quota of rewards or when you do not like the individual. Your heart must be in it. If an employee feels that handing out the reward is a chore for the employer, he or she will not appreciate the reward, no matter how well it has been chosen.

Do not do individual competitions. Competitions are great for sports and athletes and anybody who chooses to compete. However, whenever we use competitions in the workplace, we create winners and losers. Usually there is one winner and scores of losers. The losers will feel underappreciated. If you absolutely need to have a competition, make sure the competition is against a set of standards rather than against other coworkers. That way everybody can win.

Do not use the "but" word. Whenever you reward somebody, you must stick to rewarding. Do not use the occasion to mention a blunder of any sort. If you need to correct your employees, do so when you need to—just make sure you praise them more often than you correct them.

Try to avoid linking the value of a reward to the value of a given performance. Doing so will create inflation and lead to a costly bonus system. There is nothing wrong with linking performance to specific outcomes. In this case, however, we are discussing performance-related pay systems, which should not be confused with a general use of rewards.

Key Concepts

Directions: The following are key concepts presented in this chapter. Write a complete definition for each one.

Organizational culture

Culture of cultivation

Value-driven culture

Service complexity

Questions

1. How is the term *culture* defined? How is the general use of the term *culture*, as it is used in *national culture*, similar to or different from the use of the term in *organizational culture*?

2. Describe two ways in which strong cultures enhance organizational performance.

3. What is the fundamental difference between managerial styles in a culture of control and a culture of competence?

4. What is the fundamental difference between managerial styles in a culture of collaboration and a culture of cultivation?

5. Think about a successful multinational company with which you are familiar. What form of cross-border management style do you think it employs? Use Baron's categories for your discussion. Justify your decision.

6. What is the single most important factor in the success of the most profitable U.S. companies? Why is this factor crucial to the organizations' success?

7. Why are norms more effective than rules in establishing and maintaining a strong corporate culture?

8. What is the role of human resources personnel during cultural change programs? Describe two specific activities these personnel could engage in to help an organization successfully achieve its desired change.

9. How can employee selection and training strengthen an organizational culture?

10. What are the main benefits of the new service leadership paradigm for today's service organizations?

Advanced Activity

Use SWOT analysis to assess the concept of service leadership from a cross-cultural perspective. (a) Assess the major strengths, weaknesses, opportunities, and threats of attempting to implement service leadership in a service company in your own country. (b) Pick another national culture you know or have access to information on and repeat the analysis. Compare the two SWOT analyses and prepare a presentation to share your findings with your class.

Search the Web

Find a case in academic or professional databases, online journals, corporate Web sites, or annual reports that allows you to identify different types of corporate cultures. (a) Identify whether the culture can best be characterized as a *control* culture, *collaboration* culture, *competence* culture, or *cultivation* culture. (b) Use information from your search to provide an argument for your analysis. Use text, pictures, or graphic illustrations to communicate your findings to the class.

Suggested Readings

Baron, A. (1994). Winning ways with culture. *Personnel Management, 26*(10), 64–68.

Chatman, J. A., & Cha, S. E. (2003). Leading by leveraging culture. *California Management Review, 45*(4), 20–32.

Schneider, W. E. (2000). Why good management ideas fail: The neglected power of organizational culture. *Strategy and Leadership, 28*(1), 24–29.

References

1. Actavis. (2004). Corporate fact sheet. Retrieved July 22, 2005, from the Actavis Corporate Web site: http://www.actavis.com/investors/corporatefactsheet.htm
2. Ajzen, I., & Fishbein, M. (1980). *Understanding attitudes and predicting social behaviour.* Englewood Cliffs, NJ: Prentice Hall.
3. Akao, Y. (1990). An introduction to quality function deployment. In Y. Akao (Ed.), *Quality function deployment: Integrating customer requirements into product design* (pp. 1-24). Cambridge, MA: Productivity Press.
4. Alinsky, S. D. (1969). *Reveille for radicals.* New York: Vintage Books.
5. Allen, N. J., & Meyer, J. P. (1990). The measurement and antecedents of affective, continuance and normative commitment to the organisation. *Journal of Occupational Psychology, 63*(1), 1–18.
6. American Customer Satisfaction Index. (2005). *The American Customer Satisfaction Index at ten years.* Ann Arbor: Stephen M. Ross School of Business, University of Michigan.
7. Anderson, E. W., Fornell, C., & Lehmann, D. R. (1994). Customer satisfaction, market share, and profitability: Findings from Sweden. *Journal of Marketing, 58,* 53–66.
8. Anderson, E. W., & Mittal, V. (2000). Strengthening the satisfaction-profit chain. *Journal of Service Research, 3*(2), 107–120.
9. Andrew, J. (2001). *Value mapping: A second generation performance measurement and performance management solution.* Aberdeen, UK: Business Excellence International.
10. Andrews, K. R. (1996). *The concept of corporate strategy.* In H. Mintzberg & J. B. Quinn (Eds.), *The strategy process: Concepts, context, cases.* Englewood Cliffs, NJ: Prentice Hall. Chap. 4, a, p. 47.
11. Ansoff, H. I. (1965). *Corporate strategy.* New York: McGraw-Hill.
12. Appelbaum, S. H., Hébert, D., & Leroux, S. (1999). Empowerment: Power, culture and leadership—a strategy or fad for the millennium? *Journal of Workplace Learning, 11*(7), 233–254. Chap. 3, p. 243
13. Appelbaum, S. H., & Honeggar, K. (1998). Empowerment: A contrasting overview of organizations in general and nursing in particular—an examination of organizational factors, managerial behaviors, job design and structural power. *Empowerment in Organizations, 6*(2), 29–50.
14. Ariely, D., & Carmon, Z. (2000). Gestalt characteristics of experiences: The defining features of summarized events. *Journal of Behavioral Decision Making, 13,* 191–201.
15. Armistead, C. G., & Clark, G. (1994). Service quality and service recovery: The role of capacity management. In C. G. Armistead (Ed.), *The future of service management* (pp. 27–39). London: Kogan Page.

16. Arthur M. Blank, chairman. (n.d.). Retrieved July 19, 2005, from the Arthur M. Blank Family Foundation Web site: http://www.blankfoundation.org/about/bio_arthur blank.html

17. Asgeirsdottir, A. G. (2004). *Leadership style: Leaders believe in their own management ability and workers' attitude towards their job and work environment.* Reykjavik: University of Iceland, Faculty of Economics and Business Administration.

18. Bach, C. L. (2001, April). U.S. international transactions, fourth quarter and year 2000. *Survey of Current Business,* 21–68.

19. Baker, K. A. (2002). Chapter 11: Organizational culture. Retrieved June 14, 2005, from http://64.233.187.104/search?q=cache:nK0XTYAqX4QJ:www.science.doe.gov/sc-5/benchmark/Ch%252011%2520Organizational%2520Culture%252006.08.02.pdf+%2Bbaker+%2B%22organizational+culture%22&hl=en

20. Balanced scorecard method. (2004). Retrieved June 20, 2005, from http://www.valuebasedmanagement.net/methods_balancedscorecard.html

21. Barker, J. R. (1993). Tightening the iron cage: Conceptive control in self-managing teams. *Administrative Science Quarterly, 38,* 408–437.

22. Barling, J., Weber, T., & Kelloway, E. K. (1996). Effects of transformational leadership training on attitudinal and financial outcomes. *Journal of Applied Psychology, 81*(6), 827–832.

23. Barney, J. (1991). Firm resources and sustained competitive advantage. *Journal of Management, 17*(1), 99–120.

24. Baron, A. (1994). Winning ways with culture. *Personnel Management, 26*(10), 64–68.

25. Baron, A. (1995, September 21). Going public with studies on culture management. *People Management, 1*(19), 60.

26. Bartlett, C. A., & Ghoshal, S. (2002, Winter). Building competitive advantage through people. *MIT Sloan Management Review, 43*(2), 34–41.

27. Bass, B. M. (1985). *Leadership and performance beyond expectations.* New York: Free Press.

28. Bass, B. M. (1990). *Bass and Stogdill's handbook of leadership: Theory, research, and managerial applications.* New York: Free Press.

29. Bass, B. M. (1997). Does the transactional-transformational paradigm transcend organizational and national boundaries? *American Psychologist, 22*(2), 130–142.

30. Bass, B. M., & Avolio, B. J. (1989). *The multifaceted leadership questionnaire.* Palo Alto, CA: Consulting Psychologists Press.

31. Bateman, T. S., & Organ, D. W. (1983). Job satisfaction and the good soldier: The relationship between affect and citizenship. *Academy of Management Journal, 26,* 587–595.

32. Bateson, J. (1985). Perceived control and the service encounters. In J. A. Czepiel, M. R. Solomon, & C. F. Surprenant (Eds.), *The service encounter* (pp. 67–82). Lexington, MA: Lexington Books.

33. Beinteinsson, G. Á., & Eiriksson, E. (2002). *International marketing and management.* Copenhagen, Denmark: Copenhagen Business School. Chap. 4, a, p. 31, b, p. 25, c, p. 28.

34. Bell, C. R., & Zemke, R. E. (1987, October). Service breakdown: The road to recovery. *Management Review, 76*(10), 32–35.

35. Bennis, W. (1989). *On becoming a leader.* New York: Addison-Wesley.

36. Bennis, W., & Nanus, B. (1985). *Leaders: The strategies for taking charge.* New York: Harper & Row.

37. Bentz, V. J. (1990). Contextual issues in predicting high-level leadership performance: Contextual richness is a criterion consideration in personality research with executives. In K. E. Clark & M. B. Clark (Eds.), *Measures of leadership* (pp. 131–143). West Orange, NJ: Leadership Library of America.

38. Bernard, L. L. (1926). *An introduction to social psychology.* New York: Holt.

39. Berry, L. L. (1995). *On great service: A framework for action.* New York: Free Press.

40. Berry, L. L. (1999). *Discovering the soul of service: The nine drivers of sustainable business success.* New York: Free Press. Chap. 10, a, p. 40, b, p. 21; chap. 11, a, p. 181.

41. Berry, L. L., & Lamp, S. K. (2000). Teaching an old service new tricks: The promise of service redesign. *Journal of Service Research, 2*(3), 265–275.

42. Bitner, M. J., Booms, B. H., & Tetrault, M. S. (1990, January). The service encounter: Diagnosing favorable and unfavorable incidents. *Journal of Marketing, 54,* 71–84.

43. Boam, R., & Sparrow, P. (1992). *Designing and achieving competency.* New York: McGraw-Hill.

44. Booz, Allen & Hamilton, Inc. (1982). *New products management for the 1980s.* New York: Author.

45. Boshoff, C., & Allen, J. (2000). The influence of selected antecedents on frontline staff's perceptions of service recovery performance. *International Journal of Service Industry Management, 11*(1), 63–90.

46. Bowen, D. E., & Lawler, E. E., III. (1992). The empowerment of service workers: What, why, how, and when. *Sloan Management Review, 33*(3), 31–39.

47. Bowen, D. E., Siehl, C., & Schneider, B. (1989). A framework for analyzing customer service orientations in manufacturing. *Academy of Management Review, 11,* 710–725.

48. Bowers, D. G., & Seashore, S. E. (1966). Predicting organizational effectiveness with a four-factor theory of leadership. *Administrative Science Quarterly, 11,* 238–263.

49. Boyte, H. C., & Riessman, B. (1986). *The new populism: The politics of empowerment.* Philadelphia, PA: Temple University Press.

50. Brief, A. P., & Motowidlo, S. J. (1986). Prosocial organizational behaviors. *Academy of Management Review, 11,* 710–725.

51. Brown, D. (1992). Why participative management won't work here. *Management Review, 81*(6), 42–46.

52. Brown, S. L., & Eisenhardt, K. M. (1998). *Competing On The Edge.* Boston, MA: Harvard Business School Press.

53. Bryant, B. E. (1995, May). Customer satisfaction by industry among demographic and socioeconomic groups (Working paper no. 9590-08). Retrieved July 22, 2005, from the University of Michigan School of Business Administration Web site: http://www.hti .umich.edu/cgi/t/text/text-idx?sid=afba80ee1d2665a4e4ea2f6ca12aabd2;c=busadwp; view=text;rgn=main;idno=b1793901.0001.001

54. Bryman, A. (1993). Charismatic leadership in business organizations: Some neglected issues. *Leadership Quarterly, 4,* 531–539. Chap. 3, p. 439.

55. Bujold, L. M. (1999). *A civil campaign: A comedy of biology and manners.* Riverdale, NY: Baen Books.

56. Burns, J. M. (1978). *Leadership.* New York: Harper & Row.

57. Cameron, K. S., & Quinn, R. E. (1999). *Diagnosing and changing organizational culture: Based on the competing values framework.* Reading, MA: Addison-Wesley. Chap. 12, a, p. 4.

58. Campbell, D. T., & Stanley, J. C. (1966). *Experimental and quasi-experimental designs for research.* Chicago: Rand McNally.

59. Campbell, A., & Yeung, S. (1991). *Long range planning.* Oxford, England: Pergamon Press.

60. Center for Army Leadership, Department of the Army. (2004). *The U.S. Army leadership field manual.* Columbus, OH: McGraw-Hill.

61. Center for Creative Leadership. (2004). [Home page]. Retrieved June 23, 2005, from http://www.ccl.org

62. Chaffee, E. E. (1985). Three models of strategy. *Academy of Management Review, 10*(1), 89–98.

63. Chandler, A. D. (1962). *Strategy and structure: Chapters in the history of the industrial enterprise.* Cambridge: MIT Press.

64. Charan, R., & Colvin, G. (1999). Why CEOs fail. *Fortune, 139*(12), 68–75.

65. Chase, R. B., & Haynes, R. (2000). Service quality in the service delivery system: A diagnostic framework. In S. Brown, E. Gummensson, B. Edvardsson, & B. Gustavsson (Eds.), *Service quality: Multidisciplinary and multinational perspectives.* Lexington, MA: Lexington Books.

66. Chase, R. B., & Stewart, D. M. (1994, Spring). Make your service fail-safe. *Sloan Management Review, 35*(3), 35–44.

67. Chatman, J. A., & Cha, S. E. (2003). Leading by leveraging culture. *California Management Review, 45*(4), 20–34.

68. Clampitt, P. G. (1991). *Communicating for managerial effectiveness.* Newbury Park, CA: Sage.

69. Coffman, C., & Gonzalez-Molina, G. (2002). *Follow this path: How the world's greatest organizations drive growth by unleashing human potential.* New York: Warner Books.

70. Cohen, A. R. (1993). *The portable MBA in management.* New York: John Wiley.

71. Collier, F., Fishwick, F., & Floyd, S. (2003). Managerial involvement and perceptions of strategy process. *Long Range Planning, 36,* 67–83.

72. Conger, J., & Benjamin, B. (1999). *Building leaders: How successful companies develop the next generation.* New York: Free Press.

73. Conger, J. A., & Kanungo, R. N. (1988). The empowerment process: Integrating theory and practice. *Academy of Management Review, 13*(3), 471–482.

74. Cook, J. (1997). *The book of positive quotations.* Minneapolis, MN: Fairview Press.

75. Cook, J., & Wall, T. (1980). New York attitude measures of trust, organizational commitment and personal need non-fulfillment. *Journal of Occupational Psychology, 53,* 39–52.

76. Cook, L. S., Bowen, D. E., Chase, R. B., Dasu, S., Stewart, D. M., & Tansik, D. A. (2002). Human issues in service design. *Journal of Operations Management, 20,* 159–174.

77. Coombs, W. T. (1995). Choosing the right words: The development of guidelines for the selection of the "appropriate" crisis-response strategies. *Management Communication Quarterly, 8*(4), 447–476.

78. Coombs, W. T. (1999). *Ongoing crisis communication: Planning, managing, and responding.* Thousand Oaks, CA: Sage.

79. Cullen, D., & Townley, B. (1994). *Autonomy and empowerment: New wine in old bottles.* Paper presented at the Annual Meeting of the Western Academy of Management, Santa Fe, NM.

80. Darling, M. (1996, June/July). Empowerment: Myth or reality? *Executive Speeches, 10*(6), 23–28.

81. Data and text mining. (2005). Retrieved July 22, 2005, from the SAS Institute Web site: http://www.sas.com/technologies/analytics/datamining/index.html

82. Davis, S. M. (1987). *Future perfect.* New York: Addison-Wesley.

83. Day, D. V. (2001). Leadership development: A review in context. *Leadership Quarterly, 11*(4), 581–613.

84. Dean, J. W., Jr., & Bowen, D. E. (1994). Management theory and total quality: Improving research and practice through theory development. *Academy of Management Review, 19*(3), 392–401.

85. Deming, W. E. (1982). *Quality, productivity and competitive position.* Cambridge: MIT Press.

86. Deming, W. E. (1986). *Out of crisis.* Cambridge: MIT Press.

87. Drath, W. H., & Palus, C. J. (1994). *Making common sense: Leadership as meaning-making in a community of practice.* Greensboro, NC: Center for Creative Leadership.

88. Dyer, J. H., & Singh, H. (1998). The relational view: Cooperative strategy and sources of interorganizational competitive advantage. *Academy of Management Review, 23*(4), 660–679.

89. Eagleson, G. (1996). *Notes for the Workshop on Leadership Development.* Unpublished manuscript, Australian Graduate School of Management, Sidney.

90. Edvardsson, B. (1998). Service quality improvement. *Managing Service Quality, 8*(2), 142–150.

91. Edvardsson, B., Johnson, M. D., Gustafsson, A., & Strandvik, T. (2002). The effects of satisfaction and loyalty on profits and growth: Products versus services. In J. W. Cortada & J. A. Woods (Eds.), *The quality yearbook: 2002 edition* (pp. 116–129). New York: McGraw Hill.

92. Eisenberg, E. M., & Goodall, H. L., Jr. (2004). *Organizational communication: Balancing creativity and constraint.* Boston: Bedford/St. Martin's. Chap. 10, a, p. 209.

93. Eisenberg, E., & Riley, P. (1991). *A closed-loop model of communication, empowerment, urgency and performance.* Unpublished paper, University of Southern California, Los Angeles.

94. Everard, R. (1996). So what is strategy? In H. Mintzberg & J. B. Quinn (Eds.), *The strategy process: Concepts, context, cases.* Englewood Cliffs, NJ: Prentice Hall. Chap. 4, p. 11.

95. Fiedler, F. E. (1996). Research on leadership selection and training: One view of the future. *Administrative Science Quarterly, 41*(2), 241–250.

96. Fitzsimmons, J. A., & Fitzsimmons, M. J. (1994). *Service management: Operations, strategy and information technology* (2nd ed.). Boston: Irwin McGraw-Hill.

97. Fornell, C. (2000, May). Customer satisfaction: Is the free market working? Retrieved July 4, 2005, from http://www.theacsi.com/related_research.htm#web

98. Fornell, C., Johnson, M. D., Anderson, E. W., Cha, J., & Bryant, B. E. (1996). The American Customer Satisfaction Index: Nature, purpose, and findings. *Journal of Marketing, 60*(4), 7–18.

99. Freire, P. (1992). *Pedagogy of the oppressed.* New York: Continuum Press.

100. Fryer, B. (2001, March). High tech the old fashioned way. *Harvard Business Review, 79*(3), 119–125.

101. Gabbard, C. E., Howard, G. S., & Dunfee, E. J. (1986). Reliability, sensitivity to measuring change, and construct validity of therapist adaptability. *Counseling Psychology, 33*, 377–386.

102. Gallup Organization. (2002a, September 26). The four disciplines of sustainable growth: The critical elements of a performance management system. Gallup Management Journal. Retrieved July 22, 2005, from the Gallup Organization Web site: http://gmj.gallup.com/content/default.asp?ci=442

103. Gallup Organization. (2002b). The Gallup path. Retrieved July 12, 2005, from the Gallup Organization Web site: http://www.gallup.com/content/default.aspx?ci=1528

104. Gallup Organizaton. (2005). [Home page]. Retrieved July 12, 2005, from http://www.gallup.com

105. Gandz, J. (1990). The employee empowerment era. *Business Quarterly, 55*(2), 74–79.

106. Gardner, J. W. (1990). *On leadership.* New York: Free Press. Chap. 3, p. 38.

107. George, J. M. (1991). State or trait: Effects of positive mood on prosocial behavior, sales performance, and turnover: A group-level analysis in service context. *Journal of Applied Psychology, 76*(2), 299–307.

108. George, J. M., & Brief, A. P. (1992). Feeling good—doing good: A conceptual analysis of the mood at work—organizational spontaneity relationship. *Psychological Bulletin, 112*(2), 310–329.

109. Godbout, A. J. (2000). Managing core competencies: The impact of knowledge management on human resource practice in leading-edge organizations. *Knowledge and Process Management, 7*(2), 237–247.

110. Godin, G., Jobin, J., & Bouillon, J. (1986). Assessment of leisure time exercise behavior by self-report: A concurrent validity study. *Canadian Journal of Public Health, 77,* 359–362.

111. Goldstein, S. M., Johnston, R., Duffy, J., & Rao, J. (2002). The service concept: The missing link in service design research. *Journal of Operations Management, 20,* 121–134.

112. Goodman, P. S., Fichman, M., Lerch, F. J., & Snyder, P. R. (1995). Customer-firm relationships, involvement and customer satisfaction. *Academy of Management Journal, 38*(5), 1310–1324.

113. Goold, M., & Campbell, A. (2004). *Parenting in complex structures.* Oxford, England: Basil Blackwell.

114. Goshal, S., Bartlett, C. A., & Moran, P. (2001). A new manifesto for management. In M. A. Cusumano & C. C. Markides (Eds.), *Strategic thinking for the next economy.* San Francisco: Jossey-Bass.

115. Graham, J. W. (1991). An essay on organizational citizenship behavior. *Employee Responsibilities and Rights Journal, 4,* 249–270.

116. Greene, J. (2003, June). A pebble at a time. *Hospitals and Health Networks, 77*(6).

117. Grönfeldt, S. (2000). *The nature, impact and development of customer oriented behaviour.* London: London School of Economics.

118. Grönfeldt, S. (2003a). *Customer oriented behavior: The nature, impact and development.* Reykjavik: University of Iceland, Faculty of Economics and Business Administration.

119. Grönfeldt, S. (2003b). *Tjonustuhegdun: Rannsokn a edli, ahrifum og troun [Service orientation: Research on antecedents, impact, and development]* (Working paper). Reykjavík: University of Iceland, Faculty of Economics and Business Administration.

120. Grönfeldt, S. (2004). *Customer oriented behaviour: Nature, impact and development.* Reykjavik: University of Iceland.

121. Grönroos, C. (1982). A service quality model and its management implication (Handout). Swedish School of Economics and Business Administration, Helsinki, Finland.

122. Gustafsson, A., & Johnson, M. D. (2003). *Competing in service economy: How to create a competitive advantage through service development and innovation.* San Francisco: John Wiley. Chap. 4, a, p. 13, b, p. 12.

123. Hackman, J. R. (1986). The psychology of self-management in organizations. In M. S. Pallack & R. O. Perloff (Eds.), *Psychology and work: Productivity, change, and employment* (pp. 89–136). Washington, DC: American Psychological Association.

124. Hackman, J. R., & Wageman, R. (1995). Total quality management: Empirical, conceptual, and practical issues. *Administrative Science Quarterly, 40*(2), 309–327.

125. Haksever, C., Render, B., Russell, R. S., & Murdick, R. G. (2000). *Service management and operations* (2nd ed.). Upper Saddle River, NJ: Prentice Hall. Chap. 2, p. 1; chap. 6, a, p. 187.

126. Halpin, A. W., & Winer, B. J. (1957). A factorial study of the leader behavior descriptions. In R. M. Stogdill & A. E. Coons (Eds.), *Leader behavior: Its description and measurement* (pp. 39–51). Columbus: Ohio State University College of Commerce and Administration, Bureau of Business Research.

127. Hamel, G., & Prahalad, C. K. (1989, May-June). Strategic intent. *Harvard Business Review, 67*(3), 63–76.

128. Hamel, G., & Prahalad, C. K. (1990). The core competence of the corporation. *Harvard Business Review, 68*(9), 79–91.

129. Hancock, M. D., Logue, J., & Schiller, B. (1991). *Managing modern capitalism: Industrial renewal and workplace democracy in the United States and Western Europe.* New York: Praeger.

130. Hardy, C., & Leiba-O'Sullivan, S. (1998). The power behind empowerment: Implications for research and practice. *Human Relations, 51*(4), 451–483.

131. Harrison, C. (2000, April). Turning customer service inside out! How poor internal customer service negatively impacts external customers. Retrieved July 22, 2005, from http://www.craigspeaks.com/InsideCS.html

132. Harrison, T. (1985). Communication and participative decision-making: An exploratory study. *Personnel Psychology, 38*, 93–116.

133. Hart, C. W. L., Heskett, J. L., & Sasser, W. E., Jr. (1990, July-August). The profitable art of service recovery. *Harvard Business Review, 68*, 148–156.

134. Haskins, W. A. (1996). Freedom of speech: Construct for creating a culture which empowers organizational members. *Journal of Business Communications, 33*, 85–97.

135. Hatch, M. J. (1997). *Organizational theory.* New York: Oxford University Press.

136. Heifetz, R. A., & Linsky, M. (2002, Fall). Leading with an open heart. *Leader to Leader, 26*, 28–33. Retrieved July 22, 2005, from the Leader to Leader Institute Web site: http://leadertoleader.org/leaderbooks/l2l/fall2002/heifetz.html

137. Heifetz, R. A., & Linsky, M. (2004, April). When leadership spells danger. *Educational Leadership, 61*(7), 33–37. Retrieved July 25, 2005, from http://www.ascd.org/authors/ed_lead/el200404_heifetz.html

138. Hemphill, J. K., & Coons, A. E. (1957). Development of the leader behavior description questionnaire. In R. M. Stogdill & A. E. Coons (Eds.), *Leader behavior: Its description and measurement* (pp. 6–38). Columbus: Ohio State University College of Commerce and Administration, Bureau of Business Research.

139. Henard, D., & Szymanski, D. M. (2001, August). Why some new products are more successful than others. *Journal of Marketing Research, 38*, 362–375.

140. Heskett, J. L. (1986). *Managing in the service economy.* Boston: Harvard Business School Press.

141. Heskett, J. L., Jones, T. O., Loveman, G. W., Sasser, L. W., Jr., & Schlesinger, L. A. (1994, March-April). Putting the service-profit chain to work. *Harvard Business Review, 72*(1), 164–174.

142. Heskett, J. L., Jones, T. O., Loveman, G. W., Sasser, L. W., Jr., & Schlesinger, L. A. (1997). *The service profit chain: How leading companies link profit and growth to loyalty, satisfaction, and value.* New York: Free Press.

143. Heskett, J. L., Sasser, W. E., Jr., & Schlesinger, L. A. (2003). *The value profit chain: Treat employees like customers and customers like employees.* New York: Free Press.

144. Hewson, W., Meekings, A., & Russell, C. (2003). *Beyond philanthropy: How improved service contributes to efficiency and profitability.* Retrieved June 13, 2005, from http://64.233.179.104/search?q=cache:qqQahoXYhgMJ:webdesign.ittoolbox.com/browse.asp%3Fc%3DDWDPeerPublishing%26r%3D%252Fpub%252FSF070903.pdf+%2Bhewson+%2Bmeekings+%2B%22beyond+philanthropy%22&hl=en

145. Hill, G. (2004, October 26). You've got new customers. Now what do you do? *Customer Think Advisor.* Retrieved July 19, 2005, from the CRMguru.com Web site: http://crmguru.custhelp.com/cgi-bin/crmguru.cfg/php/enduser/std_adp.php?p_faqid=1382&p_created=1098810060&p_sid=cvNNASKh&p_lva=&p_sp=cF9zcmNoPTEmcF9zb3J0X2J5PSZwX2dyaWRzb3J0PSZwX3Jvd19jbnQ9MTEwOCZwX3Byb2RzPSZwX2NhdHM9Jn

BfcHY9JnBfY3Y9JnBfcGFnZT0xJnBfc2VhcmNoX3RleHQ9IllvdSd2ZSBHb3QgQ3V zdG9tZXJzLiI*&p_li=&p_topview=1

146. Hill, S., & Wilkinson, A. (1995). In search of TQM. *Employment Relations, 17*(3), 8–26.

147. Hodge, T. K. (2002). *Linking learning and performance: A practical guide to measuring learning and on-the-job application.* Boston: Butterworth-Heinemann.

148. Hogan, R. T., Curphy, G. J., & Hogan, J. (1994). What do we know about personality: Leadership and effectiveness? *American Psychologist, 49,* 493–504.

149. Home improvement store chain: Employee engagement and customer loyalty. (2005). Retrieved July 22, 2005, from the Gallup Organization Web site: http://gallup.com/content/?ci=1480&pg=1

150. Honold, L. (1997). A review of the literature on employee empowerment. *Empowerment in Organizations, 5*(4), 202–212.

151. Horner, M. (1997). Leadership theory: Past, present and future. *Team Performance Management, 3*(4), 270-287. Chap. 3, a & b, p. 270, c, p. 271.

152. House, R. J. (1977). A 1976 theory of charismatic leadership. In J. G. Hunt & L. L. Larson (Eds.), *Leadership: The cutting edge* (pp. 189–207). Carbondale: Southern Illinois University Press.

153. House, R. J., & Aditya, R. N. (1997). The social scientific study of leadership: Quo vadis? *Journal of Management, 23*(2), 409-473. Chap. 3, a, p. 410, b, p. 429, c, p. 410.

154. Howard, G. S. (1994). Why do people say nasty things about self-reports? *Journal of Organizational Behavior, 15,* 299–404.

155. Howardell, D. (2003). How to improve customer service. Retrieved July 23, 2004, from the ACA Group Web site: http://www.theacagroup.com/customerservice.htm

156. Huck, S. W., & Cormier, W. (1996). *Reading statistics and research.* New York: Harper Collins.

157. Hughes, R. L., Ginnett, R. C., & Curphy, G. J. (2002). *Leadership: Enhancing the lessons of experience.* New York: McGraw-Hill. Chap. 4, a, p. 78, b, p. 40.

158. Hutton, P. (2004, May 14). How to focus on the customer and keep shareholders happy. Retrieved July 25, 2005, from the MORI Web site: http://www.mori.com/pubinfo/pfh/how-to-focus-on-the-customer.pdf

159. Ishikawa, K. (1985). *What is total quality control? The Japanese way.* Englewood Cliffs, NJ: Prentice Hall.

160. Íslenska ánægjuvogin kynnt [The Icelandic Customer Satisfaction Survey introduced]. (2004, March 24). Retrieved July 22, 2005, from the IMG Web site: http://img.is/index.jsp

161. Ittner, C. D., & Larcker, D. F. (1996). Measuring the impact of quality initiatives on firm financial performance. In S. Ghosh & D. Fedor (Eds.), *Advances in the management of organizational quality* (Vol. 1, pp. 1–37). Greenwich, CT: JAI Press.

162. Jablin, F. (1979). Superior-subordinate communication: The state of the art. *Psychological Bulletin, 86,* 1201–1222.

163. Jack, A. (2004). Value mapping—A second generation performance measurement and performance management solution. Retrieved June 20, 2005, from http://www.valuebasedmanagement.net/articles_jack_value_mapping_second_generation_performance_management.pdf

164. Jeffrey P. Bezos. (2005, March 6). Retrieved July 15, 2005, from the Academy of Achievement Web site: http://www.achievement.org/autodoc/page/bez0bio-1

165. Johnson, M. D., Herrmann, A., & Gustafsson, A. (2000). *Customer satisfaction over industries, countries and time* (Working paper). Ann Arbor: Ross Business School, University of Michigan.

166. Johnson, R. D., & Thurston, E. K. (1997). Achieving empowerment using the empowerment strategy grid. *Leadership and Organization Development Journal, 18*(2), 64–73.

167. Johnston, R. (1995). The zone of tolerance: Exploring the relationship between service transactions and satisfaction with the overall service. *International Journal of Service Industry Management, 6*(2), 46–61.

168. Johnston, R. (1999). Service transaction analysis: Assessing and improving customers' experience. *Managing Service Quality, 9*(2), 102–109.

169. Johnston, R., & Fern, A. (1999). Service recovery strategies for single and double deviation scenarios. *Service Industries Journal, 19*(2), 69–82.

170. Jones, M. (2004, May/June). Facility of the month: Circle of life. *Healthcare Construction & Operations.*

171. Juran, J. A. M. (1989). *Juran on leadership for quality.* New York: Free Press.

172. Kahneman, D., Fredrickson, B. L., Schreiber, C. A., & Redelmeier, D. A. (1993). When more pain is preferred to less: Adding a better end. *Psychological Science, 4*(6), 401–405.

173. Kanter, R. M. (1968). Commitment and social organization: A study of commitment mechanisms in utopian communities. *American Sociological Review, 33,* 499–517.

174. Kaplan, R. S., & Norton, D. P. (2001). *The strategy-focused organization: How balanced scorecard companies thrive in the new business environment.* Boston: Harvard Business School Press.

175. Karlsson, T. (2003). Surveys: Construction, phrasing and drawbacks. In S. Halldórsdóttir & K. Kristjánsson (Eds.), *Handbook in methodology for research in health sciences.* Akureyri, Iceland: University of Akureyri.

176. Karmarkar, U. (2004). Will you survive the service revolution? *Harvard Business Review, 82*(6), 100–110.

177. Katz, D., & Kahn, R. L. (1978). *The social psychology of organizations.* New York: John Wiley.

178. Kelley, S. W. (1993, Spring). Discretion and the service employee. *Journal of Retailing, 69,* 104–126.

179. Kelley, S. W., & Davis, M. A. (1994). Antecedents to customer expectations for service recovery. *Journal of the Academy of Marketing Science, 22*(1), 52–61.

180. Kingman-Brundage, J. (1989). The ABC's of service system blueprinting. In M. J. Bitner & L. A. Crosby (Eds.), *Designing a winning service strategy* (pp. 30–33). Chicago: American Marketing Association.

181. Kingman-Brundage, J. (1991). Technology, design and service quality. *International Journal of Service Industries Management, 2*(3), 47–59.

182. Kirkpatrick, D. (1979). Techniques for evaluating training programs. *Training and Development Journal, 33*(6), 78–92.

183. Klaus, P. (1985). Quality epiphenomenon: The conceptual understanding of quality in face-to-face service encounters. In J. Czepiel, M. Solomon, & C. Surprenant (Eds.), *The service encounter: Managing employee/customer interaction in service businesses.* Lexington, MA: Lexington Books.

184. Koene, H., Pennings, H., & Schreuder, M. (1993). Leadership, culture, and organizational effectiveness. In K. E. Clark & M. B. Clark (Eds.), *The impact of leadership* (pp. 215–223). Greensboro, NC: Center for Creative Leadership.

185. Koh, W. L., Terborg, J. R., & Steers, R. M. (1991). *The impact of transformational leadership on organizational commitment: Organizational citizenship behavior, teacher satisfaction and student performance in Singapore.* Paper presented at the meeting of the Academy of Management, Fontainebleau, FL.

186. Kotter, J. P., & Heskett, J. L. (1992). *Corporate culture and performance.* New York: Free Press.

187. Kouzes, J. M., & Posner, B. Z. (1993). *Credibility: How leaders gain and lose it, why people demand it.* San Francisco: Jossey-Bass. Chap. 10, p. 21.

188. Krebs, D. L., & Miller, D. T. (1985). Altruism and aggression. In G. Lindzey & E. Aronson (Eds.), *Handbook of social psychology: Special fields and applications* (Vol. 2, pp. 1–71). New York: Random House.

189. Langeard, E., Reffiat, P., & Eiglier, P. (1986). Developing new services. In M. Venkatesan, D. M. Schmalennee, & C. Marshall (Eds.), *Creativity in services marketing: What is new, what works, what is developing?* Chicago: American Marketing Association.

190. Legge, K. (1995). *Human resource management: Rhetorics and realities.* London: MacMillan.

191. Levitt, B., & March, J. G. (1988). Organizational learning. *Annual Review of Sociology, 14,* 319–340.

192. Levitt, T. (1972). Production line approach to service. *Harvard Business Review, 60*(5), 41–52.

193. Lichtenstein, N., & Howell, J. H. (1993). *Industrial democracy in America.* Cambridge, England: Cambridge University Press.

194. Linsky, M. (2004, October 1). *Why CEOs don't always lead, or why CEOs do not exercise leadership more often.* Cambridge, MA: Cambridge Leadership Associates. Retrieved July 25, 2005, from http://www.cambridge-leadership.com/images/WhyCEO%27s Don%27tAlwaysLead.pdf. Chap. 3, p. 1.

195. Linsky, M., & Heifetz, R. (2003). *Leadership on the line.* Boston: Harvard University Press.

196. Louis, M. (1980). Surprise and sensemaking: What newcomers experience in entering unfamiliar organizational settings. *Administrative Science Quarterly, 25,* 226–251.

197. Lucas, R. W. (2002). *Customer service: Skills and concepts for success* (2nd ed.). New York: Glencoe McGraw-Hill.

198. Mahmoud, S., Lazarus, H., & Cullen, J. (1992). Developing self-managing teams: Structure and performance. *Journal of Management Development, 11*(3), 34–43.

199. Manz, C. C., & Sims, H. P., Jr. (1991). SuperLeadership: Beyond the myth of heroic leadership. *Organizational Dynamics, 19,* 18–35. Chap. 3, a, p. 18.

200. Martin, J. E., Dubbert, P. M., Katell, A. D., Thompson, K., Raeynski, J. R., Lake, M., et al. (1984). Behavioral control of exercise in sedentary adults: Studies 1 through 6. *Journal of Consulting Clinical Psychology, 52,* 795–811.

201. Masie, E. (2004, September 30–October 1). *Leadership, learning, knowledge and technology.* Keynote session presented at the Friends of the Center Leadership Conference, Jersey City, NJ.

202. Mathieu, J. E., & Zajac, D. M. (1990). A review and meta-analysis of the antecedents, correlates, and consequences of organizational commitment. *Psychological Bulletin, 108*(2), 171–194.

203. McCollough, M. A., & Bharadwaj, S. G. (1992). The recovery paradox: An examination of customer satisfaction in relation to disconfirmation, service quality, and attribution based theories. In C. T. Allen (Ed.), *Marketing theory and application.* Chicago: American Marketing Association.

204. McDonald, D. (2004, May 6). Roll out the blue carpet: How Ritz-Carlton can teach you to serve your customers better. *Business 2.0.* Retrieved July 22, 2005, from the CNNMoney Web site: http://money.cnn.com/2004/05/06/technology/business2_ritz-carlton/

205. McGill, M. E., & Slocum, J. W., Jr. (1998). A little leadership, please? *Organizational Dynamics, 26*(3), 39–49.

206. Menor, L. J., Tatikonda, M. V., & Sampson, S. E. (2002). New service development: Areas for exploitation and exploration. *Journal of Operations Management, 20,* 135–157.

207. Messmer, M. (1990). How to put employee empowerment into practice. *The Woman CPA, 52*(3), 25.

208. Michael, S. (2001). Analyzing service failures and recoveries: A process approach. *International Journal of Service Industry Management, 12*(1), 20–28.

209. Milkovich, G. T., & Boudreau, J. W. (1997). *Human resource management.* Chicago: Times Mirror Higher Education Group.

210. Mills, P. (1986). *Managing service industries.* Cambridge, MA: Ballinger.

211. Mintzberg, H. (1987, Fall). The strategy concept II: Another look at why organizations need strategies. *California Management Review, 30*(1), 25–32.

212. Mintzberg, H. (1999, Spring). Reflecting on strategy process. *Sloan Management Review, 40*(3), 21–30.

213. Mintzberg, H., & Quinn, J. B. (1996). *The strategy process: Concepts, context, cases* (3rd ed.). Englewood Cliffs, NJ: Prentice-Hall. Chap. 4, a, p. 4, b, p. 5, c, p. 14.

214. "Model" employees rewarded for outstanding customer service. (2004, February 9). Retrieved June 17, 2005, from the Roke Manor Research Web site: http://www.roke.co .uk/news/article.asp?id=66

215. Mowday, R. T., Porter, L. W., & Steers, R. M. (1982). *Employee-organizational linkages: The psychology of commitment, absenteeism, and turnover.* New York: Academic Press.

216. Mullins, L. J. (1996). *Management and organizational behaviour.* London: Pittman.

217. Naisbitt, J. (1982). *Megatrends.* New York: Warner.

218. Normann, R. (2002). *Service management: Strategy and leadership in service business.* Chichester, West Sussex: John Wiley. Chap. 2, a, p. 19, b, p. 8, c, p. 14, d, p. 15, e, p. 7, f, p. 2.

219. Nunnally, J. (1978). *Psychometric theory* (2nd ed.). New York: McGraw-Hill.

220. O'Connor, E. S. (1995). Paradoxes of participation: A literary analysis of case studies on employee involvement. *Organization Science, 16*(5), 769–803.

221. Odgers, P. (2004). *The world of customer service.* Boston: Pearson Education.

222. O'Keefe, M. (2000). *New directions in corporate strategy.* St. Leonards, Australia: Allen & Unwin.

223. Oliver, R. W. (2001). Real-time strategy: What is strategy, anyway? *Journal of Business Strategy, 22*(6), 7–10.

224. O'Reilly, C., & Chatman, J. (1996). Cultures as social control: Corporations, cults, and commitment. In L. Cummings & B. Staw (Eds.), *Research in organizational behavior* (Vol. 18, pp. 157–200). Greenwich, CT: JAI Press.

225. Organ, D. W. (1988). *Organizational citizenship behavior: The "good soldier" syndrome.* Lexington, MA: Lexington Books.

226. Organ, D. W. (1990). The motivational basis of organizational citizenship behavior. In B. M. Staw & L. L. Cummings (Eds.), *Research in organizational behavior* (pp. 43–72). Greenwich, CT: JAI Press.

227. Otely, T. (2004, July/August). British Airways' new sleeper service, New York–London. *Business Traveler.*

228. Parasuraman, A., Zeithaml, V. A., & Berry, L. L. (1985). A conceptual model of service quality and implications for future research. *Journal of Marketing, 49,* 41–50.

229. Parker, M. (1993). Industrial relations myth and shop floor reality: The team concept in the auto industry. In N. Lichtenstein & J. H. Howell (Eds.), *Industrial democracy in America* (pp. 249–274). Cambridge, England: Cambridge University Press.

230. Paul, R. J., Niehoff, B. P., & Turnley, W. H. (2000). Empowerment, expectations, and the psychological contract: Managing the dilemmas and gaining the advantages. *Journal of Socio-Economics, 29*(4), 471–485.

231. Peccei, R., & Rosenthal, P. (1997). The antecedents of employee commitment to customer service: Evidence from a UK service context. *International Journal of Human Resource Management, 8,* 66–86.

232. Pereira, D. (1987). *Factors associated with transformational leadership in an Indian engineering firm.* Paper presented at the meeting of the Administrative Science Association of Canada, Vancouver, BC.

233. Peters, T. J. (1987). *Thriving on chaos.* New York: Alfred A. Knopf.

234. Peters, T. J. (1992). *Liberation management.* New York: MacMillan.

235. Peters, T. J., & Waterman, R. H., Jr. (1982). *The politics of organizational decision making.* London: Tavistock.

236. Pettigrew, A. M., & Fenton, E. M. (Eds.). (2000). *The innovating organization.* London: Sage.

237. Phillips, J., & Stone, R. D. (2002). *How to measure training results: A practical guide to tracking the six key indicators.* New York: McGraw-Hill.

238. Phillips, R. (n.d.). Complaints welcome here. *Retailer News.* Retrieved June 20, 2005, from http://retailernews.com/898/phill898.html

239. Pilat, D. (2000, October). No longer services as usual. *OECD Observer, 223,* 52–54. Chap. 2, p. 52.

240. Pine, B. J., II, & Gilmore, J. H. (1998, July-August). Welcome to the experience economy. *Harvard Business Review, 76*(4), 97–105.

241. Pine, B. J., II, & Gilmore, J. H. (1999). *The experience economy.* Boston: Harvard Business School Press.

242. Pocock, P. (1989, November). Is business ethics a contradiction in terms? *Personnel Management,* 60–63.

243. Porter, M. E. (1980). *Competitive strategy: Techniques for analyzing industries and competitors.* New York. Free Press.

244. Powers, V. (2004, November). Finding workers who fit. *Business 2.0, 5*(10), 74.

245. Prahalad, C. K. (1997). Strategies for growth. In R. Gibson (Ed.), *Rethinking the future: Business, principles, competition, control, leadership, markets and the world* (pp. 63–75). London: Nicholas Brealey.

246. Pruyne, E. A. (2002). *Historical outline of the leadership literature.* Boston: Kennedy School, Harvard University.

247. Quinn, J. B. (1996). Strategies for change: Logical incrementalism. In H. Mintzberg & J. B. Quinn (Eds.), *The strategy process: Concepts, context, cases.* Englewood Cliffs, NJ: Prentice Hall. Chap. 4, a & b, p. 3.

248. Quinn, J. B., Baruch, J. J., & Paquette, P. C. (1987, December). Technology in services. *Scientific American, 257*(6), 50–58.

249. Quinn, R. E., & Spreitzer, G. M. (1997). The road to empowerment: Seven questions every leader should consider. *Organizational Dynamics, 26*(2), 37–49.

250. Raelin, J. A. (2003). *Creating leaderful organizations: How to bring out leadership in everyone.* San Francisco: Berrett-Koehler.

251. Rappaport, J. (1987). Terms of empowerment/exemplars of prevention: Toward a theory for community psychology. *American Journal of Community Psychology, 15*(2), 121–148.

252. Raynor, M., & Bower, J. L. (2001, May). Lead from the center: How to manage divisions dynamically. *Harvard Business Review, 79*(5), 92–105.

253. Redelmeier, D. A., & Kahneman, D. (1996). Patients' memories of painful medical treatments: Real time and retrospective evaluation of two minimally invasive procedures. *Pain, 66,* 3–8.

254. Reichheld, F. F. (1996). *The loyalty effect.* Boston: Harvard Business School Press.

255. Richins, M. L. (1983, June). An analysis of consumer interaction styles in the marketplace. *Journal of Consumer Research, 10*, 73–82.

256. Rinke, W. J. (2004). *Don't oil the squeaky wheel and 19 other contrarian ways to improve your leadership effectiveness.* New York: McGraw-Hill.

257. Rinke, W. J. (2000, October/November). Pizza in the sky: Lessons learned from service failures. *Winning Manager, 3*(5). Retrieved June 20, 2005, from http://www.wolfrinke .com/WMNEWSLETTER/wm1000.html

258. Roese, J. N., & Olson, J. M. (1995). Counterfactual thinking: A critical overview. In J. N. Roese & J. M. Olson (Eds.), *What might have been: The social psychology of counterfactual thinking* (pp. 1–56). Mahwah, NJ: Lawrence Erlbaum.

259. Rose, S. M., & Black, B. L. (1985). *Advocacy and empowerment: Mental health care in the community.* Boston: Routledge & Kegan Paul.

260. Rumelt, R. P. (1996). A teaching plan for strategy alternatives for the British motorcy- cle industry. In H. Mintzberg & J. B. Quinn (Eds.), *The strategy process: Concepts, con- text, cases* (3rd ed.). Englewood Cliffs, NJ: Prentice Hall.

261. Rust, R. T., Moorman, C., & Dickson, P. R. (2000). *Getting returns from service quality: Is the conventional wisdom wrong?* (Working paper, Report No. 00-120). Boston: Marketing Science Institute.

262. Sandrick, K. (2003, September). A higher goal: Evidence-based design raises the bar for new construction. *Health Facilities Management, 16*(9).

263. SAS customer intelligence: In fashion at The Limited. (2005). Retrieved July 22, 2005, from the SAS Institute Web site: http://www.sas.com/success/limited.html

264. SAS Institute [Home page]. (2005). Retrieved July 8, 2005, from http://www.SAS.com

265. Schein, E. H. (1992). *Organizational culture and leadership* (2nd ed.). San Francisco: Jossey-Bass. Chap. 3, pp. 373–374.

266. Scheuing, E. E., & Johnson, E. M. (1989). A proposed model for new service develop- ment. *Journal of Service Marketing, 3*(2), 25–34.

267. Schlesinger, L., & Heskett, J. (1991). The service driven service company. *Harvard Business Review, 69*(5), 71–81.

268. Schnake, M. (1991). Organizational citizenship: A review, proposed model and research agenda. *Human Relations, 44*, 735–759.

269. Schneider, B. (1973). The perception of organizational climate: The customer's view. *Journal of Applied Psychology, 57*, 248–256.

270. Schneider, B. (1980). The service organization: Climate is crucial. *Organizational Dynamics, 9*, 52–65.

271. Schneider, W. E. (2000). Why good management ideas fail: The neglected power of organizational culture. *Strategy and Leadership, 28*(1), 24–29.

272. Schonberger, R. J., & Knod, E. M., Jr. (1994). Operations management continuous improvement (5th ed.). Burr Ridge, IL: McGraw-Hill Education.

273. *Second generation performance management: Value mapping.* (2004). Retrieved June 20, 2005, from the Value Based Management.net Web site: http://www.value basedmanagement.net/methods_jack_value_mapping.html

274. Seitel, F. P. (2004). *The practice of public relations* (9th ed.). Boston: Pearson Education.

275. Selden, L., & Colvin, G. (2003, July 7). What customers want. *Fortune, 148*(1), 122.

276. Senge, P. M., Kleiner, A., Roberts, C., Roth, G., Ross, R., & Smith, B. (1999). *The dance of change: The challenges to sustaining momentum in learning organizations.* New York: McGraw-Hill.

277. Sessa, V. I. (2003, Autumn). Raelin: *Creating leaderful organizations: How to bring out leadership in everyone* [Book review]. *Personnel Psychology, 56*(3), 762–765.

278. Shelton, K. (1991). People power. *Executive Excellence, 8*(12), 7–8.

279. Shinkle, G., Gooding, R., & Smith, M. (2004). *Transforming strategy into success. How to implement a lean management system.* New York: Productivity Press.

280. Shostack, G. L. (1984). Service design in the operating environment. In W. R. George & C. Marshall (Eds.), *Developing new services* (pp. 27–43). Chicago: American Marketing Association.

281. Shostack, G. L. (1987). Service positioning through structural change. *Journal of Marketing, 51*(1), 33–43.

282. Shrivastava, P. (1986). Is strategic management ideological? *Journal of Management, 12*(3), 363–377.

283. Sidorowicz, R. (2001). Customer obsession—service recovery. *CEO Refresher.* Retrieved June 20, 2005, from http://www.refresher.com/!obsession3.html

284. Silvestro, R., & Cross, S. (2000). Applying the service profit chain in a retail environment challenging the "satisfaction mirror." *International Journal of Service Industry Management, 11*(3), 244–268.

285. Six sigma—What is six sigma? (2005). Retrieved July 15, 2005, from the iSixSigma LLC Web site: http://www.isixsigma.com/sixsigma/six_sigma.asp

286. Skanska/Beers General Contractors. (2003). Beers Skanska builds the hospital of tomorrow today. *Building Florida, 1,* 13.

287. Solomon, B. B. (1976). *Black empowerment: Social work in oppressed communities.* New York: Columbia University Press.

288. Spector, P. E. (1987). Method variance as an artifact in self-reported affect and perceptions at work: Myth or significant problem? *Journal of Applied Psychology, 72*(3), 438–443.

289. Stauss, B. (1993). Service problem deployment: Transformation of problem information into problem prevention activities. *International Journal of Service Industry Management, 4*(2), 41–62.

290. Stauss, B., & Weinlich, B. (1995, May 11). Process-oriented measurement of service quality by applying the sequential incident method. In *Proceedings From a Workshop on Quality Management in Service, V.* Tilburg, The Netherlands: Tilburg University.

291. Staw, B. M., Sandelands, L. E., & Dutton, J. E. (1981). Treat-rigidity effects in organizational behavior: A multilevel analysis. *Administrative Science Quarterly, 26,* 501–524.

292. Stewart, D. M. (2003). Piecing together service quality: A framework for robust service. *Production and Operation Management, 12*(2), 246–265.

293. Stewart, R. (1991). Chairmen and chief executives: An exploration of their relationship. *Journal of Management Studies, 28,* 185–208.

294. The strategic role of customer service offerings. (2003, September). Retrieved July 23, 2005, from the LiveWire Logic Web site: http://www.inst-informatica.pt/v20/cid/biblioteca_digital/crm/CRM_The%20Strategic%20Role%20of%20Customer%20Service%20Offerings.pdf

295. *Strategy maps—strategic communication.* (2004). Retrieved June 20, 2005, from http://www.valuebasedmanagement.net/methods_strategy_maps_strategic_communication.html

296. Strother, J. B. (2002a, April). An assessment of the effectiveness of e-learning in corporate training programs. *International Review of Research in Open and Distance Learning, 3*(1). Retrieved June 21, 2005, from the Athabasca University Web site: http://www.irrodl.org/content/v3.1/strother.html

297. Strother, J. B. (2002b). A contrast in responses to the unspeakable events of September 11: American Airlines vs. United Airlines. In *Proceedings: 2002 IEEE International Professional Communication Conference* (pp. 423–436). Piscataway, NJ: Institute of Electrical and Electronic Engineers.

298. Strother, J. B. (2004). Crisis communication put to the test: The case of two airlines on 9/11. *IEEE Transactions on Professional Communication, 47*(4), 290–300.

299. Stuart, F. I. (1998). The influence of organizational culture and internal politics in new service design and introduction. *International Journal of Service Industry Management, 9*(5), 469–485.

300. *Study shows customer service in banks is still not up to standard.* (2004, December 2). Retrieved July 7, 2005, from the eCustomerServiceWorld.com Web site: http://www.ecustomerserviceworld.com/eresearchstore_research.asp?id=701&action=display&type=research

301. Swan, J. E., & Comb, L. J. (1976). Product performance and consumer satisfaction. *Journal of Marketing, 40,* 17–30.

302. Tax, S. S., & Brown, S. W. (1998, Fall). Recovering and learning from service failure. *Sloan Management Review, 40*(1), 75–88.

303. Teece, D. J., Pisano, G. P., & Schuen, A. (1997). Dynamic capabilities and strategic management. *Strategic Management Journal, 18*(7), 509–533.

304. Thomas, K. W., & Velthouse, B. A. (1990). Cognitive elements of empowerment: An interpretative model of intrinsic task motivation. *Academy of Management Review, 15*(4), 18–40.

305. Tichy, N. M. (1997, Fall). The mark of a winner. *Leader to Leader, 6,* 25–28.

306. Toffler, A. (1980). *The third wave.* New York: Collins.

307. Tribewala, V. (2004). *Critical commentary.* Retrieved June 16, 2005, from the Manageris Web site: http://www.manageris.com/all_en/uk/goulp/pro/com96b.html

308. Umiker, W. D. (1992). Empowerment: The latest motivational strategy. *Health Care Supervisor, 11*(2), 11–16.

309. United Nations Economic Commission for Europe. (2003). *Trends in Europe and North America: The statistical yearbook of the Economic Commission for Europe 2003.* Retrieved June 13, 2005, from http://www.unece.org/stats/trends/Welcome.html

310. Van Dyne, L., & Cummings, L. L. (1990, August). *Extra role behaviors: In pursuit of construct and definitional clarity.* Paper presented at the annual meeting of the Academy of Management, San Francisco.

311. Varey, C. A., & Kahneman, D. (1992). Experiences extended across time: Evaluation of moments and episodes. *Journal of Behavioral Decision Making, 5,* 169–185.

312. Verma, R., Fitzsimmons, J., Heinke, J., & Davis, M. M. (2002). New issues and opportunities in service design research (Editorial). *Journal of Operations Management, 20,* 117–120.

313. Volberda, H. W., & Elfring, T. (2001). *Rethinking strategy.* London: Sage.

314. Von Dran, G. M. (1996). Empowerment and the management of an organizational transformation project. *Project Management Journal, 27*(1), 12–17.

315. Waldman D. A. (1994). The contributions of total quality management to a theory of work performance. *Academy of Management Review, 19*(3), 510–536.

316. Waldman, D., Ramirez, G., & House, R. J. (1996). *The effects of U.S. CEO leader behavior on firm profits under conditions of environmental certainty and uncertainty: A longitudinal investigation* (Working paper). Philadelphia: Reginald H. Jones Center for Management Policy, Strategy, and Organization, Wharton School, University of Pennsylvania.

317. Welch, J. (2001). *Jack: Straight from the gut.* New York: Warner Business Books.

318. Welch, J., & Welch, S. (2005). *Winning.* New York: Harper Business.

319. Wells, L. D. (1961). *Techniques of value analysis and engineering.* New York: McGraw-Hill.

320. Wigger, H. (2004, June 16). *Customer benefits through total solutions and innovation.* Retrieved July 19, 2005, from the Siemens Web site: http://www.siemens.com/index .jsp?sdc_rh=null&sdc_flags=null&sdc_sectionid=0&sdc_secnavid=0&sdc_ 3dnvlstid=&sdc_countryid=0&sdc_mpid=0&sdc_unitid=14&sdc_conttype=8&sdc_ contentid=1197941&sdc_langid=1&sdc_pnid=&

321. Wilcox, D. L., Cameron, G. T., Ault, P. H., & Agee, W. K. (2003). *Public relations: Strategies and tactics* (7th ed.). Boston: Pearson Education.

322. Wilson, A. (2003). *Marketing research: An integrated approach.* London: Prentice Hall.

323. Wilson, J. M., & Wellins, R. S. (1994). *Leadership trapeze: Strategies for leadership in team-based organizations.* San Francisco: Jossey-Bass.

324. Wruck, K., & Jensen, M. C. (1994). Science, specific knowledge and total quality management. *Journal of Accounting and Economics, 18,* 247–287.

325. Zaltman, G. (2003). *How customers think.* Boston: Harvard Business School Press.

326. Zeithaml, V. A., & Bitner, M. J. (2003). *Service marketing: Integrating customer focus across the firm.* New York: McGraw-Hill Higher Education. Chap. 2, a, p. 7, b, p. 5.

327. Zeithaml, V., Parasuraman, A., & Berry, L. (1990). *Delivering quality service: Balancing customer perceptions and expectations.* New York: Free Press.

328. Zemke, R., & Schaaf, R. (1989). *The service edge: 101 companies that profit from customer care.* New York: NAL Books.

329. Zook, C., & Allen, J. (2001). *Profit from the core.* Cambridge, MA: Harvard Business School Press.

Index

About the Authors

Svafa Grönfeldt is Chief Executive of Strategy and Organizational Development for Actavis Group, one of the world's top 10 generic pharmaceutical companies. She received her Ph.D. in Industrial Relations from the London School of Economics and Political Science, where her major focus was on service orientation and management. For the past 8 years, she has also been a member of the faculty of economics and business administration at the University of Iceland. Currently her work takes her throughout the world and is mainly focused on aligning strategy, structure, and the talent of key Actavis personnel on five continents and in 28 countries. Prior to her Chief Strategist role at Actavis, she held the position of Country-Managing Partner for Deloitte Consulting in Iceland and was a member of Deloitte's EMEA leadership team. Before that, she was a partner in and Director of Research and Development for IMG Gallup. Her consulting career has mainly been focused on leadership coaching and service strategic formulation, and her research projects include numerous occupational and benchmarking studies for companies in the private and public sectors, including longitudinal and cross-cultural studies.

Judith B. Strother is Professor of Applied Linguistics and Chair of the graduate program in Technical and Professional Communication at Florida Institute of Technology, where she has developed and taught a number of courses, including customer service, public relations, and communicating in the global economy. She holds M.A. and M.B.A. degrees and earned her Ph.D. at Technische Universiteit Eindhoven in the Netherlands, where she is Visiting Professor for Special Lectures in Managerial and Technical Writing. She has conducted research in management areas such as crisis communication as well as in communication and applied linguistics, including specific psycholinguistic elements in reading and writing business and scientific and technical English. She has also studied sociolinguistic issues, such as the impact of regional dialects on first and second language speakers and the effect of cross-linguistic and cross-cultural communication issues and their impact on aviation safety. She has written two books and numerous articles, and she has delivered papers at many international conferences. In the private sector, she serves as an officer in Virtual Languages Learning Academy (ViLLA), which designs and delivers Web-based business English and aviation English courses for international corporate training programs.